Fighting for the News

The Adventures of the First War
Correspondents from Bonaparte
to the Boers

Fighting for the News

The Adventures of the First War
Correspondents from Bonaparte
to the Boers

Brian Best

FRONTLINE BOOKS

FIGHTING FOR THE NEWS
The Adventures of the First War Correspondents from Bonaparte to the Boers

This edition published in 2016 by Frontline Books,
an imprint of Pen & Sword Books Ltd,
47 Church Street, Barnsley, S. Yorkshire, S70 2AS.

ISBN: 978-1-84832-437-4

CIP data records for this title are available from the British Library

Printed and bound by CPI Group (UK) Ltd, Croydon, CR0 4YY
Typeset in 10.5/13 point Palatino

For more information on our books, please email:
info@frontline-books.com,
write to us at the above address, or visit:
www.frontline-books.com

Contents

Contents

Introduction

It is now two centuries since a newspaper conceived the idea of sending a reporter overseas to observe, gather information and write about war. With no experience to draw upon, both newspaper and correspondent gradually worked out a procedure that has evolved into today's incredibly sophisticated form.

Man's fascination with wars is as old as war itself. Memoirs and first-hand accounts have always found a ready public from the time of Ancient Greece. Until printed books became available, tales of warfare were imparted by storytellers and minstrels. Even today there are parts of the world beyond the reach of television and newspapers where the storyteller still relates tales of old battles as though they were only recently fought. On the route of Alexander the Great, for instance, the storyteller still recounts to the inhabitants of some remote village the battles fought during the Greek conquest.

With Johann Gutenberg's invention of the moveable-type press in 1456 and its development over the following centuries, a literate public could have access to current information. Thus the daily newspaper began to evolve. By the early nineteenth century there was a need for more accurate and immediate reporting of overseas events, particularly the exploits of Napoleon Bonaparte, the man who dominated European affairs for so long.

At first, newspapers relied on the accounts of serving army officers. The problem with accepting a soldier's version of war was that it was couched in favour of the soldier's own institution, limited in its view of the 'larger picture' and unlikely to give any insight into the realities of war. For overseas news, the newspapers also relied on accounts from diplomats, travellers and sailors, as well as government bulletins, which were often published long after the event.

It was *The Times* that led the way, as it has so often done, with the employment of the first special overseas correspondent. This undertaking was to cover the Napoleonic Wars and, although not altogether successful, it created enough interest for the experiment to be repeated in later conflicts. At the high water mark of Victorian power, 'Specials' were the stars of journalism, and what they wrote sold newspapers. The reports of William Russell and Archibald Forbes markedly increased the circulation of both *The Times* and the *Daily News*. Russell's reports from the Crimean War are credited with bringing down Lord Aberdeen's Government and an improvement, however marginal, in the conditions of the ordinary soldier. George Steevens's accounts from the Sudan put the infant *Daily Mail* and its proprietor, Alfred Harmsworth, on the road to success. The artist reporters like Melton Prior and Frederic Villiers brought great success to *The Illustrated London News* and *The Graphic* respectively and, even today, their drawings are still used to embody the steadfast British Tommy holding back the heathen hordes.

Photography, which started in the Crimean War, became increasingly used as the century progressed. By the Boer War, cinematography began to be employed despite the clumsy equipment.

The military establishment hated this new phenomenon as they were now open to public scrutiny. Unwieldy and bureaucratic, the military were slow to control the specials, who were free to wander the camps, picking up scraps of information and gossip. They became close observers of fighting and critics of incompetent commanders. Rather than try to embrace this new breed in order to influence what was written, the military establishment sullenly tolerated newsmen because their political masters ordered they should do so. By the end of the century, thanks almost entirely to Lord Kitchener, the beginnings of censorship began to hamstring this freedom and, by the First World War, the Golden Age was a faded memory.

These war reporters were a tough and resourceful band, whose adventures made a read as exciting as the wars they reported. They were often physically unprepossessing, being overweight and balding like Melton Prior, or short and elderly like Frederic Villiers, who was still travelling to wars into his late seventies. Appearances, however, could be deceptive, for both Prior and Villiers had enormous reserves of grit and determination which overcame any physical shortcoming. Pioneers like Russell and Archibald Forbes, had to learn as they went along. Without back-up teams and shunned by the military, they had to provide for themselves. Armed with little more than writing materials, a bag of sovereigns and a revolver, these men had to rely on their guile and stamina to obtain their news. Most were excellent horsemen and they thought little of riding 100 miles to reach the nearest telegraph, filing their report and then riding back to the fighting. With their flamboyant quasi-military garb, often displaying foreign medal ribbons, they cut dashing figures. It is small wonder that they attracted adventure-seeking young men to their ranks; men like Frank Power and Hubert Howard, both destined to die in the Sudan on their first assignments.

The Victorian Specials saw themselves not only as viewers of war but also participants, acting with the same patriotism and heroism as the soldiers. In order to get good stories, they had to be close to the fighting and many were killed or wounded trying to achieve 'the scoop'. They also took risks in getting their stories back to their papers ahead of their rivals. In spite of the competition, there was a camaraderie fostered by common dangers and hardships, often resulting in the sharing of resources and services.

This Golden Age was short-lived as set-piece battles became a thing of the past. The twentieth century dawned with the outbreak of the Anglo-Boer War, a new style of conflict with fighting that covered vast areas. Now newspapers sent teams of reporters and, although they still enjoyed freedom of movement, censorship was starting to restrict freedom of writing. There were still plenty of the old school of Specials around, but scoop-hungry new men like Edgar Wallace were imposing themselves. The demise of the glamorous swashbuckling correspondent began in earnest during the Russo-Japanese War of 1904-5, when the Japanese employed a most effective censorship which acted as a model for the British during the First World War.

In 1914, after initially trying to seek and report the truth, newspapers effectively became part of the government propaganda machine. By choosing to boost morale on the Home Front and give all support to the military leaders, costly blunders and horrific casualties were glossed over or concealed. The reporters were generally decent men who managed to convince themselves that compromising their calling in the name of patriotism was the right thing to do. Some, like Philip Gibbs and William Beach Thomas, later wrote of their shame and remorse for misleading the public. The public and the common soldier, however, were in no mood to forgive, and reporters were held in low esteem for many years after the war.

The way the Second World War was reported was virtually a repeat of the First, with its heavy censorship and a strong sense of patriotism. Several of the correspondents did write books immediately after their experiences, in which they gave vent to their criticism of recent campaigns. An example was that of Ian Morrison, who thought that the Malay retreat and Singapore surrender had been avoidable disasters. The Second World War also saw the war correspondent dressed in official military uniform, praised by generals and given every assistance by the well organised military Public Relations Unit. The result was that the public were fed a diet of upbeat and patriotic stories with all blunders, scandals and injustices suppressed until they were revealed years later.

The aftermath of the Second World War brought great changes to attitudes and a clamour for change. The old colonial powers, weakened and distracted by huge domestic priorities, saw their former empires crumble away. A series of wars for independence broke out, with Africa learning the hard way that freedom does not automatically bring peace and stability. Fifty years on, reporters are still travelling to countries whose populations have known nothing but civil war.

The Korean War was the only time Communism and the West actually went to war. It also marked the end of another step in the way wars were reported. Typewriters, telegraphs and telephones were about to be succeeded by television, satellite communications and celebrity journalists. The Vietnam War was the first conflict where special correspondents had a free hand to witness and report what they liked. The American military blamed unfettered news coverage for undermining the country's will to fight, although it is now accepted that the media were just reflecting the public's disenchantment with a war they could never win. Proving that a genie can be put back in a bottle, the media have since been placed under increasing restrictions and censorship by the military establishment. The ultimate example of this was the coverage of the Gulf War, which was so tightly managed that it resulted in a news vacuum.

With all the state of the art 'gizmos' that made reporting easier came a dark downside. Journalists are now targets in their own right. In some conflicts they are no longer viewed as neutral observers but spies and propagandists; an increasing number of war correspondents have been killed, wounded or kidnapped. Media organisations now send their budding war correspondents on special courses to prepare them for the dangers that await them. With weapons becoming ever deadlier and more readily available, life at the sharp end has never been more dangerous.

As we entered the new millennium, the public took for granted the almost instant reports shown nightly on TV news programmes. Newspapers still print reports of wars in remote areas of the world, although these are usually relegated to an inside foreign page and no longer sell newspapers. Despite the seemingly declining interest, men and women are still willing to endure great discomfort and risk their lives to bring wars that still plague our planet to the public's attention. These are often in the most inaccessible places where the infrastructure has been destroyed and where the reporter is truly out on a limb.

They are a breed apart who answer their calling for all sorts of motives. Whatever their reason for following the sound of Russell's 'noisy drums and trumpets', they live out the maverick lifestyle that many of us secretly aspire to, while we do not have to suffer the anguish of witnessing the appalling sights they see on our behalf. The Golden Age may have passed over a century ago, but its spirit still lives on in the courage and determination of reporters who put their lives in danger to keep the public aware of the conflicts that still bedevil our world.

This book is a homage to those intrepid British war correspondents who, for two centuries, have earned the title, 'Special'.

Brian Best,
Rutland, 2016

Chapter 1

In the Beginning

The first special correspondent employed by a newspaper to gather information about a current war was Henry Crabb Robinson. In 1807, the proprietor of *The Times*, John Walter II, employed this thirty-two-year-old lawyer to act as their 'man in Germany', ostensibly to follow and report on the movements of Napoleon's *Grande Armée*. Robinson, known as 'Old Crabby', was a gregarious bachelor with a gift for languages who was able to fit into any sort of company or situation; this made him the archetypal foreign correspondent.

Robinson was born in Bury St Edmunds in 1775 and articled as an attorney. Between 1800 and 1805, he spent three years as a student at Jena University and studying elsewhere in Germany, where he met with the flower of German literature including Johann Goethe, Friedrich Schiller, Johann Gottfied Herder and Christopher Martin Wieland. John Walter recognised that Robinson was not only literate but could pass himself off as a German and would therefore be able to pick up more accurate information about Napoleon's advance through Prussia and Poland. It was not expected that the fledgling correspondent would accompany the *Grande Armée*, but he could learn more about their movements by being stationed on the border with Germany, something no other British newspaper had considered. He travelled to Altona, the capital of Holstein on the left bank of the River Elbe. Facing Altona on the right bank was the German port of Hamburg, then occupied by the French. Nowadays, Altona is a suburb of Hamburg but, until 1864, the provinces of

Schleswig and Holstein were ruled by Denmark. The Danes enjoyed uneasy neutrality with Bonaparte's France who threatened a take-over once their war with Russia was ended.

Crabby recalled: 'In January 1807 I received, through my friend J.D. Collier, a proposal from Mr Walter that I should take up residence at Altona, and become *The Times* correspondent. I was to receive from the editor of the *Hamburger Correspondenten* all the public documents at his disposal, and was to have the benefit also of a mass of information of which the restraints of the German press did not permit him to avail himself ... I gladly accepted the offer, and never repented having done so.'[1]

Crabby soon made friends but was under no illusion about how long his situation in Holstein would last. 'I am of the opinion that it cannot possibly last long. In all probability we shall soon hear of a peace with Russia, or a general engagement, which is ten to one, will end in the defeat of the Allies. In either event I have no doubt the French will take possession of Holstein ... the northern maritime powers will be forced to shut up the Baltic and perhaps arm their fleets against us.'

In June, his first report appeared in *The Times* with a romantic-sounding introduction: 'From the Banks of the Elbe: In my attention to the incidents of the day I was unremitting. I kept up a constant intercourse with England. On my arrival I learned that, notwithstanding the affected neutrality of Denmark, the post from Altona to England was stopped, and in consequence, all letters were sent by Mr Thornton, the English minister there [*Altona*].' Crabb Robinson's reports were included in Thornton's letters to the Foreign Office which had to be sent via Copenhagen.

On 20 June, Crabby received news of Napoleon's overwhelming victory at the Battle of Friedland on 14 June and sent a lively account, albeit second-hand, of the French victory.

Ten days later he learned of the armistice and, on 7 July, the peace signing at Tilsit. The political settlements at Tilsit were regarded as the height of Napoleon's empire because now there was no longer any continental power challenging French dominance in Europe.

Intelligence was received in London that convinced the Government that the French intended to occupy Holstein in order to use Denmark against Britain. Some reports suggested that the Danes had secretly agreed to this. This was largely reinforced by the Tilsit Treaty in which Napoleon tried to persuade Tsar Alexander to form a maritime league with Denmark and Portugal against Britain.

Spencer Perceval, the Chancellor of the Exchequer wrote a memorandum setting out a case for sending forces to Copenhagen: 'The intelligence from so many and such varied sources that Napoleon's intent to force Denmark into war against Britain could not be doubted ... Under such circumstances it would be madness, it would be idiotic to wait for an overt act.'

The British demanded that the Danes surrender their fleet until Napoleon had been defeated. The Danes were caught in between two determined protagonists but decided against the humiliation of surrendering their fleet; this amounted to a declaration of war. Crabby wrote: 'I find it was on the 12th that Lord Cathcart, with a force of 20,000 men, joined the Admiral off Elsinore, and on the 16th, the army landed on the island of Zealand, eight miles from Copenhagen.'

The Second Battle, or Bombardment, of Copenhagen lasted from 16 August to 5 September 1807, during which the Royal Navy seized or destroyed the Danish fleet. Having given the population prior warning, the British ships began bombarding the city, destroying over 1,000 buildings and killing 195 citizens. The British Army kept any Danish reinforcements reaching the capital before re-embarking and returning to England. The destruction of the Danish fleet was an act which would bear similarities to the destruction of the French fleet at Mers-el-Kebir, Algeria, in 1940. Although the British had prevented Napoleon seizing the Danish ships, they had turned a potential ally into an enemy.

With the withdrawal of Mr. Thornton, Robinson's conduit for sending his reports was now closed and daily his position became increasingly precarious. Despite reassurances from a friendly Danish officer, Crabby started to prepare for a swift departure.

With the news of the bombardment of Copenhagen, the Altona Bürgomeister ordered the arrest of all Englishmen. 'Disguising myself by borrowing a French hat,' Robinson later recalled, 'and having arranged my own little matters, I resolved to give notice to all my fellow-countrymen with whose residences I was acquainted. And so effectual were my services in this respect, that no one whom I knew was arrested.'

Finally, Crabby made his escape across the Elbe to Hamburg, where he was less likely to be known. After a few days of anonymously fitting in with the citizens, he was recognised by the postman who carried letters between Hamburg and Altona. The Bonapartist mailman promptly alerted some nearby French *gendarmes* who pursued Crabby into a market place, where he was able to lose them. Crabby realised that he was regarded as a spy and it was now obviously time to quit Hamburg. Through his connections he obtained a passport that would take him to Sweden. An overnight ride brought him to Rostock on the Baltic coast, where he had to wait over a week before he could find a vessel to take him to Stockholm. After a dreadful voyage of five days, he arrived at a port near the Swedish capital. Even here he was not entirely safe: 'This anti-English feeling was so general in Sweden at this time that I was advised to travel as a German through the country.' On 21 September, Crabby set off for Gothenburg, which he reached on the 27th. Two days later, he boarded a ship for England and reached Harwich on 7 October.

John Walter had been impressed by Crabby's reports and his efforts to obtain accurate information, despite the verbose and leaden style of writing which was typical of the period. Walter was one of the great innovators of British press history. He was still only thirty years old when he inherited *The Times* from his father in 1803. The daily circulation at the time was only 1,500 copies but, through his determination and innovative ideas, he would increase this figure to 30,000 by the time he retired in the 1820s.

Soon after Crabby's return, Walter offered him the job of foreign editor, which largely required Robinson to translate foreign newspapers and write about European politics. His period in London proved to be fruitful for his future involvement with the literati. He met and became friendly with writers and poets such as William Wordsworth, Charles Lamb, Robert Southey and Samuel Taylor Coleridge. This pleasant interlude was, however, interrupted when, in 1808, John Walter once again called upon his special correspondent to go travelling again:

'The Spanish revolution had broken out, and as soon as it was likely to become a national concern, *The Times*, of course, must have its correspondent in Spain; and it was said who so fit to write from the shores of the Bay if Biscay as he who had successfully written from the banks of the Elbe? I did not feel at liberty to reject the proposal of Mr Walter that I should go, but I accepted the offer reluctantly …

'I left London by the Falmouth mail on the night of July 19th, reached Falmouth on the 21st, and in a lugger belonging to the Government – the Black Jake. The voyage was very rough and, as I afterwards learnt, even dangerous. We were for sometime on a lee shore and obliged to sail with more than half the vessel under water; a slight change of wind would have overset us; but of all this I was happily ignorant. I landed at Corunna on the evening of Sunday, July 31st and was at once busily employed. I found the town in a state of great disorder; but the excitement was a joyous one, the news having just arrived of the surrender of a French army in the south under Marshal Dupont.'[2]

Crabby's job was to collect news and forward reports to his paper by every vessel that left the port. His first report was dated 2 August and was upbeat to the extent of believing the French were on the point of being pushed out of Spain.

'When we consider, as is officially stated, that not a Frenchman exists in all of Andalusia save in bonds; that in Portugal, Junot remains in a state of siege; that all the South of Spain is free; and that in the North the late victories of the patriots in Aragon have broken the communication between the French forces in Biscay and Catalonia, we need not fear the speedy emancipation of the capital, and the compression of the French force within the provinces adjoining Bayonne.'

These reports were followed up on 4 August with news of Dupont's surrender and on 8 August with the flight of Joseph Napoleon from Madrid.

In October, a small force of British soldiers commanded by General Craufurd arrived in Corunna. They soon marched off to the interior to join the British army, under the command of Sir John Moore, who had crossed the Portuguese border into Spain. He set about attacking the French lines of communication, attempting to rally and co-ordinate the fragmented Spanish resistance. The French were forced to leave the subjugation of the country and go in pursuit of the British.

Crabby had been several months in Corunna and news was thin at best. Deciding to travel to Madrid he learned through his military contacts 'the information, that is a great secret, that it was not advisable to advance, for the English army was on its retreat! This was 22nd November.'

This was followed by worsening news which he reported to *The Times*: 'The intelligence brought by the Lady Pellow packet is of an unfavourable complexion, yet such as we might perhaps have expected from the first appearance of Bonaparte upon the theatre of war. General Blake's army, after sustaining repeated attacks, is said at last to have been completely defeated, while the advanced body of the French have even reached Valladolid.

'The news from the English army on its way from Portugal is no less distressing. It is said that 3,000 of the men under Sir John Moore are sick.'

On 10 December, Crabby wrote: 'A tale is current which, if not true, has been invented by an Arragonese, that Bonaparte has sworn that on the 1st of January his brother shall be in Madrid, Marshal Bessieres at Lisbon and himself at Saragossa.'

In dreadful winter conditions and heavily outnumbered, the British retreated north and managed to reach Vigo. They then had to stagger on to the north-western port of Corunna where evacuation ships were waiting. Moore's men were ill-equipped and starving. Their boots had fallen apart and they had resorted to wrapping their frozen feet in rags. In an epic fighting retreat, the British managed to fend off the French and reach their destination. Old Crabby had remained in Corunna, but he could see the results of this ill-planned British expedition. His reports were reflected decades later in William Russell's stinging attacks from the Crimea on the inefficiency and failure of the commissariat and the indifference to the common soldier's plight.

By 11 January 1809, the British were dug in at Corunna. In his report of the same day, Crabby wrote: 'In the course of this day the whole English army has either entered within, or planted itself before the walls of this town. The French army will not fail to be quick in the pursuit; and as the transports which are so anxiously expected from Vigo are still out of sight, and according to the state of the wind, not likely soon to make their appearance, this spot will most probably become the scene of a furious and bloody contest.

'The late arrivals have, of course, made us far better acquainted than we possibly could be before with the circumstances of this laborious and dishonourable campaign, which has had all the suffering, without any of the honours of war. Without a single general engagement – having to fight an enemy who always shunned the contest – it is supposed that our army has lost upwards of 3,000 men, a larger number of whom perished by the usual causes, as well as labours of a retreating soldiery.'

The Times reported on 15 January: 'The last two days have materially changed the appearance of things. Yesterday evening, the fleet of transports, which had been dispersed in their passage from Vigo, began to enter the harbour, and the hearts of thousands were relieved by the prospect of deliverance. I beheld this evening the beautiful bay covered with our vessels, both armed and mercantile, and I should have thought the noble three-deckers, which stood on the outside of the harbour, a proud spectacle, if I could have forgotten the inglorious service they were called to perform.'

Transport ships waited in the harbour to evacuate the army, while the Royal Navy offered protection outside. The French army held back and waited for the British to begin embarkation before launching their attack.

On the afternoon of the 16th, Crabby decided to walk out of the town towards the gunfire. 'I noticed several French prisoners, whose countenances expressed rather rage and menaces than fear. They knew very well what would take place. I walked with some acquaintances a mile or more out of the town and remained there until dark – long enough to know that the enemy was driven back; for the firing evidently came from a greater distance.'

The cannonading seemed to be in the hills some three miles distant. It was during this phase of the Battle of Corunna that Sir John Moore was killed.

Robinson boarded his vessel at about five o'clock, which did not then leave the bay but waited until the last minute before sailing. The expected arrival of the French did not materialise the following morning.

'Early in the forenoon my attention was drawn to the sound of musketry, and by a glance it could be ascertained that the soldiers were shooting such of their fine horses as could not be taken on board. This was done, of course, to prevent their strengthening the French cavalry. One very large explosion brought us all on deck. There was on the shore a large powder magazine, which had often been the boundary of my walk. When the cloud of smoke which had been raised was blown away, there was an empty space where there had been a solid building a few moments before; but this was less exciting than when, about one o'clock, we heard a cannonading from the shore at the inland extremity of the bay. It was the French army. They were firing at the ships which were quietly waiting for orders. I remarked the sudden movement in the bay – the ships before lying in anchor were instantly in motion. I myself noticed three vessels which had lost their bowsprits. The Captain told me that twelve had cut their cables.

'We were not anxious to quit the spot and therefore sailed about in the vicinity all night. Two vessels were on fire and next day I was shocked at beholding the remains of a wreck.'

Robinson has been criticised by later generations of reporters for not remaining in Corunna and sending home second-hand reports of the campaign. In fact, there was little else he could have done. With no fixed battle lines, atrocious roads and appalling weather conditions he would not have been able to get his reports away even if he could have made sense of the chaos and confusion that beset the retreating army. Instead, he was able to piece together the jigsaw and his reports are now a primary source for this harsh campaign. The fact that he remained within French artillery range until the last moment spoke of his courage and determination to observe the battle until it was obviously time to depart.

On the following day, and against the odds, the British inflicted a defeat on the French and managed to board the transports which brought them safely to England. Robinson's account of this 'early Dunkirk' was published without any reference to the outcome of the final battle or the death of the British commander, Sir John Moore, who was later immortalised in Charles Wolfe's poem. Despite missing this scoop, the report was well received and, importantly to John Walter, the reputation of *The Times* soared.

Despite Crabby's criticism of the British campaign, he was lavish in his praise of the British soldier. The Duke of Wellington, however, was appalled at this new phenomenon that had appeared in a war zone and expressly forbade any future correspondents from accompanying the army in his Peninsular campaign or, to the impoverishment of posterity, the Battle of Waterloo. The Duke wrote to the Secretary for War: 'I beg draw your Lordship's attention to the frequent paragraphs in the English Newspapers describing the positions and numbers, the objects, the means of attaining them possessed by the Armies in Spain and Portugal … This intelligence must have reached the enemy at the same time it did me, at a moment at which it was most important that he should not receive it.'

This really set the tone for all future relationships between the military and the press. Each had fundamentally opposed objectives inasmuch as the military wished to protect their operational security, which included the lives of its soldiers. The newsmen, on the other hand, sought to achieve the public's right to know and, in so doing, to increase the circulations of their publications. During the nineteenth century there was certainly another motive for military leaders to shun the press. A victorious general would want to announce his triumph officially through Parliament. Similarly, he would wish to play down any defeat and not to have some 'civilian scribbler' probing for shortcomings and exposing any ineptitude in the military leadership.

With no further prospect of reporting wars, Henry Crabb Robinson, Britain's first war correspondent, quit journalism and studied for the Bar. He kept a diary right up to his death at the age of ninety-one in which he wrote about the contemporaries he knew and corresponded with, including William Blake, Samuel Taylor Coleridge, William Wordsworth, Robert Southey, Johann Goethe and Friedrich Schiller. As a Nonconformist, he had been unable to study at either Oxford or Cambridge and became one of the founders of the University of London (University College, London). He died in 1867, having seen his torch passed to the most influential of all war correspondents, William Howard Russell.

The defeat of Napoleon was followed by nearly four decades of peace for Britain. There were still wars and campaigns being fought during that period but these were mostly in far-off places on the edge of the expanding Empire, too difficult to access and too limited in public interest to warrant sending special correspondents.

There were some conflicts nearer home that were reported and, following *The Times*'s lead, some newspapers did cover them. One such was thirty-year-old Charles Lewis Gruneison of the *Morning Post*, who reported on the protracted and complex Spanish Civil War of 1833-39, fought between factions over the succession to the throne. The two main claimants to the throne were the regent, Maria Christina, and the late king's brother, Don Carlos de Borbon. The opposing sides were thus called the Cristinos and the Carlists.

Gruneison managed the foreign news department of his paper and, in March 1837, was sent to cover the Carlist army in Spain. Attached to the headquarters of Don Carlos, he reported various small actions and was present at the victory of Villar de los Navarros on 24 August. Gruneison was the first correspondent to write his reports from the actual scene of the fighting and, because of his neutral position, saved the lives of many captured Cristino prisoners who would have been murdered by the Carlists.

He remained with the army when it advanced to Madrid in September and in its retreat soon afterwards. Gruneison endured hardship and several times ran risks of being killed. After the Battle of Retuerta on 5 October, he prepared to leave Spain but was taken prisoner by some Cristino soldiers. He was on the point of being executed as a Carlist spy and it was only the intervention of Lord Palmerston that secured his release, enabling him to return to England in January 1838. Gruneisen later became the paper's Paris correspondent and instituted a communication system with London using homing pigeons.

The Carlist War, however, did little to excite the limited number of newspaper readers and the employment of Specials had to wait until Britain was again involved in a war.

Chapter 2

The Father of
the Luckless Tribe

The technological advances of the nineteenth century changed the way news was reported. No longer did the reporter have to rely on the vagaries of the postal system, which was still in its infancy. During the 1840s the invention of the telegraph and its swift installation in most countries over the following decade revolutionised overseas reporting. The telegraph's impact was as revolutionary in the industrial age as the computer is in the information age. Printing technology also improved so that newspapers could be produced quickly and in greater numbers. It is no coincidence that this was also a fruitful time for English literature, with exceptional and popular authors like Dickens, Thackeray, Trollope, George Eliot and the Bronte sisters publishing enduring novels in a burst of creativity.

At this period *The Times'* circulation was around 40,000 copies per day, while its nearest rival was just 7,000. With the advent of better education, greater numbers of the public were stimulated to read, whilst the abolition of the high newspaper tax in 1855 made reading papers available to a wider public. All this influenced journalism, which developed a more literate and direct style of writing. The public were becoming increasingly sophisticated and demanded immediate and clear reporting. From this early Victorian literary flowering, there emerged a man who has come to be regarded as the 'Father of War Correspondents' or, as he put it, 'the Father of a Luckless Tribe'.

William Howard Russell was born at Lily Vale, Jobestown, County Dublin on 28 March 1820. As an impoverished law student at Trinity College, he acquired his first taste of journalism through his cousin, Robert Russell, who had been sent by *The Times* to cover the Irish elections of 1841. Unable to penetrate the complexities of local politics by himself, Robert enlisted the help of his young cousin to unravel and write about the machinations of Irish affairs. This led to an invitation from the newspaper to contribute more reports on Irish matters. Russell joined at a fortuitous time, for a new editor had recently been appointed who was to have a great influence on his career.

John Thadeus Delane was a fellow Irishman who had been elevated from a staff reporter to editor at the age of only twenty-four. He was an energetic and tireless worker who was instrumental in transforming the dull *Times* into a crusading and investigative newspaper. Much to Delane's chagrin, his protégé resigned in 1846, joined the *Morning Chronicle* and reported on the Irish Potato Famine.

After two years, Russell sought to rejoin *The Times* and it says much for Delane's admiration for Russell that he broke with the convention of never taking back anyone who resigned. Russell then moved to London as a staff reporter, writing about such events as the Great Exhibition of 1851 and the Duke of Wellington's funeral, as well as day to day parliamentary matters. William Russell's first introduction to war was the brief conflict between Prussia and Denmark in 1851 over the border area of Schleswig-Holstein. He was slightly wounded while observing at the Battle of Indstedt, the first of several in his career. Denmark's victory in the war was to be followed thirteen years later with her humiliation in the 1864 war against a rejuvenated Prussia under Count Otto von Bismarck.

It was an obscure incident in a holy place in Bethlehem that led to the outbreak of the Crimean War and the realisation of Russell's true vocation.[1] Cracks had appeared in the Turkish edifice known as the Ottoman Empire, whose influence spread from the borders of Hungary in the north, to North Africa in the south and Persia in the east. Unwieldy, creaking and corrupt, Turkey had become known as 'the Sick Man of Europe'.

Nicholas I, the Tsar of Russia, felt the time was right to push his expansionist plans to add the Balkans to his burgeoning empire and to gain ice-free ports in the Aegean and Asia Minor. His overtures to the Sultan were successfully countered by the diplomatic efforts of Britain and France, who managed to thwart the Tsar's attempts to increase Russia's influence on Turkey and, by stealth, achieve his goals. Angered by the Sultan's rebuff, Nicholas sought an excuse to make war against Turkey and found it in a squabble that had broken out between some clerics in the Holy Land, then part of the Ottoman Empire. The monks of the Greek Orthodox Church were demanding the same privileges over the guardianship of the Christian Holy Places as those enjoyed by the Roman Catholic priests. This was basically about who should be the sole holder of the keys to the shrines in Bethlehem. Taking up their cause, the Tsar proclaimed himself as the Protector of all Greek Christian subjects in the Ottoman Empire, which the Sultan rejected. The Tsar achieved his aim and war was declared.

Both Britain and France put aside their mutual animosity and jointly offered their support of Turkey by declaring war on Russia. Here was a cause that seemed just and it was enthusiastically supported by the newspapers and public alike. In the first real step to popularise the daily press, Editor Delane chose Russell to accompany the first wave of soldiers as they sailed to Turkey and cheerfully promised him that he would be back home within a few weeks. Apart from a short break, Russell did not return for another two-and-a-half years!

After a farewell dinner with friends who included Charles Dickens, William Makepeace Thackeray and Wilkie Collins, Russell travelled to Southampton with written permission from Lord Haldane to sail with the Guards. There, he received the first of many rebuffs from the military when he was refused passage by the commanding officer. Instead, he had to travel through France to Marseille in order to catch a ship to take him to Malta. Here he remained for three weeks until he managed to get a berth with the Rifle Brigade and Sir George Brown's staff. Disaster struck when his Maltese servant made off with his baggage and tent.

Upon arrival in Turkey, Russell began to write about the incompetent way the British were mishandling everything, from embarking and disembarking, to the lack of transport and medical facilities. He compared the British unfavourably with their French allies, who were better organised and equipped. On 4 April, he wrote:

'On Saturday the troops were landed and sent to their quarters. The force had to lie idle two days and a half watching the seagulls, or with half-averted eye regarding the ceaseless activity of the French, the daily arrival of their steamers and admirable completeness of all their arrangements in every detail – hospitals for the sick, bread and biscuit bakeries, wagon trains for carrying stores and baggage – every necessary and every comfort, indeed, at hand, the moment their ships came in ...

'The French had a perfect baggage train and carried off all their stores and baggage to their camps the moment they landed, while the English were compelled to wait till a proper number of araba carts had been collected, instead of having an organised administration and military train to do what was required.

'The men suffered exceedingly from the cold. Some of them, officers as well as privates, had no beds to lie upon. None of the soldiers had more than their single regulation blanket. They therefore reversed the order of things and dressed to go to bed, putting on all their spare clothing before they tried to sleep. The worst thing was the continued want of comforts for the sick. Many of the men labouring under diseases contracted at Malta were obliged to stay in camp in the cold, with only one blanket under them, as there was no provision for them at the temporary hospital.'

Russell did not hold back in his criticism of individual commanders. He had travelled with the Rifle Brigade and Lieutenant-General Sir George Brown, a veteran of the Peninsular War, and saw first-hand the hidebound attitude regarding dress and appearance:

'If Sir George Brown had his way, the whole race of bear's-grease manufacturers and pomade merchants would have scant grace and no profit. His hatred of hair amounted to almost a mania. "Where there is hair there is dirt, and where there is dirt there will be disease." The stocks, too, were ordered to be kept up, stiff as ever. On the march of the Rifles to their camp at least one man fell out of the ranks senseless; immediate recovery was effected by the simple process of opening the stock. The general would not allow the little black pouches hitherto worn on the belt by officers. They are supposed to carry no pockets, and are not to open their jackets; and the question they very naturally ask is, "Does the general think we are to have no money?"'

These observations did little to enamour him to the Establishment and he was setting himself up to feel the full cold shoulder treatment from the army. When his reports began to be read by the British officers in the camps, he was positively vilified. On one occasion, his tent was pulled down and thrown outside the camp lines.[2]

The Russians then began to advance through Moldavia towards Bulgaria in a move that would threaten Constantinople. To counter this, the Turkish army marched north to check the Russians, while the Allies sailed for Bulgaria to give support.

Once more, ineptitude and chaos accompanied the Allies as they landed at Varna. There was now a more deadly element to contend with – a virulent outbreak of cholera. The disease swept through the camps and in one night alone, 600 men died. After a visit to the main British hospital at Scutari, on the opposite side of the Bosphorus to Constantinople, where the sick were sent, Russell was appalled at the conditions and wrote a letter to Delane outlining the almost total lack of medical care or essential supplies. Although he is often credited with improving conditions at Scutari, it was fellow reporters Thomas Chenery, *The Times'* Constantinople reporter, and Edwin Lawrence Godkin, of the *London Daily News*, who wrote extensively and critically of the conditions at Scutari.

Thomas Chenery, who eventually succeeded Delane as editor of *The Times*, witnessed the disembarkation of the first wounded from the Battle of the Alma. In reports dated 9 and 13 October, he wrote:

'A few of the wounded were well enough to walk, and crept along, supported by a comrade, one with his arm in a sling, another with his trousers cut open from the hip to the knee and the thigh swathed in bandages, another with his hair clotted with blood and a ghastly wound on the face or head. On many the marks of approaching death were set ... It is with feelings of surprise and anger that the public will learn that no sufficient preparatios have been made for the cure of the wounded. Not only are there not sufficient surgeons – not only are there no dressers and nurse ... but what will be said when it is known that there is not even linen to make bandages for the wounded ...

'Can it be said that the battle of the Alma has been an event to take the world by surprise? Has not the expedition to the Crimea been the talk of the last four months? And when the Turks gave up to our use the vast barracks to form the hospital and depot, was it not on the ground that the loss of English troops was sure to be considerable? And yet, after the troops have been six months in the country there is no preparation for the commonest surgical operations! Not only are the men kept, in some cases, for a week without a hand of a medical man coming near their wounds – not only are they left to expire in agony, unheeded and shaken off, though catching desperately at the surgeon whenever he makes his rounds through fetid ships, but now, when they are placed in the spacious building where we were led to believe that everything was ready which could ease their pain and facilitate their recovery, it is found that the commonest appliances of a workhouse sick ward are wanting and that a man must die through the medical staff of the British army having forgotten that old rags are necessary for the dressing of wounds.'

Delane used the furore the reports caused within the British public to launch an appeal for money and clean linen. There was an exceptional response to the appeal and more than £20,000 was raised.

Significantly, the publicity prompted a single-minded nursing superintendent named Florence Nightingale to volunteer for duty. She managed to recruit thirty-eight nurses and, despite much opposition from the Establishment, sailed for Scutari. There she found the sick and wounded soldiers dying in the most appalling conditions. Overcoming hostility from the military, she set about organising the huge barracks hospital and, with discipline and sanitary practices, drastically reduced the mortality rate. Of the 18,058 who died in the Crimea, only 1,761 died from enemy action. Of the 16,297 who died from disease and neglect, 13,150 perished in the first nine months of the war.

Russell's reports took the form of letters to his editor; by turns conversational, rambling, punchy and witty. During the dreary period spent at Varna, Russell resorted to writing some lighter pieces. Tongue in cheek, he wrote of wild Irishmen and Highlanders running amok amongst their French and Turkish allies. He told of a French general whose party trick was to feed his favourite Arab charger with a lump of sugar in his mouth but it went horribly wrong when the horse seized the unfortunate officer by the chin and lip, and gave him a good shaking leaving the general's pride injured and his features rearranged.

While the French and British were wasting away on the Bulgarian coast, their Turkish ally was inflicting a series of defeats on the invading Russians, engagements which effectively ended the fighting. Now with the war concluded without a shot being fired, the British and French felt they could not just pack up and ingloriously return home. It was decided to launch a punitive expedition cross the Black Sea to destroy the main Russian naval base at Sebastopol on the Crimea Peninsula. Without accurate maps and with a complete ignorance of the area, a vast armada carried over 60,000 soldiers, stores, horses and artillery across 350 miles of sea and landed them on a beach at a place prophetically named Calamita Bay. Russell was not the only one to remark on the ominous name.

The usual chaos accompanied the landing on a surf-beaten open shore. Other vessels had joined the invasion fleet and Russell was overjoyed to be greeted by Delane who had sailed especially to meet with him. Despite the loss of his baggage, Russell was in good spirits. He had begged, borrowed and stolen a curious mixture of clothing which included a Rifleman's patrol jacket, cord trousers, butcher's boots with huge brass spurs and the whole ensemble was topped with a Commissariat officer's forage cap. Leaving words of encouragement and more gold sovereigns, Delane re-embarked and sailed back to England. Using twenty of his sovereigns, Russell bought a locally obtained horse from a staff officer, Captain Louis Nolan, who later gained fame as the man who carried the order that sent the Light Brigade to its destruction at Balaklava. Russell described the horse as 'a fiddle-headed, ewe-necked beast – great bone – but not much else'.[3] After a miserable night spent on the open beach in torrential rain without tents, the Allied army lumbered its way towards Sebastopol, twenty-five miles to the south.

With bands playing, the tightly-packed formations of men made a colourful spectacle as they marched across the gently undulating countryside in the autumn sunshine. Unfortunately cholera had followed them from Varna, and soon men were collapsing, to be laid out in jolting locally-obtained carts. Soon the bands ceased playing and the flags lay limply in the breathless air as the vast cavalcade slowly trooped onwards. As it breasted yet another ridge, the men overlooked a valley with the hills in the distance covered with the grey masses of the Russian army. The British commander, Lord Raglan, gave just one order and that was to advance across the River Alma and carry the heights.

Russell recorded in his diary that he felt totally alone because he was not attached to any group and felt very vulnerable. He was also aware that, unlike the soldiers, his wife would not receive a pension should he be killed. In fact his concern was unfounded for *The Times* had invested £500 into a fund for just such a contingency.[4]

The battle began with an artillery duel. Russell was seized with panic. Where should he best position himself to see the action, for the front was several miles wide? Lord Raglan had made it clear that he was not permitted to stand with the Staff, so he took up a position with the Light Division under Sir de Lacy Evans. Soon he came under fire from the Russian batteries and sharpshooters.

Taking shelter in a farmhouse, he began writing – until a shell hit the roof, covering him in broken tiles and mortar. He then rode to a knoll from where he could see much of the battlefield, despite the thick smoke from cannon and burning buildings. With whizz and whoosh of bullet and shot passing him, Russell wrote the first report of a battle by a correspondent under fire. He described the Rifles skirmishing with Russian sharpshooters amongst the vineyards that lined the Alma. He then wrote: 'Up rose these serried masses, and passing through a fearful shower of round, case shot, and shell, they dashed into the Alma, and floundered through its waters, which were literally torn into foam by the deadly hail.'[5] As the walking wounded made their way back to the rear, Russell came upon two severely wounded officers. He led them to the farmhouse he had recently vacated and then rode off to fetch a surgeon. This kind of humanitarian act was often to be repeated by later generations of war reporters.

Meanwhile, the British had managed to cross the river and struggle up the steep banks. 'I heard a tremendous roll of musketry on my left front, and looking in that direction, I saw lines of our red jackets in the stream, and swarming over the wooden bridge. A mass of Russians were on the other side of the stream, firing down on them from the high banks, but the advance of the men across the bridge forced these battalions to retire; and I saw, with feelings which I cannot express, the Light Division, scrambling, rushing, foaming like a bloody surge up the ascent, and in a storm of fire, bright steel, and whirling smoke, charge towards the deadly epaulement [a barricade of earth], from which came roar and flash incessantly. I could distinctly see Sir George Brown and several mounted officers above the heads of the men, and could detect the dark uniforms of the rifles scattered here and there in front of the weaving mass. The rush of shot was appalling and I recollect that I was particularly annoyed by the birds, which were flying about distractedly in the smoke, as I thought they were fragments of shell.'[6]

The Guards and Highlanders were then released to advance steadily up the heights with perfect dressing. Russell recorded:

'But the enemy had not yet abandoned their position. An enormous division of infantry, consisting of several battalions, came in sight from the rear of the hill, and marched straight upon the Brigade of Guards, which it exceeded in numbers by three to one. The Guards advanced to meet them in perfect order. Some round shot struck the rear of the Russian columns, and immediately they began to melt away from the rear, and wavered for an instant; still they came on slowly, and began file-firing from their fronts instead of charging, as their officers evidently intended them to do. The distance between them was rapidly diminishing, when suddenly the whole brigade poured in on their dense masses a fire so destructive that it annihilated the whole of their front ranks in an instant, and left the ridge of killed and wounded men on the ground. The enemy, after a vain attempt to shake off the panic and disorder occasioned by that rain of death, renewed their fire feebly for a few seconds, and then without waiting for a repetition of our reply, turned as our men advanced with bayonets at the charge, retreated over the brow of the hill, and marched off to join the mass of the Russian army, who were retreating with all possible speed … It was near five o'clock; the Battle of the Alma was won.'

After the euphoria of the hard won victory came frustration as no attempt was made to drive on to take Sebastopol, which was at the Allies' mercy. According to Russell, this was what Lord Raglan wanted, but the French commander, Saint Arnaud, was against it. Instead, there was the usual indecision and chaos, resulting in a long diversion to take up position to the south of the city where the Allies intended to bombard the Russians into submission.

On the morning of 26 September, Russell halted on top of a hill: 'Looking down saw under my feet a little pond closely compressed by the sides of high rocky mountains; on it floated some six or seven English ships, for which the exit seemed quite hopeless. The bay is like a highland tarn, some half mile in length from the sea, and varies from 250 to 120 yards in breadth. The shores are so steep and precipitous that they shut out as it were the expanse of the harbour, and make it appear much smaller than it really is.'

This was the tiny village of Balaklava which the British chose as the totally inadequate harbour for their supply base. 'The town was in a filthy, revolting state. Lord Raglan ordered it to be cleansed, but there was no one to obey the order, and consequently no one attended to it.' From there it was a difficult three-mile climb to reach the British trenches dug before Sebastopol. Soon the track became a quagmire made repulsive by the bloated and decomposing bodies of dead horses and draught animals that had died by the wayside; travellers followed this noisome route with trepidation.

Russell wrote: 'On the night of October 10th, soon after dark, 800 men were marched out silently on our left front and commenced making the first British trenches before Sebastopol. A party of 2,000 Turks were also engaged in casting up earthworks for redoubts. These poor fellows worked most willingly and indefatigably, though they were exposed to the greatest privations.'

The Turkish government had sent these men without supplies of food except for a couple biscuits which were soon consumed. The Turks were thus reduced to begging for food, until the ordinary British soldiers spontaneously shared their rations.

Russell reported on the bombardment of Sebastopol that started on 17 October. Before measures to properly protect the powder magazines were implemented, there were four huge explosions in the city and the Allied lines. The biggest occurred just after firing began: 'The French magazine in the extreme right battery of twelve guns blew up with a huge explosion, killing and wounding 100 men. The Russians cheered, fired with renewed vigour, and crushed the French fire completely.'

Billy Russell had now become a familiar figure in the British camp and, whilst not accepted by many senior commanders, he had made some friends amongst the middle-ranking officers. His genial attitude and his Irish sense of humour made him a welcome guest. One friend in particular was Captain Louis Nolan serving on Lord Raglan's staff. He was regarded as one of the outstanding cavalry horsemen of his day and had written books about training horses and cavalry tactics. Nolan was vocally contemptuous of both cavalry commanders, the Lords Lucan and Cardigan, and was joined by Russell who noted: 'Lord Lucan is a hard man to get on with. But the moment the Government of the day made the monstrous choice of his brother-in-law, Lord Cardigan, as the Brigadier of the Light Brigade of the Cavalry Division, knowing well the relations between the officers and the nature of the two men, they became responsible for disaster; they were guilty of treason to the Army – neither more nor less.'

Nolan was frustrated that the Light Brigade had been held back from any fighting, not because of the squabbling lords, but by Lord Raglan who insisted in keeping his cavalry 'in a bandbox'. In a most tragic manner, he would soon get his way.

Chapter 3

Balaklava

With most of the Allies involved in the siege, a smaller force guarded the rear and Balaklava itself. It was from this secondary theatre that Russell's most memorable report came. Although persistent rumours should have alerted Lord Raglan that a Russian army was marching from the interior towards Balaklava, the British were unprepared. On the evening of 24 October 1854, Russell visited the camp of the Light Brigade and, as he left, was joined by his friend, Captain Louis Nolan. As the night was cold and Russell was only wearing a thin coat, Nolan insisted he borrow his cloak with the provision that he return it the following day as he had no use for it that night: 'Nor did he next night or ever after.'

Captain Nolan of the 15th Hussars served as a staff officer during the Crimean War. He had been brought up in Italy, where his father was British Vice-Consul, and had attended a military academy. He had developed such an aptitude for riding that he was presented with a commission into a crack Austrian cavalry regiment. He was persuaded to join the British Army and was soon recognised as the foremost horseman in the cavalry. Nolan took his career very seriously and was dismissive of his aristocratic and inept superiors, many of whom had only gained their position through privilege. During the war he had become outspoken at the way that the cavalry had been under-used and he was desperate to see them in action. Fate made him the instrument that sent him and the Light Brigade to their destruction.[1]

At dawn on 25 October, the Russians crossed the Tchernaya River and occupied the Fedoukhine Heights overlooking the North Valley. Their cavalry and infantry crossed the valley and advanced along the Woronzoff Road which ran east to west along a chain of hills called the Causeway Heights. This outpost of the British line was defended by a few Turkish-manned earthworks armed with some naval guns. It was the firing from these guns that sent Russell riding towards the sound of battle. He arrived at the edge of the Sapoune Heights, a position which gave him a panoramic view down the North Valley to where the main body of Russians was assembled. He saw the line of earthworks along the Causeway Heights and, to his right, the South Valley leading into Balaklava itself. Below he could see the cavalry camp sited amongst some vineyards at the base of the Causeway Heights. The only infantry he could make out was the 93rd Regiment of Highlanders, drawn up under the heights above Balaklava and supported by some Royal Marine artillery.

Russell arrived just as the Russians overwhelmed Number 1 Redoubt, the furthermost earthwork, and put the Turks to flight. The next two redoubts quickly fell and the plain leading to Balaklava was filled with Turks running for their lives pursued by Russian cavalry. As the latter came within range, the two ranks of the 93rd, under the command of Sir Colin Campbell, fired a volley. Together with the Marines' artillery rounds, this caused the Russians to turn about and return to the Causeway Heights. Russell immortalised this action in a phrase, now misquoted and beloved of headline writers. He wrote: 'The ground flies beneath their horses' feet; gathering speed at every stride, they dash towards that thin red streak topped with a line of steel.'[2] For some reason, it has been altered to 'the thin red line' and taken into the English language to mean any last-ditch defence against overwhelming odds.

'As the Russian come within six hundred yards, down goes the line of steel in front, and out rings a rolling volley of musketry. The distance is too great; the Russians are not checked, but still sweep onwards through the smoke, with the whole force of horse and man, here and there knocked overt by the shot of our batteries above. With breathless suspense every one awaits the bursting of the wave upon the line of Gaelic rock; but ere they come within two hundred and fifty yards, another deadly volley flashes from the levelled rifle, and carries terror among the Russians. They wheel about, open files right and left and flee faster than they came.'

With the Russians deflected by the Highlanders, they retreated to the main body of cavalry on the Causeway Heights. The next phase of the evolving battle happened as the British Heavy Brigade, under the command of the myopic General James Scarlett, was forming up at the base of the Causeway Heights preparing to go to the aid of the 93rd. Suddenly, the mass of grey Russian cavalry appeared on the skyline above them. With just 500 yards separating the two sides, the Russians began to descend the slope towards the greatly outnumbered Heavy Brigade, which was still trying to deploy to counter the attack. Then, with just 100 yards to go, the Russian commander ordered a halt. Scarlett squinted at the massed ranks of grey and ordered his men to charge. Russell saw what looked like certain defeat for the British as the first two regiments cantered uphill and disappeared into the centre of the massed ranks of Russians.

'There is a clash of steel and a light play of sword-blades in the air, and then the Greys and the red coats disappear in the midst of the shaken and quivering columns. In another moment we see them emerging with diminished numbers, and in broken order, charging the second line … By sheer steel and sheer courage Enniskillener and Scot are winning their desperate way right through the enemy's squadrons, and already grey horses and red coats appear right at the rear of the second mass, when, with irresistible force, like one bolt from a bow, the 4th Dragoon Guards, riding straight at the right flank of the Russians, and the 5th Dragoon Guards, following close after the Enniskilleners, rush at the remnants of the first line of the enemy, go through it as though it was made of pasteboard, and put them to utter rout.'

The result was a heaving tussle in which the Russians were almost passive. Finally, the British fought their way through and the Russians began to retreat up the slope until they disappeared over the summit of the Causeway Heights. Russell wrote that 'a cheer burst from every lip ... officers and men took off their caps and shouted with delight'.[3]

The battle was not yet over, for fifteen minutes later a misunderstood order sent the 600 men of the Light Brigade charging up the North Valley to their destruction and immortality. From his perch high above the battle, Russell observed what Lord Raglan and his staff had seen; the Russians retreating along the Causeway Heights and dragging away the naval guns from the captured redoubts. Raglan gave orders for the Light Brigade to advance, harry the retreating Russians and prevent them carrying away these guns. Down on the floor of the valley, the Light Cavalry could not see what was happening on top of the Causeway Heights and the only guns they could see were those lined up at the far end of the North Valley in front of the main Russian army.

Uncertain of the meaning of the series of confusing orders, Lord Lucan, the cavalry commander, delayed any movement. Impatiently, Raglan wrote a fourth cryptic note and handed it to Russell's friend, Nolan. Russell watched as the headstrong officer plunged his horse down the steep escarpment and delivered the order to Lucan. Still unable to understand the purpose of Raglan's instructions, Lucan asked where were the guns he was supposed to prevent being carried away. Contemptuous of Lucan, Nolan threw his arm in the vague direction of the Russian guns and pointed down the North Valley saying, 'There, my Lord, is your enemy; there are your guns'. Stung into action by Nolan's insolence, Lucan gave the fatal order to his brother-in-law, Lord Cardigan, to advance down the North Valley and capture the Russian guns. The combination of an ambiguously written order from Lord Raglan and Nolan's ill-concealed impatience caused the Light Brigade to advance up the North Valley towards the main Russian army instead of veering right up the Causeway

Heights to prevent the captured British guns being carried away from the redoubts.

Even from his position on the Sapoune Heights, Russell clearly heard in the still air the commands given to advance. With a soft jangling of harness and scraping of unsheathed swords, the colourful cavalcade moved off. Russell noted that the Light Brigade had been so reduced by sickness that it scarcely made a regiment.

It soon became apparent that they were not going to swing right and climb the Causeway Heights, but were heading into the part of the North Valley covered on three sides by the Russians. The same thought must have occurred to Nolan, for he spurred forward across Lord Cardigan's path in an attempt to divert the Brigade towards the Causeway Heights. At the time, Russell thought Nolan was cheering on the command. As he did so, the first shot was fired by the Russians. By a tragic fluke, a steel splinter from this random bursting shot penetrated Nolan's chest and killed him. Now, with the last chance of saving the Light Brigade gone, Lord Cardigan led his men into Tennyson's 'Valley of Death'. Russell's report appeared in *The Times* on Tuesday, 14 November, almost twenty days after the event. It is indicative of how much the presentation of news has changed since then. After turning five pages of advertisements, births, deaths, marriages and stock market news it was not until page six that the main news was printed.

Under the headline 'The Cavalry Action at Balaklava', Russell wrote: 'The whole brigade scarcely made one effective regiment (607 sabres), according to the numbers of continental armies; and yet it was more than we could spare. As they passed the front, the Russians opened on them from the guns in the redoubt on the right, with volleys of musketry and rifles. They swept proudly past, glittering in the morning sun in all the pride and splendour of war. We could scarcely believe the evidence of our senses! Surely that handful of men are not going to charge an army in position? Alas! it was but too true – their desperate valour knew no bounds, and far indeed was it removed from its so-called better part – discretion. They advanced in two lines, quickening their pace as they closed towards the enemy. A more fearful spectacle was never witnessed than by those who, without the power to aid, beheld their heroic countrymen rushing to the arms of death. At the distance of 1,200 yards the whole line of the enemy belched forth, from 30 iron mouths, a flood of smoke and flame, through which hissed the deadly balls. Their flight was marked by instant gaps in our ranks, by dead men and horses, by steeds flying wounded or riderless across the plain. The first line is broken, it is joined by the second, they never halt or check their speed an instant; with diminished ranks, thinned by those 30 guns, which the Russians had laid with deadly accuracy, with a halo of flashing steel above their heads, and with a cheer which was many a noble fellow's death-cry, they flew into the smoke of the batteries, but ere they were lost from view the plain was strewed with their bodies and with the carcasses of horses. They were exposed to an oblique fire from the batteries on the hills on both sides, as well as to the direct fire of musketry. Through the clouds of smoke we could see their sabres flashing as they rode up to the guns and dashed between them, cutting down the gunners as they stood. We saw them riding through the guns, as I have said; to our delight we saw them returning, after breaking through a column of infantry, and scattering them like chaff, when the flank fire of the battery on the hill swept them down, scattered and broken as they were. Wounded men and dismounted troopers flying towards us told us the sad tale – demi-gods could not have done what they had failed to do. At the very moment they were about to retreat an enormous mass of Lancers was hurled on their flank. Colonel Shewell, of the 8th Hussars saw the danger, and rode his few men straight at them, cutting his way through with fearful loss. The other regiments turned and engaged in a most desperate encounter. With courage too great almost for credence, they were breaking their way through the columns which enveloped them.'[4]

This report, for all its archaic and flowery turn of phrase, captured the essence of another heroic British failure. Its impact on the British public was immense. For the first time ever, a reporter had been in the position to observe the unfolding of a complete battle. With the panorama of the battlefield spread below him, Russell was able to write in comfort and with little danger to himself. Although historians have been able to fill in the details of the famous charge, Russell was accurate with the duration of twenty-five minutes and its progression. His reporting had a similar impact on the British public that television coverage of the Vietnam War had on American viewers. With his graphic and hard-hitting reports, Russell had invented a new pattern of reporting, one which is taken as normal today.

After the charge, Billy Russell descended into the North Valley and talked with some of the survivors, who seemed unaware that they had taken part in an event that lives in the memory despite being a pointless and wasteful failure. *The Times* refused to blame Nolan's impulsiveness for the destruction of the Light Brigade and Russell paid tribute to his friend, writing: 'A braver soldier than Captain Nolan the army did not possess. A matchless horseman and first rate swordsman. God forbid I should cast a shade on his honour.'

A few days later Russell was joined by another *Times* correspondent, a Hungarian named Ferdinand Eber, who has been described as writing English like a native but speaking like an Hungarian. Both Specials were under fire nine days later as they tried to make sense of the Battle of Inkerman, fought in swirling mist and dense scrub. It was a most confusing and savage contest, largely fought by small pockets of men acting instinctively and with no one person in overall command. The heavily outnumbered British managed to repel the dense ranks of Russians, but at a high cost. Unlike the Alma and Balaklava, where he could safely view a battle, Russell wrote of the confusion and danger he encountered as he tried to make sense of the Inkerman assault:

'Let me say, it is – for a man who has no orders to obey, no orders to give, to find himself under fire, a strange position – very uncomfortable to say the least of it. He cannot if he cares for his own good opinion, or for those around him, gallop off ventre a terre [at full speed]. If a bullet finds its billet in his body corporate, he knows that the general verdict will be 'Serve him right', what business had he to get in the way?'

Sickened by the sights that he had witnessed, Russell turned to Eber that evening and exclaimed, 'God! Wasn't it an awful day?' Eber, who relished the sound of gunfire and who would later seek out further wars, replied, 'Awful, no, a most bewdiful day: fine baddle as ever vos. No men ever fide bedder. De Generals should all be shot.'[5]

Eber was one of those individuals who got a buzz from being under fire and preferred fighting to writing. In 1860 he was sent by *The Times* to cover Garibaldi's invasion of Sicily and, to the consternation of the editors, ended up being appointed a general commanding a brigade in the insurgent army.

Arguably, it was during this War of Italian Unification that the first female war correspondent emerged. She was an English woman named Jessie Meriton White, who was married to one of Garibaldi's officers. She served mostly as a nurse, but did send reports of Garibaldi in Sicily and his march to Naples to the *Daily News*. The Italians feted her as a heroine and after the war she continued to write freelance for the *Daily News* and the New York papers, the *Tribune, Times* and *Evening Post*.

It was, however, Russell's graphic description of the Inkerman battle and the terrible wounds suffered by both armies that had a shock effect on *The Times*' readers. Russell saw his old adversary, Sir George Brown, carried from the battlefield with wounds to his arm and side: 'I saw with regret his pale and sternly composed face, as he was borne by me on a litter early in the day, his white hair flickering in the breeze, for I knew we had lost the services of a good soldier that day.' The sixty-five-year-old Sir George was made of stern stuff and returned to duty by the following spring.

Two days later, while walking the battlefield with the burial parties, Russell was almost killed by a Russian shell which tore a hole in his coat.

Despite the continued hostility shown Russell by the high command, his easy-going, clubbable manner made him popular with most officers and he began to find life a little easier as he became more accepted. Indeed, as a result of his campaigning journalism, supplies, clothing and accommodation improved during 1855. It can be said that he was indirectly responsible for the instigation of the Victoria Cross, for his reports of bravery and fortitude by junior officers and the ordinary soldier had an effect with MPs like Captain George Scobell who raised the subject of a gallantry award in Parliament.

The winter of 1854-55 was one of the most severe on record, and was endured by the ill-prepared British. By the spring of 1855, they had all but ceased to be a functioning force.

Russell himself wrote under the greatest physical difficulties. Irregular meals often meant he was cold and hungry as he tried to write by the flickering light of a single candle in a draughty tent. Sometimes he resorted to manufacturing ink from gunpowder, something soldiers were still doing twenty-five years later during the Zulu War. Another result of Russell's exposure of the mismanagement of the army was that the Government of Lord Aberdeen lost a vote of confidence and was forced to resign in January 1855.

At the end of April 1855, the Allies embarked on an attack on the Russian coastal bases 150 miles northeast of the Crimean Peninsula. This was the main supply route for the Russian army and a successful disruption would greatly hamper the enemy's efforts. Billy Russell managed to secrete himself onboard the transport *Hope* against the orders of the expedition's commander, General Sir George Brown, who must have wished he had been more diligent in banning this troublesome newsman.

Although the expedition was a success, with military stores and supplies destroyed, it was the wanton destruction of civilian property that appalled Russell and he did not hold back in his description of these acts of vandalism:

'When the troops marched into Kertch the following morning, the population (left behind) made their submission, and offered bread and salt to the conquerors, in accordance with the Russian custom, and they were assured that they would be protected, and that their lives and property should be spared.

'The troops marched onto Yenikale, leaving behind them a few sailors and soldiers to guard Kertch ... in the afternoon ... the crews of some merchant ships landed and began to break into three or four houses, which had been closed and fastened up, and to pillage the contents. As they couldn't remove the heavy furniture they smashed it to atoms. Towards the evening Turkish stragglers from the camp, and others who had fallen out of the line of march, flocked into the town and perpetrated the most atrocious crimes. To pillage and wanton devastation they added violation and murder.'

The indigenous Tartars welcomed the Turkish stragglers as liberators united in their hatred of the Russians, and led them to the houses of those they particularly didn't like. Soon killing was added to pillage.

'The French patrols endeavoured to preserve order ... but not until they had killed and wounded several Turks and Tartars. One miscreant was shot as he came down the street in triumph waving a sword wet with the blood of a poor child whom he had hacked to pieces.'

The next day some British merchantmen joined in the destruction by entering an ancient temple and destroying the contents.

'One might well wonder how the fury of a few men could effect such a prodigious amount of ruin in so short a time. The floor is covered for several inches in depth with the debris of broken glass, of vases, urns, statuary, the precious dust of their contents and charred bits of wood and bone, mingled with the fresh splinters of the shelves, desks and cases in which they had been preserved.'

By the time the vandals had finished, there was virtually nothing left of the town. Although the violence had not been perpetrated by British soldiers, Russell was scathing that General Brown had not left a force to secure and protect its streets and buildings.

When Russell returned from what remained of Kertch, he found that his temporary replacement, thirty-year-old William Stowe, was dying of cholera in his hut. Stowe was almoner and distributor of *The Times* Benevolent Fund at Scutari and was a devoted supporter of Florence Nightingale and the Sanitary Commission. He also reported on events at Scutari for *The Times*. Sir John Hall, Inspector of Hospitals and Chief of the Medical Staff of the Army, resented any criticism of his inefficient and chaotic methods at the Scutari Barrack Hospital and described Stowe as a 'miserable penny-a-line youth'. Stowe had written: 'Florence Nightingale arrived and order out of chaos sprung.' He died at the Balaklava Hospital on 22 June 1855.

Such was the interest in the war that there were many civilian travellers and tourists who visited the Allied positions. Around the time of the fall of Sebastopol in June 1855, a certain Indian gentleman named Azimullah Khan, whom Russell had met briefly in Constantinople, visited the British lines. Russell gave him a conducted tour and found his guest somewhat disparaging about the British in comparison with the French, which coming from Russell was a bit rich. Good host that he was, Russell gave up his bed and tent for a night and the next day bade his Indian guest goodbye. It later transpired that Khan was gathering intelligence and, encouraged by the weakened state of the army, recommended to his fellow conspirators a move to overthrow British rule in India. This came about two years later with the outbreak of the Indian Mutiny. Azimullah Khan was secretary and military adviser to Nana Sahib, one of the leaders of the Indian Mutiny. Khan had a fierce hatred for the British and it was he who ordered the killing of the British survivors of the siege at Cawnpore.

William Russell was not the only correspondent to be employed by the British press, but he was the only one to make a deep impression with the British public. Russell was dismissive of his fellow correspondents remarking: '*The Morning Herald* correspondent [Nicholas Woods] lives on board the *Caradoc*, and comes ashore now and then after the battle to view the ground. The *Daily News* [Edwin Lawrence Godkin] lives on board another ship and never I believe comes on shore at all.'[6]

Russell was unjustly critical of fellow Irish reporter Godkin, who more than Russell brought the conditions of the Scutari hospital to the public's attention. Godkin wrote as early as January 1854: 'One would imagine that thousands of young surgeons who are starving in England and France would flock here to fill up the vacancies which exist in every regiment.' He described the conditions of the army as winter approached: 'With common care our troops might have been hutted before the setting in of the rainy season. With common care, field hospitals of wood and straw work might have been erected for the reception of the wounded. With common care, medicines would not be allowed to rot in bulk in Constantinople, while brave men die and doctors despair for the want of them.'

In his despatch of 25 November 1854, Billy Russell had also described the worsening conditions:

'It is now pouring rain, the skies are black as ink, the wind is howling over the staggering tents, the trenches are turned into dykes, in the tents the water is sometimes a foot deep, our men have not either warm or waterproof clothing, they are out for twelve hours at a time in the trenches, they are plunged into the inevitable miseries of a winter campaign, and not a soul seems to care for their lives.'

The *Morning Advertiser* employed George Alfred Henty, who had volunteered with his brother Frederick for active service at the outbreak of the war. They were employed as part of the hospital commissariat but sadly Frederick died of cholera at Scutari and George was later invalided home. When he recovered, he was promoted to the Army Purveyors Department. Although he made little impact with his Crimean despatches, he did report on other conflicts, including the Franco-Prussian War for *The Standard*. He went on to fame and fortune as a writer of ripping historical yarns for boys.

The Crimean War was also the first conflict in which war artists were used. William Simpson was an illustrator who managed to persuade the print publisher Colnaghi to send him to the war zone so he could capture the conditions and terrain at Sebastopol. The results were well received and made Colnaghi a handsome profit, but Simpson had to be content with some spin-off commissions. Although he arrived after the main battles of 1854, he accurately conveyed the fighting by closely questioning those who had taken part. One of those was Lord Cardigan, who was recuperating on his luxury yacht in Balaklava harbour. It took three attempts by Simpson to depict the Charge of the Light Brigade before Cardigan was satisfied with its accuracy. Besides showing the heroic action, Simpson also drew scenes such as the 'Embarkation of the Sick and Wounded at Balaklava', that conveyed the reality of war to the British public.

The most popular pictorial weekly, *The Illustrated London News*, sent its own correspondent/artist, Joseph Archer Crowe, to the Crimea, as well as half a dozen other special artists. On his return from the Crimea, Crowe received an offer to direct an art school in India. When he arrived in India, the post did not materialise and he turned to journalism again, becoming *The Times'* correspondent during the start of the Indian Mutiny. Illness cut short his time in India and he was replaced by Billy Russell. He returned to England and was *The Times'* correspondent during the Austro-Italian War, being present at the Battle of Solferino. Crowe eventually entered the diplomatic service, and served in the Berlin and Vienna embassies before retiring with a knighthood in 1890.

In the same way that Russell's reports eventually lead to an improvement in the soldier's lot, so war photography can also be said to have started with *The Times'* despatches. Prince Albert found Russell's reports so critical that he suggested a photographer be sent to the Crimea in order to show that conditions were not as bad as they were described. Roger Fenton was commissioned by a Manchester print-dealer, Thomas Agnew, to travel to the Crimea to take a series of photographs. He was ordered to photograph healthy-looking, warmly clothed and well-fed soldiers posed around camp fires, as well as images of commanding officers and their staffs, distant shots of tented camps and regiments on parade. Great care was taken not to show dead bodies.

Photography was still in its infancy, but it had captured the public's imagination. The combination of this fascinating new medium and a 'popular' war was irresistible. Despite the cumbersome equipment and difficulties of processing in the field, it was considered as both in the public's interest and commercially viable to travel to this remote and rugged seat of war to photograph it for posterity.

Roger Fenton is sometimes credited with being the first war photographer. There are, however, several others who could make this claim. One was James Robertson, an amateur photographer working for the Turkish Imperial Mint, who covered the beginning of the war with photographs of the British arriving at Scutari and embarking at Varna. Like Fenton, he photographed posed groups of soldiers and scenes around the Allied lines. Unlike Fenton, whose three-month stay in the Crimea was cut short by cholera, Robertson photographed Sebastopol and its fortifications after its fall. Even there he was not allowed to photograph any distressing images. His famous photograph of the interior of the Redan after its capture was taken after the removal of all dead bodies. Despite his more extensive coverage, Robertson's efforts were overshadowed by those of Fenton, who was presented to Queen Victoria and Prince Albert and, later, Napoleon III.

When the war broke out, the War Office decided to send an official photographer named Richard Nicklin, together with a couple of Royal Engineers specially trained in photography. They photographed throughout 1854 but sadly the results of Nicklin's efforts have been lost to posterity. During the Great Storm which hit the area on the night of 14 November 1854, he, his assistants and all the plates and equipment went down with their ship, *Rip Van Winkle*.[7]

Because of the limitations of early photography, moving subjects could not be captured. Instead, both Fenton and Robertson have left us with a wonderful portfolio of stiffly posed groups, tented camps, distant parades as well as some excellent views of the overcrowded Balaklava harbour, the interior of the Redan after the fall of Sebastopol and a panoramic view from Lord Raglan's viewpoint on the Sapoune escarpment of the Balaklava battlefield.[8]

With the war settling into the unglamorous routine bombardment of Sebastopol, Russell continued to send long despatches back to Editor Delane. Although conditions were difficult, he had the freedom to go where he liked and talk with whom he liked. He worked for the most influential newspaper in the world and for an editor who gave him unlimited space and support and who had turned him into a celebrity in his own right. Russell's reports were of some 6,000 words, which were accepted by mid-Victorian readers but would be too long by later standards.

He continued to expose the failures of the High Command and to attack the Government. It was these attacks and Delane's scathing editorials that were instrumental in the downfall of Aberdeen's Government, as well as an improvement in supplies and clothing for the troops. Years later, Field Marshal Sir Evelyn Wood acknowledged that Russell's revelations saved what was left of the army. It was at the onset of the 1854 winter that Russell got into his stride with his criticism of Lord Raglan's leadership and, with the death of Lord Raglan on 28 June 1855, Russell was accused of part-responsibility for his demise. Indeed, Russell had written his opinion of Raglan as early as the Alma battle:

'That Lord Raglan was brave as a hero of antiquity, that he was kind to his friends and to his staff, that he was unmoved under fire, and unaffected by personal danger, that he was noble in manner, gracious in demeanour, of dignified bearing, I am ready to admit; that he had many and great difficulties to contend with I believe; but that this brave and gallant nobleman had lost, if he ever possessed, the ability to conceive and execute large military plans – and that he had lost, if he ever possessed, the faculty of handling great bodies of men, I am firmly persuaded.' Russell had seen nothing since to change his mind.

Delane told him six months after Raglan's death that 'It is believed that you killed Raglan'. Indeed, William Legge, the Earl of Dartmouth, believed so and carried on a vitriolic correspondence with Russell for a further twenty-one years.

Russell was also taken to task for providing the Russians with information, mostly about shortages and declining morale. In early November 1854, he wrote that the army's weakest point was its thinly defended eastern flank which caused great consternation with Raglan's staff. Tsar Nicholas stated: 'We have no need of spies; we have *The Times*.'

At the end of the war in 1856, Russell returned to England and great acclaim. Delane, no doubt in an effort to keeps his protégé's feet on the ground, then sent him off to cover the new Tsar's coronation in St Petersburg. When he did return to London he embarked on a highly successful lecture tour which included London, Glasgow, Edinburgh and Dublin. It was at one of these lectures that he fired the imagination of a young cavalry trooper named Archibald Forbes, a man destined to become almost as famous as Russell himself.

To the veterans of the Crimea, Russell was regarded as their champion. One Irish trooper, who had ridden down the North Valley with the 4th Light Dragoons, left the army and sought a new life in the United States. On arriving in New York, he gave his name as William Russell Parnell, a combination of the men he admired the most. He enlisted into the Union Army and ended the American Civil War as a lieutenant-colonel. He later won the Congressional Medal of Honour during the US-Indian Wars.

William Simpson, the special artist, also enhanced his reputation, if not his pocket. He had enjoyed a good relationship with Lord Raglan, who allowed the use of his own post-bag to send back his sketches to Colnaghi's. Upon his return to London, he found that he had gained the approval of the Establishment and, in particular, Queen Victoria. A steady stream of commissions gave him independence to act as a freelance but, in 1866, he succumbed to a generous offer and joined the *Illustrated London News* as a permanent staff artist.

The reporting of the Crimean War established the polarisation between the military and the media which was present in every subsequent conflict. The military obviously wished to keep their plans and the conditions of their men secret from the opposition, while the press believed that the facts should be published, even at the risk of giving comfort to the enemy. Russell's writing inspired the Poet Laureate, Alfred Lord Tennyson, to compose his poem *The Charge of the Light Brigade,* further establishing the gallant failure in the nation's psyche.

Despite some inaccuracies and unfair criticism, Russell single-handedly put war reporting on the map. A radical by nature, his Irish charm allowed him to disarm most of his critics and he was to enjoy the confidence of many in the Establishment. Although he went onto report other wars, Russell's life was to be conditioned by his Crimean experience and, as will be seen, he was unable to adapt to new technology and competitive news gathering.

Chapter 4

Eastern Troubles

Britain at the zenith of her power enjoyed great prosperity as the world's leading nation. As if to undermine her complacency, however, there occurred an event that shook her confidence and altered her outlook forever. The country was at peace after the Crimean War – apart from a largely naval operation in China and a small-scale expedition against Persia, neither of which were regarded by the newspapers as important enough to send their Specials.

Chinese resentment of European traders in the five ports ceded to the British after the First China War of 1840-42, led to the Second China War (1856-57), during which the Royal Navy easily destroyed a force of Chinese junks. A treaty was signed in 1858, which opened eleven more ports open to European trade, a significant cargo being opium. This fuelled further resentment resulting in the Third China War of 1860.

The Anglo-Persian War (1856-57) was fought because the Afghan city of Herat had been annexed by Persia. Britain wished to keep Afghanistan as a buffer state against the perceived threat from Russian expansion and sided with the Afghans in this dispute. The British launched a successful amphibious attack in the Persian Gulf which resulted in the Persians withdrawing from Herat and opening up Persia for British trade.

In 1857, India was ruled by the Honourable East India Company (HEIC), which had originally been established as a trading company a century before by Robert Clive. A hundred years later its role had shifted as, one by one, the many Indian principalities were either defeated in battle or peacefully submitted until the Company controlled the vast area from the Himalayas to the southernmost tip of the sub-continent. Although Britain benefited through trade and taxes, the HEIC ran the country as the British Government's representative. It had its own civil servants, judiciary, administrators and, fatally, her own army.

The HEIC Army was in fact made up of three separate commands: Madras, Bombay and Bengal. Of this trio, the Bengal army was regarded as the most expensive, inefficient and poorly led. The white officers were generally contemptuous of their native soldiers, while the sepoys had little respect for their commanders. The Bengal sepoys were mostly high-caste Brahmins, who saw themselves as superior to the more tolerant soldiers of the other two armies. They made demands that became increasingly difficult to keep; one of which was a refusal to be sent on service overseas. Through neglect and ignorance, the Bengal army had declined to the point where its loyalty could not be relied upon. With resentment simmering just below the surface, the time was ripe for a release of anger and hatred. It only needed a spark to set a tragic chain of events in motion.

By May 1857, there had been plenty of signs that trouble was brewing, but a combination of arrogance and weakness overrode the advice of clearer heads. It took the insensitive action of the colonel of the 34th Native Regiment at Meerut to set off the uprising. The new Enfield cartridge was rumoured to be coated with animal fat, which was an anathema to both Muslim and Hindu alike; in fact, it was actually lubricated with vegetable oil. The fact that the cartridge did not infringe religious sensibilities was not explained and as far as the white officers were concerned the native sepoys were guilty of disobedience in refusing to accept the new cartridge. The heavy-handed colonel humiliated his men by calling a parade and ordering those who refused the new cartridge to be manacled and marched off to prison. The outcome was that the sepoys turned their arms against their officers and then, joined by local civilians, slaughtered the officers' wives and children.

With no clear objective, the mutineers set out for Delhi, gathering more supporters along the way. Like a brush fire, news of the outbreak at Meerut spread to other garrisons where more regiments mutinied until those Europeans who had escaped the initial bloodletting took refuge together in hastily prepared defensive enclaves. There they became besieged for weeks and months, waiting in vain for relief to be sent by the British Government.

The Times did have a correspondent in Calcutta: Cecil Beadon, who was Home Secretary to the Indian Government. Beadon had to be very circumspect, as it was forbidden for employees of the HEIC to communicate with the press. Although he reported on the transfer of British troops out of India, thus weakening the British presence, he has been criticised for failing to recognise the approaching storm. Even when the mutinous 19th Native Infantry had been ceremoniously disarmed and disbanded in April he wrote reassuringly that 'the Empire is in no danger. There is, so far as we know, no real disaffection among the great body of the Army.'[1] The following month the Great Mutiny began, but it was still regarded by the Establishment as a little local difficulty. Because of the vast distances and poor communications, news of the Bengal army's mutiny and the shocking massacre at Cawnpore took weeks to reach Britain.

The nearest British regiments had just completed fighting in the Anglo-Persian War (1856-57) and were either still in Persia or on their way to Calcutta. Other British regiments were en-route to fight the Chinese and had to be diverted from Singapore or Hong Kong. When they arrived, these regiments were hurried to the seat of the Mutiny, the state of Oude in central northern India. Though heavily outnumbered, they managed to hold on with the support of loyal troops, mostly from the Punjab, until the British Government was able to send a strong force to stamp out the rebellion and lift the many sieges, the largest of which was at Lucknow. The man they chose for the task was Sir Colin Campbell, who had commanded the Highland Brigade in the Crimea and had stood with the 'Thin Red Line' at Balaklava. Joseph Crowe had been sent as *The Times'* correspondent but ill-health forced his return. Delane somewhat reluctantly decided to interrupt William Russell's successful lecture tour and sent him to report on Campbell's progress and to provide an impartial account of events.

Leaving on Boxing Day, 1857, Russell travelled overland and by sea, reaching Calcutta four weeks later. His impressions of the British he encountered along the way were not favourable. He particularly hated the attitude they took toward the Indian population and was sceptical about the horror stories of massacres that were rife. There was an unhealthy thirst for revenge and retribution, regarding all those with brown skins as the enemy. As he travelled to join Campbell at Cawnpore, he saw evidence of this as he passed bodies hanging from trees and slogans daubed on walls proclaiming, 'Revenge your slaughtered countrywomen'. The worst aspect of the infamous Cawnpore massacre was not so much that Britons had been killed but that 'the deed was done by a subject race – by black men who dared to shed the blood of their masters,' Russell wrote, after visiting the Bibigarh where 206 women and children were butchered in cold blood. 'One fact is clearly established; that the writing behind the door, on the walls of the slaughterhouse, on which so much stress was laid in Calcutta, did not exist when [Sir Henry] Havelock entered the place, and therefore cannot be the work of any of the poor victims … God knows the horrors and atrocity of the pitiless slaughter needed no aggravation. Soldiers in the heat of action need little excitement to vengeance.'[2]

In contrast to the ostracism he had experienced at the hands of the military in the Crimea, Russell was warmly welcomed by Sir Colin Campbell and his staff. General Sir Colin Campbell (1792-1863), whose real name was Colin McIver, was the eldest son of a Glasgow carpenter. He fought under Wellington during the Peninsular War and served all over the world including America, China, India and the West Indies. When the Crimean War broke out he was on half-pay and returned to take command of the Highland Division. Of all the brigade commanders who served in the Crimea, Campbell was the most respected and capable. He had a reputation for steadiness and hard discipline and gained public fame because of his command of the 93rd Sutherland Highlanders at Balaklava, the regiment having been described by Russell as 'the thin red streak tipped with steel'. Then his caution and lack of dash during the Indian Mutiny earned him the nickname of 'Sir Crawling Camel'. Nevertheless, he remained a hero with the public and a favorite of Queen Victoria. After the Mutiny had been suppressed, Campbell was honoured and retired as Field-Marshal Lord Clyde.

Billy Russell was placed in the charge of Lieutenant Patrick Stewart, who was the Deputy-Superintendent of the Indian Telegraphs, a most happy arrangement for a correspondent. Being the only journalist in the column, Russell enjoyed both exclusivity and executive help in getting his reports telegraphed back to Calcutta. By the end of his stay in India, Russell had managed to run up a telegraph bill of £5,000, which the management swallowed in the knowledge that *The Times* virtually had the campaign to itself.

Russell joined Campbell's column as the men completed their preparations to mount an expedition to recapture Lucknow. With a force of 20,000 men and 54 heavy guns, Campbell was determined not to suffer the fate of the previous relief expeditions under Sir Henry Havelock and his own second relief in November.

Russell kept up a flow of lengthy detailed reports which were noticeably free of racism or stories of atrocities. Russell was troubled by the many stories he had heard of violence against women and children but could not find any concrete evidence. He saw slogans and messages scrawled on walls such as: 'We are at the mercy of savages who have ravished young and old' and 'Remember the 15th of July, 1857 … Oh! My Child! Countrymen, revenge!' These had not been written at the time of the early outrages but long afterwards and aimed at inflaming passing soldiers. Both his reports and Delane's editorials helped to calm the British public's anger and thirst for revenge. Campbell's mission, as he saw it, was to try to surround Lucknow and prevent the rebels escaping, while keeping his line of retreat safe.

Campbell had evacuated the Residency in November and left a force under Sir James Outram to hold the walled palace and grounds of the Alambagh just south of Lucknow. Although it was attacked, the 5,000-strong force kept the rebels at bay. When Campbell reached them, the enemy had pulled back allowing the British to occupy the Dilkusha and its parkland to the east of the city, but the closer they got to Lucknow, the more intense the fighting became.

Russell witnessed the desperate fighting, in which no prisoners were taken. He described the taking of the Begum Kothie: 'The fight was very close and desperate for some time; but the strength of the 93rd and the fury of the Sikhs carried everything before it. From court to court, and building to building, the sepoys were driven, leaving in each hundreds of men bayoneted and shot. The scene was horrible. The rooms in which the sepoys lay burning slowly in their cotton clothing, with their skin crackling and their flesh roasting literally in its own fat, whilst a light-bluish, vapoury smoke, of disgusting odour, formed a veil through which the dreadful sight could be dimly seen, were indeed chambers of horrors ineffable. It was before breakfast, and I could not stand the smell.'

First the Martinière School was taken and then the Imamabarra Mosque. It was when the large palace called the Kaiserbargh was overrun that Russell witnessed the senseless destruction of the mob. With adrenaline pumping, the victorious soldiers went on an orgy of looting. Despite the ever-present threat of armed mutineers, the British soldiers became indifferent to danger in their quest for booty. What could not be carried away was smashed or torn. Russell described the unedifying scene:

'It was one of the strangest and most distressing sights that could be seen; but it was also most exciting. Discipline may hold soldiers together till the fight is won; but it assuredly does not exist for a moment after the assault has been delivered …

'Lying amid the orange-groves are dead and dying sepoys; and the white statues are reddened with blood. Leaning against a smiling Venus is a British soldier shot through the neck, gasping, and at every gasp bleeding to death! Here and there officers are running to and fro after their men, persuading or threatening in vain. From the broken portals issue soldiers laden with loot or plunder. Shawls, rich tapestry, gold and silver brocade, caskets of jewels, arms, splendid dresses. The men are wild with fury and lust for gold – literally drunk with plunder.'

It did not, however, prevent the man from *The Times* from helping himself to a few modest and portable baubles, but the chance of obtaining valuable booty narrowly eluded him.

'Enter three or four banditti of Her Majesty's – Regiment. Faces black with powder; cross-belts specked with blood; coats stuffed out with all sorts of valuables …. The men emerged with caskets of jewels, iron boxes and safes, and wooden boxes full of arms crusted with gold and precious stones. One fellow, having burst open a leaden-looking lid, which was in reality of solid silver, drew out an armlet of emeralds, and diamonds, and pearls, so large, that I believed they were not real stones, and that they formed part of a chandelier chain. "What will your honour give me for these?" said he, "I'll take a hundred rupees on chance."

'Oh wretched fate! I had not a penny in my pocket, nor had any of us … I said, "I will give you a hundred rupees; but it is right to tell you if the stones are real they are worth a great deal more".'

The soldier was still happy to sell for his asking price, but when Russell said he would send the money to him, the soldier replied: 'How do I know where I'd be this blessed night? It's may be dead I'd be, with a bullet in me body … With that, the soldier put the chain of great nobbly emeralds, and diamonds, and pearls, into the casket and I saw my fortune vanish.'[3]

Russell witnessed so many gruesome sights that they became almost a routine occurrence. On 13 March he wrote: 'A battery of heavy guns and mortars was established outside the Martinière Park and, whilst the tents were being moved, I went down and stayed by it for some time, watching the shot and the bombs flying into the town. Many of our shells fell short. Just as I was turning to go away, I heard an exclamation of alarm from the men at one of the mortars. As the smoke of the gun cleared away, I saw the headless trunk of a naval officer on the ground. It was a horrid sight. He had been killed by the shell which was discharged just as he rode before the muzzle. He will be buried this evening and forgotten tomorrow.' The unfortunate sailor was Mate Henry Garvey of the Naval Brigade, who was riding fast to deliver a message and did not see that the quick-matches were alight.

It was during the latter period of fighting that Russell had yet another narrow escape. He had previously avoided being hit by a cannon shell which had brushed past him only to kill a group of officers standing behind him. A little while later, Russell recalled: 'Our further progress down the street was stopped by some bullets from badmashes in the houses. Separating from Stewart for a moment, I came across five of them, who were as much startled as I was; however, they all blazed away at me within a few yards distance and immediately dashed around the corner, whilst I retreated in the opposite direction.'

Once Campbell's men had occupied Lucknow, Russell wandered around the deserted ruins of the Residency, which had been refuge for 1,600 men, 700 non-combatants and 600 women and children for five months. Amongst the belongings left behind was an album of photographs which was presented to him. These salt-print photographs had been taken by a local Indian photographer and were a unique record of the local residents. Many were named together with their fate: 'Killed in Siege'.

The plan to surround Lucknow to prevent the rebels escaping was not effective and thousands streamed out from the west of the city. Russell wrote: 'It is evident most of them have escaped … It must be admitted that it is unfortunate we could not inflict on the rebels such a severe punishment as would ensure their complete discomfiture and prevent their assembling in other strongholds to renew their opposition to our rule. In the evening I saw Sir Colin. He seemed satisfied – "The runaways will go home to their homes".' As the Mutiny rumbled on for another year, Sir Colin's prediction proved false.

After clearing Lucknow, Russell accompanied Campbell as he marched north in pursuit of the mutineers. It was while crossing the River Ganges that Russell suffered an injury that was to plague him for the rest of his life. His mare was in season and attracted the attention of some stallions. During the melee that followed, Russell was kicked in the stomach and thigh and was severely wounded. In great pain, he had to be carried in a *dhooly* (litter) as Campbell's column advanced on the rebel position at Bareilly. The rebels' first line fled at the sight of the British, but Campbell's men were taken by surprise by a charge from a group of fanatical Rohilla *ghazis*. All around the prostrate Russell, men were being dragged from their horses and slaughtered. Barely able to move and deserted by his bearers, Russell was caught in the middle of a scrum of terror-stricken camp followers, screaming women and stampeding elephants and camels. Fortunately, his *syce* (groom) came to his rescue, manhandling him onto his horse. Wearing nothing but a shirt and semi-delirious, Russell found himself in the path of some *ghazi* horsemen bearing down on him. One of them took a swipe with his *tulwar* (sword), which narrowly missed. The heat, terror and his weakened state caused Russell to faint and fall from his horse as the *ghazis* rode over him, leaving him untouched except for some additional bruises.

It took many more months of hard marching and skirmishes before the Mutiny was finally suppressed. Russell spent much of that time recuperating, but was still able to send back trenchant despatches to Delane. The Mutiny was essentially a slave revolt and he found little glory but much shame in this dark episode. The British learned little from this experience and added hatred to indifference in their dealings with their Indian subjects. They did reorganise the Indian Army and tended to favour the more martial subjects from the Punjab who had remained loyal. The British Government replaced the rule of the HEIC and the era of the Raj began.

Russell could be moved by acts of heroism but was more impressed by the horrors and futility of war, the sufferings of the soldiers and the debasing effect on man's humanity. He later wrote that 'Queen Victoria's reign has been an incessant record of bloodshed'. As he grew older he took the unpopular view that colonialism was evil when it was supported by claims of racial and religious superiority. Without doubt, his experience during the Indian Mutiny influenced his subsequent outlook on British Imperialism.

The Mutiny was photographed by James Robertson, of Crimean War fame, and his brother-in-law, Felice Beato. Together, they had formed a partnership and can be regarded as the first true war photographers. In contrast to the sanitised photos of the Crimea, in which no corpses were shown, their Indian photographs show hanged mutineers and skeleton-strewn courtyards. They captured images of the extensive damage caused by artillery-fire at the Lucknow Residency; the confined area of the Satischaura Ghat, where the defenders from Wheeler's garrison were slaughtered; and the extensive damage to Delhi and the Ridge. For the first time, photographs captured the grimness and pity of war.

While Britain was absorbed in the Indian Mutiny, she was also waging a mainly naval war against China in what became known as the Second Opium War. A treaty had been made in 1858, but the Chinese had not adhered to the terms to open up their country for further trade, principally opium. In 1860, an Anglo-French expedition was launched to implement the treaty by force.

The Times sent Thomas William Bowlby, the only correspondent to accompany the expedition. He observed the bombardment and capture of the Taku Forts at the mouth of the Pei Ho River and the occupation of Tsientsin. When the Chinese began to make overtures of peace, a small party was instructed to travel to Tungchow under a flag of truce to arrange the preliminaries of peace.

Bowlby managed to join the party, which included the consul and Lord Elgin's private secretary. When they reached Tungchow, hostilities broke out again and the party was taken prisoner. The three dignitaries were soon released but the remaining fourteen were not so fortunate. Two of the Britons were decapitated while the remainder had their hands and feet tightly bound and water poured on their bonds preventing circulation. Further torture followed when they were put in chains, kicked and beaten. They were then thrown in carts and left out in the open for three days and nights. Finally they were locked in a filthy room in an old fort where their wounds became severely infected. The Indian soldiers of the escort managed to survive but Bowlby died. When the British reached Peking, they found his body greatly disfigured by quicklime as his captors sought to hide their crimes.

Thomas Bowlby was buried in the Russian cemetery with full military honours. He was arguably the first Special to be killed on assignment. On 18 October 1860, the Summer Palace, which had been looted by the French, was burnt as a reprisal for the killing of Bowlby and his comrades.

Chapter 5

The American Civil War

In 1861 the fragile bonds that bound together the emerging United States of America were torn asunder when the central government tried to impose its authority over those of individual states, who had enjoyed virtual autonomy. The argument had rumbled on for years and had polarised into one of pro, and anti, slavery. The largely anti-slavery industrial northern states opted to keep the Union intact and allow greater federalisation. There was also a powerful church-led body that called for the emancipation of all slaves. The southern states, whose agriculture-based economy was entirely reliant on slave-labour, voted to secede from the Union and to form themselves into a Confederation. With battle-lines being drawn and attitudes hardening, civil war was becoming inevitable.

Britain's attitude towards America was a mixture of condescension and hostility. It had been just eighty-five years since the humiliation of the War of Independence, an event that still rankled with many Englishmen, who now regarded themselves as the world's leading race. Despite this, Britain was heavily dependent on cotton grown in the southern states to feed the insatiable mills in Lancashire. As such, any event that threatened the supply of raw material to a vital British industry was of public concern and Delane of *The Times* understood this. He once again called upon his star writer, William Russell.

Since his return from India, Russell had started to edit his new publication called the *Army and Navy Gazette*. In its early years it was recognised as a crusading service periodical, which exposed many naval abuses and was instrumental in producing several reforms. Delane offered Russell the irresistible sum of £1,200 a year plus expenses – which he readily accepted as he was going through one of his periodical financial troughs. Russell was the highest paid news reporter of his generation. Despite this, he was frequently short of money. Besides his large and demanding family, Russell enjoyed gambling and carousing with his friends. Later, he began to move in elevated circles that put a further strain on his pocket, exacerbated by his friendship with the Prince of Wales.

Russell duly sailed for America in March and upon his arrival in Washington interviewed the new president, Abraham Lincoln. In common with many observers, Russell had not been impressed by Lincoln's appearance. He rather patronisingly wrote: 'A person who met Mr. Lincoln in the street would not take him to be what – according to the usages of European society – is called a gentleman.' After the interview, however, Russell changed his opinion: 'I left agreeably impressed with his shrewdness, humour and natural sagacity.'[1]

In the company of other correspondents, Russell made an extensive tour of the South. In Montgomery, Alabama, he wandered into a slave auction, which filled him with disgust and confirmed his preference for the Northern cause.[2]

It was on 12 April, in South Carolina, that the long anticipated war began. A small Union Army garrison in Fort Sumter, on an island at the entrance to Charleston Harbour, came under fire from all sides and was forced to surrender. The *New York Herald* correspondent, Captain Bradley Sillick Osbon, was in Charleston and was able to witness this prelude to the four-year-long Civil War:

'Civil War has at last begun. A terrible fight is at this moment going on between Fort Sumter and the fortifications by which it is surrounded. The batteries of Sullivan's Island, Morris Island and other points were opened on Fort Sumter at four o'clock this morning. Fort Sumter returned the fire, and a brisk cannonading has been kept up. The military are under arms, and the whole of our population are on the streets. Every available space facing the harbour is filled with anxious spectators. The firing continued all day without intermission ... The thunder of the artillery can be heard for fifty miles around, and the scene is magnificently terrible.'[3]

Russell visited the site not long after and found a universal belief that Britain would side with the Confederacy: 'They assume that the British crown lies on a bale of cotton.'[4] Both sides began to mobilise in earnest and a popular war-fever gripped the divided nation as Russell returned to Washington. Having seen slavery in action, Russell's sympathies lay with the North, which ran counter to those of the management of *The Times*. For almost the entire duration of the war, *The Times* showed a marked bias in favour of the South and this was undoubtedly due to Russell's early exclusion from reporting the conflict.

Thousands thronged the recruiting offices to volunteer for the army. Wealthy men and politicians, with no military experience, raised regiments, some of which aped the more exotic European units and gave themselves titles like Fire Zouaves, Garibaldi Guards and New York Highlanders. Barely trained and equipped, but high on confidence, Northern volunteers regarded war as a great adventure before disillusion set in.

Under pressure and with some reluctance, the Union commander, General Irwin McDowell, led his army of 35,000 raw recruits and a sprinkling of regular soldiers across the Potomac River into Virginia. They were accompanied by hundreds of spectators from Washington's society including Senators, Representatives and many ladies conveyed in carriages and prepared to picnic while watching the coming spectacle. In the midst of this festive crush of humanity was *The Times'* correspondent wondering, no doubt, where he should place himself to watch the war's first battle. In the event, he and his two companions were held up in the hamlet of Centreville, from where he could hear the sound of gunfire coming from the direction of the small stream called Bull Run.

At first, all seemed to be going the way of McDowell's men. Gallopers brought back reports of Union advances and the civilian spectators cheered. As the day lengthened, the Confederates counter-attacked and the Union line wavered and broke. Panic quickly spread and the whole army turned and ran for the safety of Washington, just twenty-three miles away. Russell belatedly managed to get clear of Centreville and rode towards the sounds of gunfire. After about three or four miles, he heard loud shouts and was surrounded by a tide of retreating Union soldiers running for their lives.

Unperturbed, Russell rode on, until it became obvious that the whole army was in full retreat. As he was forced to return towards Centreville, the retreat became a panic-stricken rout. He wrote graphically: 'The ground over which I had passed going out was now covered with arms, clothing of all kinds, accoutrements thrown off and left to be trampled in the dust under the hoofs of men and horses. The runaways ran alongside the wagons, striving to force themselves in among the occupants, who resisted tooth and nail. The drivers spurred, and whipped, and urged the horses to the utmost of their bent. I felt an inclination to laugh, which was overtaken by disgust, and by that vague sense of something extraordinary taking place which is experienced when a man sees a number of people acting as if driven by some unknown terror.'

Russell tried to calm those near him by saying, 'There is no enemy to pursue you. All the cavalry in the world could not get at you. But I might as well have talked to the stones.'[5] All semblance of order had evaporated. If the Confederates had but known they could have marched into Washington unopposed.

In this confusion, Russell had become separated from his two companions and rode back alone to Washington amongst the disorganised rabble. At one point, he was confronted by a soldier who tried to commandeer Russell's horse at gun-point. From close range, he aimed and pulled the trigger of his rifle but fortunately it misfired, which allowed Russell to dig in his spurs and escape.

The correspondent finally reached his hotel in Washington at eleven o'clock that night. Pausing only for a light supper, he wrote all night and sent off his despatch the following day. William Russell's report appeared in *The Times* on 6 August and filled seven columns. In his usual perceptive but impartial style, he told the truth about the shortcomings of the Union Army. It was in marked contrast to the eulogistic and wildly inaccurate reports that had appeared in the American press. Delane was prophetic when he wrote to Russell: 'My fear is only that the United States will not be able to bear the truth so plainly told.'[6] He was told a similar thing by the pragmatic General Sherman, who said, 'Of course you will never remain when once all the press are down on you. I would not take a million dollars and be in your place.'

When copies of his report filtered back to America, a veritable storm broke about his head. Russell was attacked verbally and in print and even received several death threats. Delane advised him to seek refuge in the British Embassy until the storm blew over. Angry and hurt, the military and politicians refused to talk to him and, worst of all for a war journalist, he was refused a press pass, thus denying him access to any military column or camp. For Russell, the war was over and there was little alternative but to return home. In 1863, Russell retired with a £300 a year pension from *The Times*. He did, however, continue to work on a freelance basis until 1879.

The Federal authorities had made a bad mistake in forcing Russell's departure for he was basically pro-Northern and anti-slavery and his reporting would have reflected these views. Instead, *The Times* sent a couple of replacements who were fervent supporters of the South and the paper became a mouthpiece for Confederate propaganda.

It was not just Russell and *The Times* who were penalised for publishing the unpalatable truth. Another British correspondent present was Frank Vizetelly, who represented both the *Illustrated*

London News as special artist and the *London Daily News* as reporter.

The *Illustrated London News* had been founded in 1842 by Herbert Ingham. The first issue sold 26,000 copies, but by 1863 its circulation had exceeded 300,000, which greatly exceeded the circulation of other British newspapers at the time, due mainly to the amount and quality of the pictorial engravings which illustrated the reports. Of Italian extraction, Frank Vizetelly had newsprint in his blood and was actually born in Fleet Street into a family of newspapermen. He studied art and lived in Paris, where he refined his artistic talent. He grew into a tall burly-looking man, tough and resourceful, and was both a talented artist and a fearless reporter. Along with Russell, Vizetelly became the leader in his field during the mid-Victorian period.

After covering the Battle of Solferino in northern Italy in 1859, the *Illustrated London News* sent Vizetelly to Sicily to follow the fortunes of Giuseppe Garibaldi in his second attempt for Italian independence from the hated Bourbon rulers. Garibaldi was an enormously newsworthy figure and was nowhere more popular than with the British public. Leading 1,072 red-shirted volunteers against the vastly superior forces of the Bourbons, Garibaldi cut an inspirational and romantic figure. Frank Vizetelly struck up a life-long friendship with the leader and chronicled his victorious Sicilian campaign.

Writing on 2 June 1860, Vizetelly reported the street fighting in Palermo: 'About half past three on Sunday morning ... I was awoken by a rapid discharge of musketry, the ringing of church bells, and loud hurrahing, shouted by thousands of lungs ... Garibaldi and his men were fighting their way into the town by the Porta St Antonino, while Neapolitan officers, surprised at the sudden appearance of the man they thought was far away and a fugitive, were galloping about, giving confused orders to the troops they had got together, and then countermanding them afterwards ... The military placed sentinels at intervals along both sides of the streets and the entrance of every thoroughfare, with instructions to fire on anyone to show themselves either at the windows or the doors of the houses. Two guns were brought up and are sweeping the Strada Nuova ... Every balcony in the street has become a fortress; citizens that were supposed to have been disarmed are now doing good service on the panic-stricken troops; while the small column of liberators are making sure progress, taking advantage of every projection that offers shelter. The men who drove the Austrians from Como and Varese know the value of every ounce of lead, and there is not one of their bullets that has not its billet on leaving the muzzles of their guns. Hurrah!'

Finally, with the help of a popular insurrection, Palermo was taken, followed soon by the rest of Sicily and then the mainland.

Arriving in America, having covered the victorious Italian campaign, Frank Vizetelly was to see a contrast between the generalship and fighting spirit of Garibaldi's makeshift army and the timidly led, ill-disciplined rabble that made up the Union Army in 1861. Vizetelly's description in the *Illustrated London News* of the unseemly Northern stampede is graphic: 'The terror-stricken soldiers threw away their arms and accoutrements herding along like a panic-stricken flock of sheep, with no order whatever in their flight ... Wounded men were crushed under the wheels of the heavy, lumbering chariots that dashed down the road at full speed. Light buggies, containing members of Congress were overturned or dashed to pieces in the horrible confusion of the panic.'

As a result of Bull Run and a string of other defeats, Frank Vizetelly, too, found increasing difficulty in getting accreditation from the military. Incensed by the unflattering portrayal of the Union Army, Secretary of War Edwin M. Stanton denied Vizetelly any further military contact.

Soon after Russell's departure, the North had set up a formal system of censorship. Stanton was given draconian powers which he did not hesitate to use. Publication was suspended of those newspapers that did not toe the line, editors were arrested and proprietors threatened with court-martial. Reporters were intimidated and one even sentenced to be shot for not handing over a despatch.

By the summer of 1862, Frank had had enough and decided to report on the war from the South's perspective. Taking a chance that he could be shot as a spy, he evaded Northern patrols and crossed the Potomac River on a raft accompanied by a black man, who dived for oysters to feed them both while they hid from Union patrols. He rode south and presented himself at the Confederate capital, Richmond, where he was warmly received.

The Civil War was covered by over 300 reporters. As most of the fighting took place near centres of population, reports of a battle could be read by its participants the very next day. On the whole, the quality of writing was both inaccurate and pure propaganda, not improved by editors like Wilbur Storey of *The Chicago Times* who instructed his reporters to: 'Telegraph fully all news you can get and when there is no news, send rumour.'[7]

Meanwhile, Frank Vizetelly accompanied General Robert E. Lee's army during his Virginian campaigns. The 100-odd drawings and reports he sent back to Britain were carried on ships that had to evade the increasingly tightening Northern naval blockade. Sometimes his drawings were taken from a captured blockade runner and ended up being published in the New York-based *Harper's Weekly* and *Frank Leslie's Illustrated Newspaper*.

Vizetelly showed his sympathy for the South's plight in his reports of shortages of weapons and clothing. He saw the war as the aggressive North trying to dominate the noble Southern underdog. Vizetelly acted as a messenger for Confederate General James Longstreet at the Battle of Chickamauga and acted as a staff aide at the Battle of Fredericksburg. He witnessed the shrinking of the Confederacy as the stronger North began to win a series of crucial battles. Liked and trusted by the Confederate High Command, he travelled with Jefferson Davis after the fall of Richmond on 2 April 1865 and even loaned him money to aid his escape. Choosing to remain, he was there at the end, when he recorded Lee's surrender on 9 April at the Appomattox Court House.

The American Civil War saw the first real battle for international support through the newspapers, with both sides engaging in overt and covert propaganda for their respective causes. It also saw the formalisation of censorship which set a pattern for future war reporting.

Once the fighting stopped, the aftermath went largely unreported by the British press. Wars sold newspapers, reconstruction did not. The Specials packed their kit, paid off their local servants and guides and headed for the next theatre of war.

Chapter 6

Prussia on the March

Joseph Crowe returned from India having suffered a long bout of sickness that had led to Billy Russell replacing him. He arrived back in London in late May 1859 and reported to Mowbray Morris, *The Times*' editor. He recalled:

'I had scarcely time to explain the cause of my leaving India before he [Mowbray Morris] asked me whether I was available for work. He said that, in consequence of an outbreak of war between France and Austria, two correspondents had been sent to headquarters in Italy; that [Ferdinand] Eber had done very well on the French side, but that Colonel Blakeley, though well recommended by Count Gyulai, [Austrian commander] had failed on the Austrian side … The pay would be £80 a month with outfit and expenses. An effort would be made to procure a uniform for me by applying for a commission in a volunteer regiment. The duty now offered me should have been performed by William Russell, who had recently returned from Bengal. But he had been temporarily disabled by an accident which prevented him from riding.'

Crowe reported to the Austrian headquarters in the Italian Po Valley and on 23 June witnessed the bloody Battle of Solferino. From a hill he was able to observe the whole front between Solferino and Lake Garda. Because of the extent of the front, he had to watch the action through a telescope:

'The sun alternately shone with brilliancy, or lay hid under clouds. Small puffs of musketry, here also were visible with a glass, yet they were lost to unassisted view in the broad expanse of the landscape. It was only when volleys of artillery followed each other in rapid succession that the smoke took a distinct shape ... But not only smoke puffs, the forms of men, too, were lost in the vast proportions of the battlefield; and it was only when large bodies lay together that they showed a definite outline. With my glass I could distinguish thousands on each side opposing each other at all points, amidst dead bodies of men and horses and a wreck of uniforms and arms which encumbered the ground. To the naked eye it seemed as if a vast ant hill had been disturbed, and the men appeared to be pygmies in a field of exceptional magnitude.'

By the afternoon it was clear that the French were gaining the upper hand and, by the end of the day, the Austrians conceded defeat. The aftermath was truly appalling, with the Austrians suffering about 13,000 killed or wounded and the French losing 14,500. With so many wounded left suffering on the extensive battlefield, Henri Dunant, a Swiss and one of the many civilian observers, began to organise the collection of the helpless wounded and their transport to hospitals. So affected was he by the casualties of the battle that he started the international relief society that became the Red Cross. The French emperor, Napoleon III, was so shocked by the bloodshed at Solferino that he chose to abandon the war and signed a truce.

Crowe wrote his report to *The Times*, but wished to avoid sending it via the Austrian military post office. Instead he managed to persuade his Veronese banker to put it in one of the bank's envelopes and send it to an agent in Augsburg, who posted it onto London. The whole process took six days but Crowe still beat his colleague, Ferdinand Eber, by twenty-four hours and earned a flattering leader in *The Times*.

While there was a general world peace throughout the 1860s, a small German state, which would dominate European events way into the twentieth century, began to flex its muscles. For years, Prussia under the guidance of its chancellor, Count Otto von Bismarck, had been reorganising its army and building a railway network capable of moving large numbers of men and supplies. Bismarck's goal was the unification of the many German states under the rule of the Prussian Hohenzollern dynasty.

The easy victory over the Danes in 1864 gained Prussia the border states of Schleswig-Holstein. Prussia had agreed to share the spoils with its Austrian ally, but it was a marriage of convenience as far as Bismarck was concerned. His aim was to exclude Austria, which was the most powerful country in Central Europe, from any German Federation, and to assert Prussia as the true leader of the German people. To this end he provoked an argument with Austria over the joint ruling of Schleswig-Holstein and, in June 1866, war was declared.

Once more the British newspapers despatched their correspondents to the seat of war, which most saw as Vienna. Amongst them was the now eminent correspondent, William Russell. How things had changed for him in just twelve years! In the Crimea he was barely tolerated. Now, when *The Times* sent him, he was entertained by the British ambassador in Vienna. He was also given an assistant; an artillery captain and Crimean veteran named Charles Brackenbury. As well as a role as military observer, Brackenbury had journalistic aspirations. He did cover the Franco-Prussian War with Russell but his later efforts as a leader writer were not a success. Despite this, he reviewed books and was still a contributor to newspapers even when he attained the rank of general.

The Seven Weeks War, as it was to be dubbed, was largely one of manoeuvre enlivened by a few skirmishes. The Prussians, with their ability to move men quickly, were winning the tactical war. It was an unsatisfactory conflict to cover for a war reporter, with both armies spread over hundreds of miles and no real action to report. Then the Prussians began to concentrate their forces in Bohemia and advance on the fortress town of Königgratz. The Austrians shadowed their enemy until a battle became inevitable. Both sides were forced into unfavourable positions with the Austrians having the better ground to defend. Thus, with Königgratz Castle to their back and flanked by the River Elbe and Bistritz Brook, the Austrians felt confident of victory.

Russell and Brackenbury hurried to Königgratz, arriving just as the battle commenced. Thanks to Russell's good contact with the Austrian commander, Ludwig von Benedek, *The Times*' men were allowed to observe the unfolding battle from the highest tower in the fortress, which gave them a grandstand view of the biggest battle Russell ever reported. He wrote: 'From a lofty tower commanding the Prague gateway, whence Josephstadt on the north and the whole position of the army were displayed as if on a raised map.'

Spread below and covering a five-mile front was the largest concentration of soldiers ever seen on a European battlefield. The Austrians were 241,000 strong but were outnumbered by the Prussians, who could field 285,000. The white uniforms of the Austrians were covered by dull grey greatcoats although the cavalry displayed their showy uniforms of azure, green and white. The Prussian army were clothed in their distinctive blue tunics and *pickelhaubes* (spiked helmet). Not only were the Austrians outnumbered, but they were also outgunned by the new Prussian breech-loading needle rifle. The Austrians were armed with old muzzle loaders and relied on their usual shock of a bayonet charge to overwhelm their opponents. In terms of firepower and numbers involved, the Battle of Königgratz (also known as Sadowa) was not to be surpassed until the First World War.

The day of the battle, 3 July 1866, dawned chilly, wet and cheerless. After an artillery duel, which caused many casualties on both sides, the Austrian infantry steadily advanced and seemed to have the better of the first three hours of fighting. Frequent heavy showers obscured Russell's view from time to time but he was able to observe almost the entire battle. Around two o'clock the Austrian frontal assaults were seen to be weakening and the Prussians began to advance and take the Austrian right flank with the huge reserves that had been kept hidden. Pressed on the left and centre, the Austrians were forced to retreat and many managed to be evacuated by a procession of trains. Others surged across the Elbe, but in doing so hundreds were drowned as they crowded onto the hastily constructed pontoon bridges.

The Prussians, too, had suffered great losses and were in no condition to follow up their victory, which allowed the Austrians to withdraw. The casualty list was horrific. The Austrians lost 40,000 men, half of whom were taken prisoner, while the Prussian losses amounted to 15,000. Both sides had fought each other to a standstill but, for Bismarck, the end did justify the means. Victory brought into the Prussian-dominated North German League the states of Hanover, Hesse, Schlesweig-Holstein, Kassel, Nassau and Frankfurt. Russell concluded in *The Times*, 'When Austria marched from the wreck of Könniggratz, she found that the sceptre of the German Caesars had been stricken from her hand.'

This short, nearly forgotten war was but a prelude to a greater conflict that had a far greater significance for the future of continental Europe: the Franco-Prussian War of 1870. It was the most widely reported European war of the century. A new style of reporting evolved and brought to the fore a correspondent who assumed the crown that William Russell had worn for so long.

Archibald Forbes, who became the acknowledged leader of 'the adventurous school of war correspondents', was born in Morayshire in 1838, the son of a Scottish minister. A restless youth, he was given a grant to study at Aberdeen University, where he stayed, 'until follies and extravagance abruptly terminated my university career'.[1] To escape his debts and the wrath of his family, Forbes took the Queen's Shilling and joined the Royal Dragoons in 1857. Life in a peacetime cavalry regiment on a home posting was monotonous and only alleviated for Forbes by the tales told by the veterans who had taken part in the Charge of the Heavy Brigade at Balaklava. His imagination was further fired when he attended a lecture in Edinburgh given by William Russell during the winter of 1857. Inspired by Russell's tales, Forbes began to write about military subjects.

A couple of years later he was appointed as servant to Major Richard Molesworth, who was married to a remarkable young woman, Louisa Molesworth. In an age when a woman's role was little more than her husband's chattel, she was an independent spirit and a talented writer. Starved of intellectual company, she obviously took an interest in Archibald Forbes, her husband's intelligent and literate batman, who was the same age as herself.

Louisa was already writing for several magazines and encouraged Forbes to submit articles for publication. Both *The Morning Star* and *The Cornhill Magazine* accepted and published his pieces, all on military matters. Forbes recalled the writing of his first article: 'It was at a table in the barrack room, amidst din and turmoil. Fellows were singing as they pipe-clayed belts or burnished sword scabbards. I was interrupted by the necessity to clear the table away to make room for a fight'.[2] Years later, when he was at the top of his profession, the editor of *The Cornhill Magazine* recalled that Forbes' first article had been smudged with chrome yellow pipe-clay, which was authentic evidence of its barrack-room origin.

Louisa also coached Forbes in both French and German. These languages, together with army-taught riding skills, were soon to stand him in good stead. When the Molesworths left the army, Forbes was speedily promoted and attained the rank of quartermaster sergeant by 1867. By now bored with army life and encouraged by the publication of his articles, Forbes had saved enough money to buy his way out of the army and to embark on a career of writing. Instead of applying for work with an established newspaper or magazine, Forbes staked his remaining money in producing a new journal called *The London Scotsman*. He was not only the proprietor but also its only contributor. He wrote everything from sketches, reviews, births, deaths and marriages.

In order to fill up the pages, he also serialised an unpublished novel he had written about the Indian Mutiny. Having no first-hand experience of either India or campaigning, Forbes employed a veteran who worked as a commissionaire outside a gentlemen's outfitters in Oxford Street. The old soldier was James Hollowell, who had won the Victoria Cross during the Siege of Lucknow in 1857. He was paid five shillings an interview for giving detailed and colourful descriptions of his experiences, which Forbes was able to weave into a very readable story.

In order to keep his ailing publication afloat, Forbes took on some freelance work for the *Morning Advertiser*. When war seemed imminent between France and Prussia, he was summoned by the editor, who offered him the job of reporting on the hostilities. It transpired that Forbes's Indian Mutiny story, with its vividly descriptive battle scenes, had greatly impressed the editor, who thought this was qualification enough to employ him. Flattered and grateful, Forbes left for the continent. With no preparation or support, Forbes headed for the eastern border between the two adversaries, equipped with little more than a rucksack, a notepad and about £20 in his pocket. Such was the casual and informal way that many correspondents with the lesser journals went to war.

William Russell, once again with *The Times*, now had a retinue of assistants to gather news as far and wide as possible from both sides. Along with the other leading newspaper correspondents, he had travelled to Berlin to obtain permission to accompany the Prussian army. Archibald Forbes knew nothing about press accreditation and just headed to where he thought the first action would occur at the border town of Saarbrücken.

He was attending the wedding of an acquaintance when the town was attacked and temporarily occupied by the French. Along with most British correspondents, Forbes was sure that victory would ultimately go to the Prussians so he chose 'the German side of the great cock-pit'.[3] He travelled everywhere on foot and sent back reports by post. After the Prussian victory at Gravelotte, he did apply for formal accreditation and, through the efforts of a friendly orderly sergeant, was given a Royal Headquarters Pass. In fact, the Prussians soon saw the value of having a 'good press' and actively encouraged reporters by giving them plenty of information and allowing the use of the military postal service to send their reports. They were also clever enough to make use of a couple of captured French journalists. After imprisoning the two for a couple of days, they then released them in Switzerland, having taken the captives through Prussian-occupied France. By impressing them just how strong they were, and certain that the journalists would report what they had seen, the Germans gained a propaganda coup.

British reporters who covered events from the French side encountered many difficulties, not least rampant 'spy-mania'. One reporter, carrying full accreditation and a pass issued by French General MacMahon, was dragged from his carriage by a wandering band of *francs tireurs*, a semi-criminal irregular militia. Despite his protests, he was found guilty of being a Prussian spy by an improvised court martial and given just fifteen minutes to prepare to meet his maker. The official documentation had meant nothing to his illiterate captors so, in an effort to delay his fate, the condemned man asked for a priest. While a priest was being sought, an old French veteran who could read appeared on the scene and confirmed the reporter's true identity and occupation. While they were debating whether or not to accept the old man's explanation, the reporter and his saviour edged their way to the carriage and made their escape, helped on their way by a smattering of shots, one of which went through the reporter's hat.

Initially, the French expelled all English correspondents from Paris. George Robinson, an art critic for the *Manchester Guardian* drafted in as a war correspondent, decided to attach himself to one of the French armies. En route he met General Bazaine's army, which was about to be caught in the unplanned Battle of Borny against a weaker Prussian force.

Robinson had no great faith in the French military high command as described in his report:

'At last the ammunition failed us, and then the generals lost their heads. Regiments were ordered into impossible places, overlapping each other in the clumsiest fashion, simply placed where they could be most conveniently killed. And then forgotten; no supplies of ammunition were brought up, and Canrobert's corps was absolutely pushing back the enemy from his position on our right, really bending him back, when the last round his artillery had was fired. At the same time, the 67th stood for three hours right in front of a wood, being leisurely shot down by the Prussians, without a single cartouche to fire; not a single non-commissioned officer came away from the wood; and two-thirds of the regiment remained with them.

'An ambulance [field hospital] was pitched at a place appointed by [General] Frossard, who, in half-an-hour afterwards, had so forgotten where it was, that he ordered some artillery immediately in front of it. Of course, the Prussian fire comes plunging into it to silence this, and over it into our ambulance to silence many there. Bursting in the midst of the poor maimed wounded and amputated men, come the shells and the horrors of war are intensified to a pitch beyond the power of the most devilish imagination to surpass.

'Good God! This is glorious – splendid work, war! The profession of arms is certainly the noblest calling when it is conducted thus; here are poor men killed over and over again, that is, they go through the horrors of death many times; and what with their generals, and what with their doctors, it is a wonder there are any left.'

General Bazaine managed to extricate his army and they retreated into the city of Metz. Robinson went with them, where he was the only English correspondent to record the 70-day siege. Over 190,000 French soldiers held out for two months, suffering starvation and disease. Robinson was determined to send out his reports and, together with a French engineer, devised a balloon method to carry them. They became known as *Papillons de Metz* (Metz butterflies). At one point he was arrested as a spy and the French commander forbade him to float out any more 'butterflies'. Robinson made several attempts to cross the Prussian lines but had to wait for the French to capitulate before giving his full account of the siege.

As the Prussians advanced into France, Archibald Forbes teamed up with another debutant reporter, a Dutchman named Jacob de Liefde, who was representing *The Glasgow Herald*. Together they walked and hitch-hiked their way towards Paris and managed to get into Sedan before the capitulation of the main French army.

The two rookie Specials were the only civilians to witness Napoleon III's surrender to Bismarck in a humble weaver's cottage on the Donchery Road. Forbes wrote: 'Now following along the road to Donchery a rather shabby open carriage, on the right of the principal seat of which I at once recognised the Emperor. He wore a blue cloak with scarlet lining, which was thrown back disclosing the decorations on his breast ... A few hundred yards had been traversed by the cortège in the direction of Donchery, when at Napoleon's insistence the carriage halted in front of a weaver's cottage on the left-hand side of the road. I saw him turn round in his seat and heard the request he made to Bismarck that he should be allowed to wait in the cottage until he should have an interview with the King [of Prussia] ...

'Bismarck accompanied him to a small room with a single window, its sole furniture a deal table and two rush-bottomed chairs. The conversation lasted about three-quarters of an hour; at the end of which Bismarck rode away to dress, and, on his return in full uniform, conducted Napoleon to the Château Bellevue [for the formal surrender].'

Napoleon was described by one witness as 'a little thick-set man, wearing jauntily a red cap with gold border, black paletot lined with red, red trousers and white kid gloves. His appearance was a little unsoldierlike. The man looked too soft, too shabby for the uniform he wore.'

Russell, too, witnessed the Sedan attack as the Prussians stormed the French ramparts and he wrote something that many reporters could relate to. 'It is not a pleasant thing to be a mere spectator of such scenes. There is something cold-blooded in standing with a glass to your eye, seeing men blown to pieces, or dragging their shattered bodies to places of safety, or writhing on the ground too far for help, even if you could render it.'[4]

Shortly after the battle, Forbes was approached by a *Times* correspondent named Sutherland Edwards, who had reported back to William Russell about his rival's exploits. Russell made an offer to recruit Forbes into his band of news gatherers. Although flattered by the offer, Forbes felt he should remain loyal to the *Morning Advertiser*, and reluctantly declined. Russell later changed his tune and wrote in his diary that, 'I have quite altered my opinion of Forbes and would not like to see him at *The Times*. He simply invents and puts false addresses etc and I find he has a bad character ... He is no doubt a good but risky reporter.' He also wrote to *The Times'* editor, Mowbray Morris, 'I am so glad we have escaped having Forbes. He is a low trooper, full of go but a drunken fellow and an audacious liar.'[5]

Shortly after Russell's offer, Forbes received a letter from his editor, which upbraided him for irregular and patchy reporting and recalled him home. Forbes had been frequently posting off reports, so he concluded that most had been misdirected or become lost. Back in London, with a notebook full of up-to-date information, Forbes was sacked by the *Morning Advertiser*. He then approached *The Times*, which would soon rue the day that they rejected his application. Standing on the pavement in Fleet Street, disheartened and about to give up, Forbes tried one more newspaper.

To his joy, he was taken on by the *Daily News* and told to write four columns immediately, for which he was paid more than he had ever earned.

Better equipped and with a large newspaper behind him, Forbes returned to France and so, after an unpromising start, began his rise as the decade's top war reporter. Learning from his experience that the postal service was unreliable, Forbes set about using the telegraph to be first with the news. He deposited a large sum of money with the telegraph master at Saarbrücken, along with an arrangement with a local bank to keep this topped up. Forbes sent his messages from the front via the daily train to Saarbrücken, where they were collected and immediately transmitted. In this manner, his reports could be published in the *Daily News* the following day. Most of the older correspondents like William Russell persisted in sending their carefully written reports by mail and, later, by a relay of couriers.

With his passable German, Forbes cultivated good contacts at the Prussian headquarters, in particular Crown Prince George of Saxony. As the Prussians encircled Paris, Prince George confided in Forbes that they were going to start the bombardment at St Denis on a certain day. Forbes amazed and baffled his rivals by having his story printed the very morning of the attack. Many years later he revealed the secret to William Russell. He wrote an imagined description of a bombardment complete with details of troop movements and sent it off to London. Here it was typeset ready for printing, waiting for Forbes's word. When the first gun fired, he immediately telegrammed his editor, 'Go ahead!'[6] This was to be a ploy he used on other occasions and gave him the reputation of being first with the news.

While Russell and Forbes were reporting from the comparative comfort of the victorious Prussian side, there was an intrepid contingent of British Specials sharing the privations of the besieged citizens of Paris. It included Henry and Frank Vizetelly of the *Illustrated London News*. Henry's son, Ernest, also contributed and later claimed that, at the age of eighteen, he was the youngest correspondent on record. The *Daily Telegraph* was represented by John Merry Le Sage and *The Standard* by Captain John O'Shea. The latter had commenced the war by reporting from the Prussian side but had decided to enter Paris, where he remained during the siege.

The final British Special was a wealthy young adventurer named Thomas Gibson Bowles. He travelled to Paris when the war broke out and offered his services to the *Morning Post*. Bowles found journalism to his taste and eventually founded *The Lady* and *Vanity Fair* magazines. He was friend and champion of the artist James Tissot, with whom he became reacquainted during the Paris siege, and was grandfather to the Mitford sisters. He later became a politician and is gratefully remembered by Winston Churchill for having supported the latter during his maiden debate. He supplied the young Churchill with a telling opening riposte against the formidable Lloyd George, in a speech with which the fledgling MP made his mark.

In the event, it was Bowles, the amateur, who alone ventured to the battlefront whenever the French attempted to break through the Prussian lines. He described a rare French success near Champigny on the banks of the Marne: 'In a minute or two the fusillade began in earnest – a rolling, rattling crackling fire, which now and then swelled into a continuous roar. The road to the right was partially hidden by an incessant curtain of white smoke, which distinguished it from the rest of the line, where the action was indicated only by little detached puffs. Suddenly the smoke of the barricade cleared off and was not renewed, and the instant after I saw a swarm of men running rapidly at and disappearing behind the barricade, which was thus taken at the point of the bayonet.'

When the Siege of Paris began, there were only seven balloons in the city. By improvising with varnished cotton many more were constructed. Despite being inflated with highly explosive coal-gas, very few were brought down by Prussian sharpshooters. In total sixty-five balloons were successfully launched. Because of the risks involved, the Specials found themselves charged £100 to send their reports. The balloon service echoed George Robinson's short-lived enterprise at the Siege of Metz.

Henri Labouchere gained fame as the 'Besieged Resident' of the *Daily News*. Aged thirty-nine, Labouchere had led a varied life. In his youth he had joined a Mexican circus because he had fallen in love with a lady acrobat. In 1865, he had been elected to Parliament as a radical and a republican, which brought much displeasure from Queen Victoria, who referred to him as 'that viper Labouchere'. His term as an MP was short-lived as he lost in the next election, but as one door closed, another opened. Labouchere inherited a fortune, part of which he used to purchase a quarter-share in the *Daily News*, then promptly assigning himself to Paris.

Labouchere found himself reporting on a Paris that showed little fighting spirit, despite the presence of some 400,000 troops, including the National Guard. They seemed more concerned with squabbling amongst themselves than resisting the Prussians who were taking their time in preparing for an assault. Labouchere described the city:

'Paris, once so gay, has become as dull as a small German capital. Its inhabitants are not in the depths of despair, but they are thoroughly bored. They are in a position of a company of actors shut up in a theatre night and day, and left to their own devices, without an audience to applaud them or to hiss at them. "What do you think they are saying of us in England?" is a question which I am asked not less than a hundred times every day. My interrogator usually goes on to say, that it is impossible that the heroism of the population has not elicited the admiration of the world. It seems to me that if Paris submits to the blockade for another month, she will have done her duty by France; but I cannot for the life of me see that she has done anything to entitle her to boast of having set the world an example of valour.'

Reports of fighting were rare as hunger continually occupied the thoughts of the residents. The accounts of food shortages and a population reduced to eating all manner of livestock from rats to the occupants of the zoo shocked British readers into a wave of pro-French sympathy. The Specials were able to get their reports and sketches away by using the balloon post, which proved highly successful in evading the Prussian noose.[6] Labouchere thought otherwise. When the armistice was restored, he found that only one in twenty dispatches had reached his paper.

Henri Labouchere wrote a rather tongue in cheek series of the hardships the population faced, particularly regarding food. On 19 October, he reported:

'Each person now receives one hundred grams of meat per day, the system of distribution being that everyone has to wait on an average two hours before he receives his meat at the door of a butcher's shop. I dine habitually at a bouillon; there horseflesh is eaten in the place of beef, and a cat is called rabbit. Both, however, are excellent, and the former is a little sweeter than beef, but in other respects much like it; the latter something between rabbit and squirrel, with a favour all of its own. It is delicious. I recommend those who have cats with philoprogenitive proclivities, instead of drowning the kittens, to eat them. Either smothered in onions or in a ragout they are excellent.'

He followed this with some more culinary advice on 31 October: 'I shall never see a donkey without gratefully thinking of a Prussian. If anyone happens to fall out with his jackass, let me recommend him, instead of beating it, to slay and eat it. Donkey is now all the fashion. When one is asked to dinner, as an inducement, one is told that there will be donkey. The flesh of this obstinate but weak-minded quadruped is delicious – in colour like mutton, firm and savoury. This siege will destroy many illusions, and among them the prejudice which has prevented many animals being used as food. I can most solemnly assert that I never wish to taste a better dinner that a joint of donkey or a ragout of cat – trust me.'

On 15 December he sent via balloon mail: 'In the rue Blanche there is a butcher who sells dogs, cats and rats. He has many customers, but it is amusing to see them sneak into the shop after carefully looking round to make sure that none of their acquaintances are near. A prejudice has arisen against rats … For my part, I have a guilty feeling when I eat dog, the friend of man. I had a slice of a spaniel the other day; it was by no means bad, something like lamb, but I felt like a cannibal. Epicures on dog flesh tell me that poodle is by far the best, and recommend me to avoid bulldog, which is coarse and tasteless.'

With the dwindling animal population being devoured by Parisians, Labouchere finally wrote on 6 January 1871:

'Yesterday, I had a slice of Pollux for dinner. Pollux and his brother Castor are two elephants from the zoological gardens, which have been killed. It was tough, coarse and oily, and I do not recommend English families to eat elephant as long as they can get beef and mutton. Many of the restaurants are closed owing to want of fuel. They are recommended to use lamps, but although French cooks can do wonders with very poor materials, when they are called upon to cook an elephant with a spirit lamp the thing is almost beyond their ingenuity. Castor and Pollux's trunks sold for forty-five francs per pound; the other parts of the interesting twins fetched about ten francs per pound.'[7]

Another danger the Specials had to face was 'spy mania'. Armed with their pencils and notepads, it was all too easy for the curious newsman to be accused of being a spy. Indeed, Henri Labouchere was forced to leap onto a café table and deliver a fiercely pro-French speech to placate a crowd who had accused him of spying. He also took to wearing a 'sugar-loaf hat of the First Republic and am consequently regarded with deference. An English doctor who goes about in a regulation chimney-pot had already been arrested twenty-seven times; I, thanks to my revolutionary hat, have not been arrested once.'

The Special artist from *Illustrated London News*, William Simpson, with his sketch pad, came in for particular attention. He had been accused of being a spy by a mob in Metz and arrested for sketching a coach at the Battle of Forbach. When he returned to Paris in 1871, he was again arrested during the paranoia of the Commune. There was certainly an anti-British feeling which came about because of the British Government's neutral stance in the conflict and generally pro-Prussian public opinion. This did change as news reports of how the French were suffering were published.

It was on 1 March 1871, when the Prussians entered Paris, that Archibald Forbes experienced his own 'spy-mania'. He had crossed from the protection of the German cordon to see what conditions were like for the Parisians. Almost immediately he was surrounded by a knot of angry men accusing him of being a spy. Tall and well-built though he was, Forbes was wrestled to the ground by the mob and dragged feet first towards a fountain where they intended to drown him. At the last moment a detachment of French National guardsmen arrived on the scene and rescued him. They marched him off to the police station where, to his dismay, he discovered that part of his greatcoat that had contained his notebook had been torn away. Forbes was more concerned with the loss of his precious notes than the predicament in which he found himself. While he was bemoaning his loss, a citizen dashed into the police station waving aloft his notebook and proclaiming that it was evidence that Forbes was indeed a spy. Ignoring the serious allegations levelled at him, Forbes was so relieved at the return of his notes that he actually tipped the astonished accuser a five franc piece. 'The implacable patriot accepted it!'

Under escort, Forbes was marched through the gathering crowd to appear before a magistrate. Examining his passport and journalistic credentials, the magistrate consulted his sister, who had lived in England, and she confirmed his bona fides. Forbes was released, with many apologies, and the magistrate's sister volunteered to accompany him safely back to his hotel. Grateful for her help, Forbes was at a loss to know how to repay her. Swallowing her pride, she asked for food, which was increasingly in short supply. Forbes and his fellow journalists filled a large hamper and employed a porter to take it and his saviour back to her house. This was probably the last decent meal she enjoyed, for the Prussians withdrew to their lines that encircled the city and the nightmare of the Commune began.

Forbes chose this time to leave Paris and the war. He was to use this piece of advice many times: 'However interesting a battle may be, you must always get away before your communications are cut, for your material will be held up or never arrive. You must not be taken prisoner, for then you will be out of business completely. You must not get wounded, for then you will become a useless expense to your paper. And if you get killed, you will an infernal fool.'[8]

Forbes had an ulterior motive for returning to London for he had entered into a contract with a publisher to write a book about the war. The *Daily News* was not impressed and urged him to return to Paris to cover the Commune. Writing flat out ten hours a day, Forbes stalled his editor and delivered his manuscript in eight weeks.

If the siege was dreadful, then the events once the Prussians had had their victory parade and withdrawn were catastrophic. A civil war raged in the streets of Paris between the revolutionary republican Commune and the conservative Versailles National Assembly, which favoured a settlement with the Prussians. Supplied and encouraged by the Prussians, the troops of the National Assembly crushed the Commune with a great loss of life. Even today there is still bitterness on the French Left over this conflict.

Archibald Forbes, having completed his history of the war, finally complied with his editor's wishes and returned to Paris to witness the last bloody days of the Commune. Other correspondents and artists were already there. William Simpson, in particular, had a torrid time. When the National Assembly troops broke through into central Paris, Simpson was pinned down by a hail of bullets. A Communard grabbed him and hauled him along to help build a barricade, something that other reporters experienced. Under threat of death if he refused, Simpson had no alternative than to start piling materials to build a rampart across the street. When the gunfire became so intense, the Special was able to slip away. Four days later, Simpson was storming a barricade with the Versailles soldiers.

As the Communards' defence perimeter shrank, Archibald Forbes found himself sheltering in the porch of a church from where he could observe three barricades. He was spotted by a Communard officer who demanded that he pick up a rifle and man a barricade. Forbes explained that he was both a foreigner and a reporter, but to no avail. Forbes still refused to fight, so the officer called on four of his comrades and put the protesting Special up against the church wall and prepared for summary execution. He was rescued by a sudden rush of Versaillist troops, which sent the firing squad scampering away. Forbes then went through the same experience with the Versaillists as he was accused of being a Communard and again put up against the same church wall. Protesting his innocence, his story was finally believed when the officer examined Forbes's hands for tell-tale gunpowder stains.

Forbes's account of the final days of the Commune vividly convey the chaos, fear and hopelessness amongst the civilian population, as it sought to escape the fighting that was in its midst. Stripped of the Victorian tendency for verbosity, his account reads as if written by a later generation of war correspondent. One can only have admiration for Forbes and, indeed, his fellow reporters as time and again they risked their necks, wandering the dangerous city streets seeking the centres of action. They were almost always alone, not having the companionship of a cameraman and sound engineer as might today's correspondents. Often under fire from both sides they ran the risk of being regarded as spies as they scribbled notes or drew hasty sketches. The wonder was that there were no fatalities amongst this tough band of Specials.

The Versaillists had sealed off the city so that none of the correspondents had been able to get their reports away. Forbes had given a copy of his despatches to a colleague, who was well acquainted with several Versaillist officers and was confident he would be allowed through the cordon. The following day Forbes visited the British Embassy and found his friend, blood-spattered and exhausted. Far from being allowed through, he had barely escaped with his life. Not for the last time Forbes resolved to try himself to get his despatches through enemy lines, despite the poor odds against success. He persuaded the embassy to allow his reports to be put in a big official red-sealed envelope bearing the address 'Her Majesty the Queen of England'.

Almost immediately, things started to go wrong. The poor starved horse that he rode collapsed on its side, pinning Forbes by the leg. Fortunately some passing soldiers rescued him and, pausing to confirm his leg was unbroken and after rewarding his rescuers with drinks at nearby café, Forbes slowly rode on. Successfully negotiating patrols and road blocks, he reached the most formidable obstacle, the Point du Jour Gate, where the colonel in charge absolutely refused him right to pass, despite producing the impressive looking envelope. Undeterred, Forbes hung around until the colonel went away. He had noticed that the major left in charge was wearing a British Crimean War medal. Sharing a cigar and dwelling on the old comradeship of the French and British during the Siege of Sebastopol, Forbes finally won over the officer, who then turned a blind eye as Forbes passed on his way.

Travelling by train and ferry, Forbes reached his London office early on the 25 May. Having submitted his report, he then retraced his steps and was back in Paris the following day to witness the retribution meted out to anyone suspected of being a Communard. Death, fear and suspicion hung over the city like the smoke from the many burning buildings. Forbes, Simpson and many of the foreign press reported their shock and disgust at the dreadful bloodletting that left some 20,000 dead.

With the conflict over, Archibald Forbes emerged as the new star of the Specials. His mentor, William Russell, was unable or unwilling to involve himself in competing to have his stories first in print. In what was his last active campaign, Russell did land a scoop, albeit a political one. He was present when the King of Prussia was proclaimed Kaiser of a united Germany in the mirrored hall at Versailles. Without a doubt, Russell enjoyed favours and access to information that were denied other correspondents, not least the German papers. This was mostly due to representing a major paper of a neutral country in the hope of producing a positive impression on British opinion. In fact, the favouritism shown to British correspondents by the Prussians caused one young German correspondent named Hoff to commit suicide. He had written an outspoken protest against the preferential treatment of English correspondents and had his accreditation revoked. Unable to bear the humiliation and disgrace, he killed himself.

Russell had become a favourite of Edward, the Prince of Wales, which was not altogether a good thing for the profligate journalist. Now moving in elevated circles, but still not abandoning his radical beliefs, Russell found himself increasingly involved with his royal friend. The Great Man had now become an anachronism, out of touch and stand-offish. He knew his day was over, but, as will be seen, he could still court unpopularity with the Establishment if he found incompetence and injustice.

Chapter 7

Into Africa's Dark Centre

The 1860s was a decade of relative peace for Britain. Apart from trouble in far-off New Zealand and the occasional unrest on the North West Frontier of India, the British Army was not involved in any major campaign. Then in 1868, the British mounted a new campaign, not of expansion, but one of rescue. The emperor of Abyssinia, Tewodros II (anglicised to Theodore), was an unstable ruler who was regarded as a friendly pro-Christian by Britain. A lost letter addressed to Queen Victoria and the subsequent lack of response drove the deeply insulted Theodore to make a captive of the British envoy, Captain Charles Cameron. In 1864, he had also imprisoned other British subjects and various other European missionaries and their families. The British sent a mission with a letter from the Queen, but they too were added to the emperor's list of captives. This breach of diplomatic immunity finally drove the British government to launch a rescue mission. In 1868, the largest and most expensive expedition involving the British Army was landed on the coast of the largely unknown Abyssinia. Led by Lieutenant-General Sir Robert Napier, Commander-in-Chief of the Bombay Presidency, a force of 13,000 fighting troops (9,000 Indian and 4,000 British) and 14,500 camp followers, scientists and a few newspaper correspondents set off to cover the 400 miles to Theodore's mountain-top fortress at Magdala.

Along with George Henty of *The Standard*, was Welsh-born Henry Morton Stanley. After an extremely unhappy childhood, a young John Rowlands ran away to sea and arrived in New

Orleans in 1859. There he was taken in by a merchant named Henry Morton Stanley, who adopted the young man and gave him his name. With the outbreak of the Civil War, Stanley volunteered for the Confederate Army but was captured and imprisoned in the North. He was given the choice of fighting for the Union side but sickness led to him being returned to England. When he had recovered he sailed back to America and volunteered for the Union Navy. After the war, he began to work as a newspaper reporter and covered the Indian Wars in the West. His flair for reporting led the proprietor of the *New York Herald*, James Gordon Bennett, to send him to report this interesting rescue the British were mounting in a wild and unknown country.

The *Illustrated London News* employed Major Robert Baigrie, who had thirty-two drawings published, all of the surrounding country, accompanied by text. He was regarded by *Illustrated London News* as their 'scenery specialist', for his talent did not run to drawing figures in a lifelike way. Finally, the *Illustrated London News* sent William Simpson, their experienced artist-correspondent, specifically to draw Abyssinians and their customs, but he arrived a week after the capture of Magdala. His drawings continued to be published as the public had an appetite for life in this faraway country. Interestingly, he was issued with an Abyssinian War Medal, despite the military's reluctance to recognize war correspondents until the Anglo-Boer War.

General Napier, an experienced Royal Engineer, planned the expedition meticulously. He installed a desalination plant and built 300-yard-long piers at the base in Annesley Bay; a telegraph line was strung and a single-line railway track was laid for part of the route. Setting off on 25 January 1868, and after fighting a series of small battles, the expedition reached Magdala on 10 April. A concerted rush by 6,500 of Theodore's warriors was met by the 4th (King's Own) Regiment and the Naval Brigade armed with a combination of the new Snider breech-loading rifle and rockets. The brief battle resulted in huge casualties on the tribesmen while the British suffered just twenty wounded. The following day, Theodore released his prisoners and later committed suicide. Before he left Magdala, Napier set charges and blew up the late emperor's lofty capital.

Henry Stanley sent his report to the *Tribune,* scooping his competitors. He had bribed the telegraph operator at Suez so his despatches were the first to be sent out. He was further helped by a fortuitous breakdown of the cable between Malta and Alexandria, making his report on the fall of Magdala the 'sole authoritative source for almost a week'. Stanley neatly summed up Napier's expedition: 'Though a little war, it was a great campaign.'

George Henty was understandably miffed by Stanley's coup and there were mutterings of fraudulent practice and vulgar behaviour from other rivals. It must be remembered that Stanley received the backing of the millionaire James Gordon Bennett, who spared no expense to obtain early news.

Bennett then backed Stanley to go in search of the missing missionary, David Livingstone. The two met up in a village on the eastern shore of Lake Tanganyika and his greeting, 'Dr. Livingstone, I presume?' became one of history's most famous catchphrases. Despite gaining fame on his return to England, Stanley was not well received by the Royal Geographical Society, who resented being upstaged by a mere newspaper reporter. At the height of his fame, he chose to return to Africa to report on the Ashanti War, but his main purpose was to prepare for a major exploration of the interior. Between 1874 and 1878 he traced the course of the Congo River, mapped Lake Victoria and wrote a book of his exploits entitled *Through the Dark Continent,* a title by which Africa has been known since. In 1892, Stanley reverted to British citizenship, was elected a Member of Parliament and later knighted.

Britain continued to enjoy peace and prosperity and was happy to have been a spectator while her old rival across the Channel was suffering defeat and civil war. The emergence of a United Germany was felt to be of little significance to Britain as she turned away from Europe to concentrate on her expanding empire around the world. Topics other than war caught the public's interest during 1872-3. The newspapers were filled with the mystery of the American barque *Marie Celeste* which had been found drifting crewless in mid-Atlantic. A significant event was the opening of the Suez Canal, which considerably cut the time it took to sail to India. Giuseppe Verdi was commissioned to write an opera and the premiere of *Aida* was performed in Cairo to mark the occasion. And, of course, there was Henry Stanley's famous meeting with David Livingstone at Lake Tanganyika on 25 November 1871. In America, meanwhile, there was a development which was to have a profound effect on the future of reporting. The arms manufacturer, Remington, started the first mass production of the typewriter.

After the end of the Civil War, America increasingly looked west and as a consequence stirred up the Indians who would have to make way for the burgeoning numbers of settlers. Although the British public was little concerned with this mass movement of Americans and the subsequent Indian Wars, the *Illustrated London News* did send William Simpson to draw illustrations of the spectacular American West. Reaching California in 1873, Simpson learned of an Indian outbreak in the north of the state. Dubbed the Modoc War, this took place amongst the bizarre moon-like landscape of the Lake Tule lava beds. Fifty-two warriors and 150 dependents took refuge amongst the jagged outcrops and held off the American army for several months. Simpson hurried north and recorded this unusual campaign which was the only one of the Indian Wars to be covered by a British publication.[1]

Meanwhile, on the West Coast of Africa there was trouble brewing from another bellicose tribe, the Ashanti, which was ruled by the barbarous King Kofi Karikari, whose name was soon anglicised to King Coffee. In a complicated arrangement, Britain held several fortified trading posts on the coast of an unhealthy spot called the Gold Coast. It was probably the least regarded of all Britain's possessions, producing little in the way of a trading return and having a deadly climate that was the original 'white man's grave'. Britain used the local coastal tribe, the Fantee, to act as their go-betweens in their dealings with the Ashanti, who traded in gold. When the Ashanti attacked the Fantees, the local authorities organised a defence force formed from the local tribes, the West Indian Regiment and the crews of Royal Navy ships in the area. For nearly a year, there were continuous skirmishes with the Ashanti who dominated the country, leaving the heavily out-numbered British barely able to keep their finger-hold on their coastal settlements. Belatedly and with some reluctance, the Government finally sent out the 23rd Royal Welch Fusiliers, the 42nd Highland Regiment and a battalion of the Rifle Brigade under the command of thirty-eight-year-old Major-General Sir Garnet Wolseley.

Garnet Wolseley was the most famous soldier of his day. Unlike many of his contemporaries, he was energetic, innovative and successful. Taking on this seemingly minor and inglorious task, he actually emerged with his reputation further enhanced. Despite his own overweening vanity, ruthless ambition and love of publicity, he came to despise war correspondents. He later described them as 'those newly invented curse to armies who eat the rations of the fighting man and do no work at all', 'a race of drones', 'that dreadful creature "One Who Knows"' and 'those twin brothers, "The Man on the Spot" and "the Man who has been There"'.[2] He seems to have made an exception, however, for war artists. Certainly for this campaign, he was well disposed to the press and placed them on the same footing as the Staff and allowed them to draw rations.

A good number of newspapers sent out their correspondents to cover this little conflict. This was a time when Africa made 'good copy'. During the middle years of Victoria's reign, British explorers had penetrated the interior of the Dark Continent and their adventures and discoveries continued to excite the public. Now a war was to be waged in the frightening and dangerous jungles of West Africa and an eager public wanted details.

Amongst those sent were George Henty, still with *The Standard,* Frederick Boyle of the *Daily Telegraph,* Winwood Reade of *The Times* and, rather surprisingly, the *New York Herald*'s celebrated correspondent, Henry Morton Stanley.[3] A twenty-eight-year old artist-reporter was also making his debut for *The Illustrated London News* – Melton Prior was about to embark on a most extraordinary career that lasted thirty years in which he covered twenty-five campaigns. In fact there was only one year in which he did not visit a seat of conflict.

Garnet Wolseley surrounded himself with similar-minded officers who worked with efficiency and energy. One of them was Henry Brackenbury, whose brother, Charles, had been with William Russell at the Battle of Königsgratz. Henry sent Wolseley-approved reports back to *The Times* brimming with praise for his chief. Amongst the forward-thinking decisions Wolseley made was for the British soldiers to be kept on board their transports some miles from the coast so as to cut the risk of tropical diseases and to clothe the men in a lighter-weight grey material instead of the usual heavy serge red tunics. They also received a daily dose of quinine and a list of 'do's and don'ts' for the tropics. During the voyage from Britain, officers were required to acquaint themselves thoroughly with the area of operations by reading all available accounts and studying the latest maps. This ran counter to the usual expectation of the British officer who took pride in his lack of professional knowledge, preferring to limit his conversation to hunting and society gossip.

Wolseley planned a swift direct thrust north to take and destroy the Ashanti capital, Kumasi, while another column of the Naval Brigade approached from the east. The advance was as arduous as any experienced by the British Army and the Ashantis proved to be a very tough nut to crack. Struggling through the curious half-light of the thick jungle, Wolseley's men were frequently ambushed and everyone suffered from the high temperatures and humidity. The men were constantly tormented by mosquitoes, ticks and leeches and suffered the ever-present threat of snakes and crocodiles as they waded through swamps and streams. Prior had six servants and bearers, one of whom was a female who carried his 60lbs of whisky and claret upon her head and a baby on her back. Going into camp one evening, Prior was alarmed to find that this bearer or, more accurately, his precious stock of alcohol, was missing. After a couple of hours, however, she appeared with an additional baby strapped to her back!

On 31 January, just outside the village of Amoaful, Prior and Henty found themselves in the thick of the fighting and unable to find suitable cover. Stumbling through the undergrowth, they managed to reach the protection of the 42nd Highlanders. Prior quickly sketched them as they made a determined charge and scattered their attackers. Having taken the advice of his more seasoned colleagues, Prior had augmented his campaign kit of sketch-pads, pencils, Lamplough's Pyretic Saline and champagne with a pistol and a double-barrelled shotgun. In the confusion of the ambush, Prior found himself confronted by two warriors. He fired and hit the first warrior in the chest and felled the other in the back as he turned to flee. He later wondered if he had committed murder as he was not a soldier, but quickly consoled himself with the fact that it had been a matter of self-defence. The close-up horror of fighting and its results nearly persuaded the fledgling Special to quit. He was pressed into service in the makeshift field hospital and had to hold down a wounded soldier as he had his leg amputated. He vowed: 'Prior, if you ever get out of this fight alive, you will never catch yourself coming of your own free will into another.'[4] He did, of course, and into many more.

Prior was not the only Special to take part in the fighting. Winwood Reade was employed by *The Times* because of his knowledge of the West Coast of Africa. On one of his explorations, a journey in present-day Sierra Leone, he had been imprisoned for three months by a local chief and set four gruelling tasks for each day of his captivity. He managed to survive and return to England to write a book of his experiences entitled *Savage Africa, a Tour*.

At Abakrampa on 6 November 1873, he fought alongside a mixed command of the Naval Brigade and West Indian Regiment as they were besieged in a church by hundreds of Ashanti warriors. Reade wrote of his experience:

'At the upper end of the village was a Wesleyan chapel, which was occupied by the blue-jackets and marines and was a perfect fortress in itself. The thatch had been taken off, and the roof or ceiling made an upper-deck, on which was placed a rocket-trough and a little Dutch gun. The windows and open sides of the roof were filled and padded with sacks, behind which lay the men, who arranged port-holes or embrasures for themselves. Shelter-trenches ran down the side of the village, which was partly enclosed by a palisade, and the houses were all of them loopholed. But the chief defence of Abrakrampa was its clearing. A large space of ground had been made open so that it afforded no cover from fire, and at the same time was littered with brushwood so that it could not be crossed at a rush. Before the Ashantees could enter the village they would have to storm this open ground under fire from the Snider, and their loss would be severe …

'The Ashantees, concealed in the bush, swarmed along the paths they had cut in a crescent facing the church. We heard their drums beating, and their ivory trumpets, and the voices of their chiefs; and then they began their war-song, which, chanted by thousands in unison, had a magnificent effect. The King of Arbra went out into the open near to the bush and cried out. "I am the king of this country; come on if you are coming!" He was answered with a fusillade [from the Ashanti]. The Ashantee kept up their fire almost without intermission through the night, ceasing only at 4 am. Lieutenant Saunders, R.A., worked the little gun … and Lieutenant Wells fired rockets, which were sometimes received with a yell, sometimes in dead silence. There was a bright moon and the enemy ventured but little beyond the margin of the bush.

'The next day they attacked the village on three sides at once, and kept it up till dusk without a moment's cessation. The sharp whistling of slugs, like that of wind through fir trees, was always in the air … Opposite the church within the clearing was some rising ground which sloped towards the bush. A party of Ashantee skirmishers, creeping out into the open, but covered by the hill, fired at the men in the church.

'Captain Grant of the 2nd West Indies Regiment was stationed with thirty soldiers to the left of the church and received permission to clear the hill. Captain Grant took his men over the open near the brow behind which the Ashantees were lying. Then, waving his sword in the air, cried "Charge" and went at the double, followed by his men and the "Times" correspondent [Reade].'

The Ashantis took to their heels and the attack petered out as they withdrew. They still kept some skirmishers to trouble the defenders and Winwood Reade went in search of one of them. 'I stalked the man in advance till I got near enough to see him when he stood up to fire. I missed him twice, and he shot back at me, so it was quite a little duel; the third time I silenced him ... The gallery applauded, or, in other words, I was cheered by the men in the church ... So ended the famous siege of Abrakrampa.'

Reade also found himself fighting alongside the 42nd Highlanders in the jungle at Amoaful. He wrote: 'It was no idle motive that induced me to thrust myself into "the forefront of the hottest battle". In a bush-battle no bird's-eye views are to be had, and a war correspondent who wishes to see anything of war must go very near the enemy ... Now hitherto we had never beaten the Ashantees in the bush.'

On 21 January 1874, Reade was breakfasting with the 42nd Highlanders when they were alerted by firing. Reade recalled: 'I snatched up my Snider. The 42nd marched along at a pace which, after four months of West Africa, and an attack of dysentery, made me pant and perspire ... as we descended a hill the battle began. The soldiers extended to the right and the left of the path in line, and we found we were in the Ashantee camp. ... A hundred yards ahead the forest was filled with smoke, and seemed to roar: tongues of flame shot forth, and these alone served as a mark, for not a man was to be seen. The slugs hummed and danced in among us, rattling against the trees, and against the pots on the fires. I was hit three times in about five minutes; but these hits were innocuous that I thought it was all going to be mere child's play. However, I was soon undeceived.

As the Highlanders slowly advanced, moving from tree to tree as directed by their officers, and lying down to shoot, we came to a thicker part of the bush, and the enemy fired at close range. Finally, we came to a swampy bit at the bottom of the hill, with a dark sluggish stream flowing through its midst; beyond this was another hill, covered, not the forest, but jungle ... I am not exaggerating when I say that for more than an hour the leaves fell just as they do on an English autumn day when there is a strong wind. At one time, which ever way I looked, I saw wounded men. One poor fellow ran past me with a strange staggering gait, his eyes fixed and his hand upon his heart, and then suddenly fell and rolled over stone dead.

'The Highlanders advanced but very slowly; the bag-pipes were playing, but even when close to could scarcely be heard for the din ... We were now at the foot of the jungle-covered hill on the summit of which was Amoaful. Up went the gun; every five minutes there was a halt; the gun was fired two or three times; the Highlanders crept into the bush on the right and on the left. Then I heard a clear cheery voice cry out "Advance!" The jungle was now so thick that the men were formed again in column; it was too thick for the Ashantees, who had not cut war-paths, and were so obliged to occupy the road, where they suffered severely. Soon we had to lie down among dead bodies marked with great red wounds: yet still the slugs sang over us, and savagely slashed the boughs above our heads.'[5]

Finally, Amoaful was captured and the Ashanti Campaign was almost over. On his return to England, Reade wrote a final book, *The Story of the Ashantee Campaign*, but his health had been badly affected and he died in 1875.

George Henty used his experiences as a reporter to write 'ripping yarns' for boys. He wrote 122 adventure novels including *By Sheer Pluck; a Tale of the Ashanti War*. A fervent supporter of the British Empire, his books became recommended reading for young boys by educationalists of the day.

It took a further five days of cautious advance, fighting and negotiating to cover the remaining ten miles to the capital,

Kumasi. A steady stream of litters conveyed the sick and wounded back to the coast. Half of Wolseley's command was incapacitated and most were later discharged from the army with permanently damaged health. The heat and humidity were debilitating and, as Prior faced another steep hill to climb, he grabbed the tail of a passing mule. The rider was Wolseley who turned and said, 'Never mind, Prior, hold on and we two will drag you in.'

As they neared the capital, they waded through pools of stagnant water strongly smelling of blood. It was soon found to be the blood of human sacrifices that had run into the water. There was one more encounter with the Ashanti before all opposition evaporated and the victorious soldiers entered a deserted Kumasi in the evening. The exhausted and feverish soldiers gave three weary cheers and Prior celebrated by sharing a bottle of warm champagne with Henty and Stanley. The light-hearted mood, however, soon turned sombre. There was a tangible atmosphere of evil about the place. Boyle, of the *Daily Telegraph*, graphically described Kumasi as 'a town over which the smell of death hangs everywhere, and pulsates on each sickly breath of wind – a town where, here and there, a vulture hops at one's feet, too gorged to join the filthy flock preening itself on the gaunt dead trunks that line the road; where blood is plastered, like a pitch coating over trees and floors and stools'.

The journalists explored the town and its surroundings and what they found was the stuff of nightmares. In a grove behind the main street they came upon the King's slaughter place where the remains of the victims of human sacrifice were deposited. There were thousands of piled-up skulls amongst the trees and the ground was thick with whitened bones. Several decapitated bodies were in various stages of putrefaction and the stench was sickening. The troops found a dungeon full of intended sacrificial prisoners who refused their freedom because they had accepted their fate as offerings to their deity.

Prior made a quick sketch of the mass slaughter area before exploring King Kofi's two storey stone-built palace. The interior was less than imposing, being furnished in trade cloths and cheap European furniture. Leaning against the bed was a British sword bearing the inscription 'From Queen Victoria to the King of Ashanti', which had been presented to the king two years earlier. This, along with other artefacts, was claimed by Wolseley as his personal war booty. Prior's own plunder was more modest; a pair of gold slipper buckles he took for his wife. This was despite Wolseley's express instructions that the correspondents should not help themselves to any booty. Wolseley forbade plunder of any kind and actually had one of the native soldiers hanged for taking a piece of cloth. The British camped that night in the streets and the following morning the general ordered an early evacuation and destruction of Kumasi. The reason for the precipitous withdrawal to the coast was the almost total breakdown of his line of supply. Prior was so engrossed in making last minute sketches that he was left behind as the town went up in flames around him.

As he retraced his steps to the coast, Wolseley sent a courier ahead with despatches to England and, magnanimously for him, included Prior's sketches and report. Although the Ashanti army had not been destroyed in battle, they had been subdued for the time being. Wolseley had further enhanced his reputation and the new Special, Melton Prior, was shown to be a worthy successor to the veteran William Simpson.

The brief campaign had exacted a heavy toll on the British, who had suffered terribly from the heat and jungle diseases. Prior himself had to be carried aboard the home-bound ship suffering from fever but, as he later reflected, 'if I am stupid enough to follow Tommy Atkins, I must share his luck. It is not all beer and skittles.'

Chapter 8

The Balkan Wars 1876-78

Following the Ashanti War, there was a lull in war reporting. True, there was yet another Carlist War in Spain during 1873, which was covered by Forbes, Prior and a few others. Henry Stanley summed up the indifference generated by this conflict as 'the most uninteresting and interminable campaign ever planned'. The newspapers soon realised this and withdrew their correspondents.

For many of the Specials there followed a pleasant break from roughing it on some uncomfortable assignment. In 1874 the Prince of Wales offered William Russell the appointment of Honorary Private Secretary, which he was obliged to accept. It seems a strange decision, given their different personalities and beliefs. Russell was good company and the Prince did enjoy mixing with some of the less conventional personalities of that time. There may also have been an element of spiting his father, the late Prince Albert, who was always critical of the British press and took particular exception to Russell's reports from the Crimea, which he felt undermined the Government and Army. He wrote to the Secretary of State for War, 'The pen and ink of one miserable scribbler is despoiling the country of all the advantages which the hearts blood of 20,000 of its noblest sons should have earned'.[1] Edward was also known to enjoy slightly raffish company. For his part, Russell, despite his anti-establishment attacks, did relish moving in such rarefied circles, even if it did hit his pocket hard and he never entirely trusted the Prince.

The following year the most elaborate tour ever undertaken by British royalty occurred when the Prince visited India. He was accompanied, not only by his new Private Secretary, but also a full complement of the gentlemen from the press. Amongst those taking time off from war reporting were Archibald Forbes, George Henty and Melton Prior. These rather rough and ready characters were dealt with somewhat harshly by Billy Russell in his diary. Besides dismissing Forbes as a low trooper, he described Prior as 'the most insufferable conceited snob I ever met'. The latter also gained the epithet of 'the screeching billiard ball', due to his round bald head and high-pitched laugh.[2]

Whilst the royal party were enjoying themselves in India, the newly elected Conservative government under Benjamin Disraeli made a purchase that was to have great significance for Britain and its future foreign policy. Britain bought nearly half the shares in the Suez Canal from the impoverished Ottoman Khedive of Egypt, thus thwarting French attempts to wholly own the canal. In so doing, Egypt fell into the category of being strategically important to Britain and so became another splash of pink on the atlas of the world. The free passage to India and the Far East was regarded as essential as four fifths of the ships that passed through the Canal were British.

It was in another part of the ailing Ottoman Empire, however, that the next significant conflict broke out. The Balkans held a fascination for the Victorians who avidly read the dozens of books that were published each year about this wild, mountainous and exotic region. By 1877, there were as many as 129 titles devoted to the subject, so any conflict in the region would be certain to have a ready readership. During the summer of 1876, the Christian Serbs in the Balkan states of Bosnia and Herzegovina rose up against Turkish rule and were quickly supported by their cousins from Serbia and Montenegro. In an unequal contest, the might of the Ottoman Empire, although greatly weakened by corruption and economic turmoil, took just four months to defeat the Serbs.

In 1875, Melton Prior was sent instructions to visit the insurgents in Herzegovina. He arrived at Ragusa (Dubrovnik) and waited until he could make contact. In the meantime, he learned the hard way to avoid sampling the local cooking. Everything was filthy and any meat obtained from the local butcher was unfit for human consumption. Taking the advice of some local ex-pats, he feasted on boiled eggs, chocolate and preserved meat.

Through contacts, he was passed through a network of insurgents until he was deep into the mountains where he met Peco Pavlovitch, the notorious Herzegovinan chief: 'He stood 6 ft. 6 in tall in his stockings, and a more magnificent specimen of the genus bandit, I should say, it would be impossible to imagine.'

The conference with fellow chiefs was interrupted by a knock at the door. 'An insurgent entered followed by a Turkish soldier who stood to attention unarmed. He brought a letter from the General in charge of the Turkish forces which were then at Gatcho, and he asked permission to pass provisions through to the starving fortress at Goronsko. This letter was read and explained to Peco, who then pretended to read it, and with a growl tore it into small pieces and cast it into the fire. "That is my answer," he said, with which he waved his hand for the man to get out of his sight. The Turk and his insurgent keepers left the room, and he had not proceeded half-way down the staircase when I heard a shriek and a thud. The Turk had been murdered.'

A few days later, Prior was to see more of this casual violence. 'We were travelling along the road on the edge of a mountain, and were examining with our glasses the fortress, when we noticed a Herzegovinian coming round the corner of the road. For some reason or other, as soon as he espied us, he turned round and seemed to stroll back again. Peco Pavlovitch said something to the man accompanying him, and without any hesitation this man brought up his rifle to his shoulder and fired, and down fell the Herzegovinian mortally wounded.

'We then hurried forward, and to my amazement and horror I found he was not quite dead, but one of our men drew his yataghan (long knife) and in an instant cut his head off. To my astonishment I found he was not a Herzegovinian but a Turk disguised.'

Prior was to witness the most appalling barbarity by both sides. From his perch on a hillside, he watched as a column of Turks were ambushed in a defile below and killed to a man. 'On came the Turks, their advance-guard passing through the defile. It was only when half of them got through that the firing began. It is impossible for me to describe it, as it seemed to occur in a dream, the whole thing was so quick. The rifle-firing from the splendid cover our men had taken up was certainly carried on for some considerable time without the Turks being able to reply. Then, when our men found they had demoralised the enemy, they threw down the rifle and cloak, drew their yatagans, and with a fiendish yell rushed in upon the Turks. The slaughter was simply terrible.'[3]

The following day he visited the scene after there had been a heavy snowfall. His attention was drawn to three mounds that reminded him of cannonballs stacked at the Woolwich Artillery Academy. Kicking away the snow, he was sickened to discover the decapitated heads of the slain neatly piled in heaps. This was just one of the many terrible sights he was to see in this cruellest of wars.

It turned out to be but a prelude to a more serious conflict the following year.

The *Daily News* sent Archibald Forbes, who reached the Serbian capital, Belgrade, in May 1877. Sitting in his hotel restaurant, Forbes pondered how he was going to cope in a country of which he had not the slightest knowledge of either topography or language. His attention was drawn to his waiter, who seemed a particularly assured individual. Upon being questioned by Forbes, the young man turned out to be fluent in English, Serbian, Russian and Turkish. Andreas, as he was named, was hired on the spot and proved to be an invaluable find.

War correspondents at that time relied on a team of servants, couriers and local representatives to gather and send their reports. The resourceful Andreas fulfilled all these functions, although Forbes did have his problems in keeping him in line.

On several occasions, when they came under fire, Andreas would grab a rifle and go charging off to join in with the Serbian attack but would always reappear, on one occasion minus an ear-lobe. He was also a good rider and Forbes would occasionally send him off with his reports, sometimes on round trips of a hundred miles or more. A great scrounger and cook, he could be relied upon to produce a chicken for the pot as long as no questions were asked. Forbes also owed him his life. During some confused and scattered fighting, Forbes rode straight into a Turkish patrol. Dragging him from his saddle, the Turks prepared to carve him up. Suddenly Andreas appeared from out of the woods, wearing a fez, waving an old parchment and shouting in Turkish that Forbes had safe passage from the Turkish commander. The ruse worked and Forbes was released with profuse apologies. Andreas explained later that he carried a fez in case of such incidents and the proffered parchment always worked because the average Turk was illiterate.

An example of Forbes's own determination and toughness occurred when he closely observed the six-hour Battle of Deligrad, then rode 120 miles, changing horses every fifteen miles. Arriving at the telegraph office, he then wrote a telegraphic report of four columns and sent it off to the *Daily News*, all in the space of thirty hours! Later in the campaign, Forbes was joined by a special artist on his first assignment for *The Graphic*. At the age of twenty-four, Frederic Villiers was destined to become one of the most distinguished recorders of war in a career that spanned fifty years. Compared with Prior and other artists, he possessed only moderate ability but he made up for it with exceptional energy and perseverance.

When he was a student at the Royal Academy, Villiers used a fellow student's French passport to travel to Paris to observe the aftermath of the Commune for a painting project. To his relief, he was never challenged as he sketched the war-scarred city. He was particularly moved by the sight of lightly buried bodies of Communards close by the wall where they had been executed by firing squad. His first effort at reporting, however, came when he submitted sketches he had made of the fire at Alexandra Palace. He had been attending an exhibition when a fire broke out which rapidly spread throughout the building. Along with other volunteers, he managed to carry to safety most of the pictures and other treasures before the fire was brought under control. Villiers then sent his sketches to *The Graphic*, who published them.

When Villiers saw the headlines that war had broken out in the Balkans, he again contacted *The Graphic* and volunteered his services. Armed with a letter of introduction, he sought out and teamed up with Forbes in a small town that served as the Serbian army headquarters. The sketch he made of Forbes at the time seems so full of life that one feels it is a true image – with a backdrop of soldiers, peasants and a priest, mingling with several pigs. In the foreground, the striking figure of Forbes: 'A tall, well-knit man in knickers and jacket of homespun with tam-o'-shanter bonnet cocked over his handsome, sunburnt face and a short cherry-wood pipe protruding beneath his tawny moustache.'[4] The next few years would see them sharing many adventures together. During the final days of this brief war, they acted as orderlies in a makeshift hospital run by a British medical team, a particularly harrowing experience as they witnessed close-up the effects of artillery on the human body.

Another correspondent, whom Forbes regarded as the most brilliant he ever met, rejoiced in the name of Januarius Aloysius MacGahan, an Irish-American who worked for the *New York Herald* and was also commissioned by the *Daily News*. It was he who exposed 'the Bulgarian atrocities' to the British public when he graphically described how Turkish irregulars had murdered 12,000 men, women and children. His graphic despatch published by the *Daily News* on 22 August 1876 caused a sensation and led Russia to declare war on Turkey. Under the headline, THE TURKISH ATROCITIES IN BULGARIA: HORRIBLE SCENES AT BATAK, he wrote:

'We formed a curious but a somewhat lugubrious procession as we wound up the steep mountainside. First there were our two zaptiehs in their picturesque costumes, bristling with knives and pistols, our guide likewise armed to the teeth, then the five persons who composed our party, mounted on mules decked out with nondescript saddles and trappings, followed by a procession of 50 or 60 women and children who had resolved to accompany us to Batak ... We at last emerged from a thick wood into a delightful little valley that spread out a rich carpet of verdure before our eyes ...

'This little valley with its rich grassy slopes ought to have been covered with herds of cattle and sheep. No one was to be seen. The pretty place was as lonely as a graveyard, or as though no living thing had trod its rich greensward for years ...

'This was the village of Batak, which we were in search of. The hillsides were covered with little fields of wheat and rye that were golden with ripeness, although in many places the well-filled ears had broken down the fast-decaying straw ... and were now lying flat, there were no sign of reapers trying to save them. The fields were deserted as the little valley, and the harvest was rotting in the soil ...

'As we approached Batak our attention was drawn to some dogs on a slope overlooking the town ... They barked at us in an angry manner, and then ran off into the adjoining fields. I observed nothing peculiar as we climbed until my horse stumbled on a human skull partly hid among the grass. It was quite hard and dry, and might, to all appearances, have been there two or three years, so well had the dogs done their work. A few steps further there was another, and a part of a skeleton, likewise, white and dry.

'As we ascended, bones, skulls, and skeletons became more frequent, but here they had not been picked so clean, for there were fragments of half dry, half putrid flesh attached to them ... At last we came to a little plateau where the ground was nearly level ... But all suddenly drew reign with an exclamation of horror, for right before us, almost beneath our horses' feet, was a sight that made us shudder. It was a heap of skulls, intermingled with bones from all parts of the human body, skeletons nearly entire and rotting, clothing human hair and putrid flesh lying there in one foul heap, around which the grass was growing luxuriantly. It emitted a sickening odour, like that of a dead horse, and it was here that the dogs had been seeking a hasty retreat when our untimely approach interrupted them.

'In the midst of this heap, I could distinguish the slight skeleton form, still enclosed in a chemise, the skull wrapped about with a coloured handkerchief, and the bony ankles encased in the embroidered footless stockings worn by Bulgarian girls. We looked about us. The ground was strewed with bones in every direction, where the dogs had carried them off to gnaw them at their leisure ... These, then were all women and girls. From my saddle I counted about a hundred skulls, not including those hidden beneath the others in this ghastly head nor those scattered far and wide through the fields. The skulls were nearly all separated from the rest of the bones – the skeletons were nearly all headless. These women had all been beheaded.'

This is just part of MacGahan's grim report, which goes on to describe even more distressing sights. Nowadays, we are subjected to reports of so many outrages (Rwanda, Srebrenica, ISIS etc.) that we have become somewhat numbed by the frequency and scale of these religious and tribal massacres. For the first time, a newspaper published MacGahan's long and detailed account of the atrocities committed against helpless civilians.

Diplomatic efforts from the major powers brought a temporary halt to the war, but in the spring of 1877, the Slavic champion, Russia, once again resolved to end Ottoman dominance in the Balkans. With two of the largest powers involved, the newspapers sent teams of correspondents to cover what was considered a major war. Once again Archibald Forbes was sent to join MacGahan and Villiers. They were teamed with two more Americans, Frank D. Millet and John P. Jackson, in the reciprocal alliance between the *Daily News* and the *New York Herald*.[5] By pooling their resources and observations, they were able to report a much wider view of the war than their rivals. Also present was the now veteran George Henty, on his last campaign before concentrating on a hugely successful career as an author of adventure stories for boys. He was accompanied by his *Standard* colleague from the Ashanti War, Frederick Boyle. *The Standard* took an anti-Russia stance, as did the *Daily Telegraph*. Both Boyle and the *Telegraph*'s man, Drew Gay, had their accreditation withdrawn by the Russians and moved to report the Turkish side.

A teenager, Frank Scudamore, was covering the first war of his long and active career. Amongst *The Times*' correspondents was George Dobson, destined to spend most of his working life in Russia before falling foul of the Communists after the Revolution and being deported. Melton Prior was sent to record the fighting from the Turkish side and annoyed his employer by insisting in taking along his wife, no doubt in an effort to placate her. Given the long and uncertain periods that war correspondents spent away from their homes, it was not surprising that there was discontent and pressure from many of the wives. Russell's own family life was miserable and Prior's ended in divorce, although both remarried later in life.[6]

With justification, the Turks had always suffered from a bad press and were highly sensitive to any critical reports. Faced with the enforcement of a strict censorship, Prior got around the problem by a head-on solution. He showed the censor's office sketches he had made of Turkish brutality and threatened to have them smuggled to London if any of his other sketches which had been rejected were not released. The official, however, got his revenge when he had Prior arrested some months later. Prior travelled to Bulgaria and met up with both Drew Gay and Coningsby of *The Times*. Together they travelled to the border areas where the Russian advance was being effectively repulsed. To avoid being mistaken for a Russian, Prior took the advice of wearing a fez rather than his bowler hat. He did not find this style of headgear to his liking as the sun baked his bald pate. Even travelling with accreditation, they were in constant danger from the wild and murderous Bashi-Bazouks, semi-criminal irregulars used by the Turkish army. They saw plenty of casual cruelty by these undisciplined thugs who took delight in cutting up women and children in the villages through which they passed. Prior later recalled that, as neutral reporters, they dared not interfere: 'I had seen Circassians attacking a convoy of fugitive women and children, whom they robbed, and, in some instances, murdered. I saw women with half a dozen sword-thrusts, children prodded with bayonets, and more than once I have seen Bulgarians chased by young Circassians and Bashi-Bazouks, stabbed and killed before my eyes, yet I was powerless to render them any protection.'

On one occasion, Prior and his companions got wind of a plot that their escort of Bashi-Bazouks was planning to rob and murder them on the road. By sticking closely together and with revolvers drawn, the reporters managed to discourage any such attack.

On the other side, the Russians did not impose any field censorship. Instead, they merely insisted that the correspondents gave their honour not to reveal troop movements or advanced plans. A copy of the newspaper had to be filed and later checked for any transgression. If any was found then a warning was issued and, if further displeasure was incurred, the guilty newsman was expelled. Also, for the first time, visual identification was issued in the form of a brass arm badge, to which the more fashion-conscious French contingent objected. It was replaced by a more discreet embroidered arm band displaying the Russian double-headed eagle. Furthermore, a stamped identification had to be carried at all times, with a duplicate copy placed in the 'Correspondent's Album' kept by the commandant of the headquarters. When Forbes saw this comprehensive album, he found it contained as many as eighty-two portraits.

Forbes and Villiers travelled to Bulgaria and were joined in Bucharest by Forbes's Serbian 'gofer', Andreas. The front they had to cover was extensive and, as the only telegraph was at Bucharest, there was much hard travelling to and from the front line. They were the only correspondents present when the Russians made a desperate and unsuccessful attempt to storm the

Turkish defences before the town of Plevna, the biggest battle of the war. Forbes wrote:

'The jagged line springs onward through the maize fields, gradually assuming a concave front. The roll of rifle fire from both sides is incessant, yet dominated by the fiercer and louder turmoil of the artillery above us. The cannon redouble the energy of their fire. The crackle of the musketry fire swells into a sharp continuous peal. The clamour of hurrahs of the fighting men comes back to us on the breeze, making the blood tingle with the excitement of the fray. A village is blazing on the left. The fell fury of the battle has entered its maddest paroxysm. The reserves which have remained behind the crest are being pushed forward over the ridge in reinforcement. The wounded are beginning to trickle back to behind the ridge – some poor fellows have already passed us. We can see the dead and the more severely wounded lying where they have fallen on the stubbles and among the maize. The living waves of fighting men are pouring over them on and on. The gunners behind us stand to their work with a will on the shell-swept ridge. The Turkish cannon fire begins to weaken from that earthwork opposite to us ... they are across the ditch in an avalanche of maddened revenge. Not many Turks get the chance to escape from the gleaming bayonet ... There is a momentary desperate struggle, hand to hand, bayonet to bayonet; and then the Russians were in possession of the Turkish redoubt.'[7]

This somewhat purple-tinged account was typical of Forbes' style with its punchy short sentences building to a climax. He and Villiers did not watch this battle unfold from some distant hillside, but were amongst the shells and bullets.

After repeated attempts to carry the Turkish positions, the Russians fell back, having suffered many casualties. The Bashi-Bazouks then left their lines to slaughter the wounded. As the Russians retreated, Forbes joined a protective line to cover the evacuation of the wounded, which went on all during the night. With the dawn, Forbes rode away to report on this costly Russian defeat, only to have his horse collapse and die on him. Carrying his saddle on his head, he struggled onto the nearest town to find another mount, before continuing on his way. During the same battle, Drew Gay witnessed the Russian attack from the Turkish position. With nightfall he managed to creep through the Russian lines and evade Cossack patrols. After a hair-raising ride, he was able to reach Constantinople and file his report.

Forbes's efforts to help the wounded at Plevna were later rewarded in a singular way. He was riding to report the fighting on the Schipka Pass when he paused at the Imperial headquarters to change horses. The commander, General Ignatieff, questioned him about the battle, as Forbes had beaten the army messengers with the news. Pausing only to grab some food and a change of horse, Forbes was anxious to be on his way. Instead, Ignatieff led him into the presence of Tsar Alexander II and made Forbes repeat his report to the Father of All Russia. So the travel-worn ex-trooper not only gave his account of the recent battle but was asked his opinion on the progress of the whole war. At the end of this audience, the Tsar said: 'Mr. Forbes, I have had reported to me your conduct on the disastrous days before Plevna, in succouring the wounded Russian soldiers under heavy fire. As the head of the State, I desire to testify how Russia honours your conduct by bestowing on you the Order of St Stanislaus with the crossed swords, a decoration never conferred save for personal bravery!'[8]

Frederic Villiers wrote that he and Forbes both received the Serbian Order of the Takova for bravery some twelve years later. He was hard-put to recall any particular incident that warranted the award, but was told it was for saving a large store of ammunition at Deligrad when they had torn off the burning thatched roof.

Hard riding, poor diet and suspect water caused Forbes to be invalided back to England suffering from fever and exhaustion. Unfortunately for him he missed the eventual fall of Plevna.

His friend Januarius MacGahan was on hand to witness the Turkish surrender but his report was the last he wrote. He had spent most of the war encased in plaster suffering from a broken ankle. Another fall from his horse broke his half-set bone but his lameness did not deter him from following the fighting through the terrible winter of 1877-78. Tragically, an outbreak of typhus hit the camp in which he was staying and claimed his life at the age of thirty-two. His death was received throughout Bulgaria with great mourning as he was regarded as their great champion for independence. Indeed, when Bulgaria did receive its independence, an annual mass was performed for many years in his memory and today there are several memorials in Bulgaria honouring MacGahan. It can be said that this was the only time that the passionate writings of a war correspondent influenced events by bringing about the Russo-Turkish War and the resultant birth of a new country.

With the revelations of the 'Bulgarian atrocities', the newspapers were unanimous in their opposition to Turkey and generally supportive of Russia. This ran contrary to the British Government's official line which was to keep Russia away from the Mediterranean even if it meant taking an unpopular pro-Ottoman line.

Chapter 9

The Afghan Wars

For over two decades, British newspaper readers had been fed accounts of other countries' wars. True there had been the Ashanti War, but that had not involved any great feats of arms or mighty battles. Now Britain entered into a period where her armed forces would be involved almost constantly in some conflict or other on the borders of her burgeoning empire. The demand for more exciting stories from a growing and impressionable young readership led to the appearance of such magazines as the *Boys Own Paper*, *Sons of Britannia*, *Young Englishman* and George Henty's contribution, the *Union Jack*. This heightened patriotism and the need for first-hand accounts brought about a change of style in war reporting.

The strident age of jingoism had dawned and with it a general decline in balanced objective writing. Now the reporter was more inclined to write about the campaign from his own perspective, bringing in events real and imagined to excite his readers and boost his reputation. War reporters were also more aware of their status and enjoyed their roles as the elite of journalism. They began to dress in a quasi-military style, draping themselves with bandoliers and binoculars and wearing revolvers on their hips. Military-style forage caps, wide-brimmed hats or pith helmets became the rage. The experienced specials like Forbes and Prior proudly wore the medal ribbons of their foreign decorations on their campaign jackets. With the notable exception of William Russell, who was permitted to wear both the Crimea and Indian Mutiny ribbons, the British Army refused to award campaign medals to newspapermen until the Anglo-Boer War.

Increasingly, war correspondents identified themselves with the British Army and imperialism. Barely tolerated by most army commanders, they were generally well accepted by the officers and were often made honorary members of the mess. They also often shared the British contempt and condescension for their native foes and believed in the absolute right of the British Empire. Although there was little contact with the lower ranks, the press presented a rosy picture of Tommy Atkins as a strong and steadfast soldier, dependable and ably led. The reality, however, was somewhat different.

In 1870 the average height for a recruit was five feet and eight inches but by 1879 it had fallen to a puny five feet and four inches. The Army was still regarded as the last resort for a desperate man, and the British soldier was generally treated as a social outcast. There was little to attract a normal healthy youth into volunteering and those who did were usually running away from poverty, boredom, family or a pregnant girl. Harsh treatment and constant drilling did, nevertheless, turn this unpromising material into well-disciplined, if unimaginative, soldiers who would behave well in battle. The newspapers were not inclined to report any criticism of the fighting calibre of the British soldiers and any disastrous reverse was heroically depicted. The reporters were not entirely uncritical and were quick to attack shortcomings in the generals and deficiencies in equipment and supplies.[1] This was the age when Victoria Cross winners became national celebrities rather than just local heroes. Officers became role models for the young, and the common soldier began to gain respect, and all largely thanks to glowing coverage provided by the increasing power of the war reporter.

Of all the regions in which Britain has been involved in conflict, the North West Frontier still epitomises all that appealed to the Victorian readers: harsh, unforgiving terrain, a formidable and cruel foe and, in the background, the threat of the Russian bear. It was just this threat that led to the Second and Third

Afghan Wars of 1878-81. After Russia's victory over Turkey, Britain was fearful that her old enemy would gain control of the Bosphorus and, therefore access to the Mediterranean. The Treaty of Berlin that followed the war blocked Russia's ambitions in that direction. Thwarted, Russia concentrated on expanding her empire in Central Asia and by 1878 she had reached the northern border of Afghanistan.

Although alarmed by Russia's expansion, Britain did not want to absorb this wild and chaotic Afghanistan into her Indian empire. Instead, she preferred to have a pro-British ruler in control who would act as a buffer between India and the Russian menace. In the summer of 1878, the Russians sent a large mission to Kabul. To counter this, the British sent a similar mission, but it was turned back at the fort of Ali Musjid near the entrance to the Khyber Pass. Smarting from this insult, the Governor-General demanded an apology and the installation of a British Resident, but when there was no response, war was declared on 21 November 1878. Conveniently, the gradual build-up to hostilities had enabled the newspapers to have their best men on the border as the invasion columns entered Afghanistan.

The army divided itself into three field commands, with the smallest, the Kurram Valley Field Force, bearing the brunt of the fighting. This was commanded by the diminutive Major Frederick Roberts of the Bengal Artillery, who was given the local rank of major-general. A winner of the Victoria Cross during the Indian Mutiny and an experienced campaigner, he had found climbing the promotion ladder a slow process. The next few years would change this and by 1885 he was appointed commander-in-chief of the Indian Army. Further campaigns and honours followed until Field Marshal Roberts retired with an earldom. From the start, Roberts made himself popular with the newspapermen by stating that he would cooperate fully. In return, all he asked was that they reported truthfully and fairly and that he should read their telegrams before they were sent. This was like a breath of spring to men used to the frustrations of dealing with remote and dismissive commanders. From then on,

'Little Bobs', as Roberts was affectionately known, could do little wrong and generally enjoyed a good press.

Archibald Forbes, Frederic Villiers and Drew Gay arrived at the border and were joined by the veteran William Simpson of the *Illustrated London News*. Another reporter was the unscrupulous Hector MacPherson of *The Standard*, soon to fall foul of the amenable 'Little Bobs'. A notable absentee was Melton Prior, who had been sent to cover an outbreak of fighting in South East Africa. The Anglo-Indian force crossed into Afghanistan and was soon confronted by a formidable obstacle, the Peiwar Kotal, a narrow and heavily defended pass. It was dominated by a steep-sided mountain, which looked impossible to carry. Roberts pulled back out of range of the Afghan guns and pitched a camp, using a few days to scout the area. A frontal attack was out of the question but he fooled the Afghans into thinking this was what he intended. Leaving the camp intact with fires burning, he marched under cover of darkness around the left flank of the mountain and attacked at dawn. The defenders were taken by surprise as soldiers charged up the pine covered slope and after a fierce exchange of fire the Afghans melted away into the surrounding mountains. Roberts secured the area, received additional reinforcements and pushed forward occupying the whole of the Kurram Valley. He established a strong line of supply including a telegraph link, which was regularly cut by the tribesmen.

Forbes recalled that there was a constant danger from Afghan sniping, so much so that one night, as he drifted off to sleep, he heard a splattering of shots and chose to ignore them. Unfortunately, one of the Afghan bullets hit one of the draught elephants in the ear and sent it stampeding about. In its frenzy, the elephant blundered into Forbes's tent, but fortunately did not step on him. The greatest danger, however, was the huge swing in temperature. During the duration of one day, a soldier died of sunstroke and another froze to death while on night sentry duty.

On 7 January 1879, there was an incident that was so misrepresented by *The Standard* that it led to the withdrawal of their correspondent and damaged the new-found trust between the military and the reporters. During the night, some tribesmen were discovered trying to creep into camp and the sentries opened fire. In the confusion, some Afghan prisoners tried to wrest the rifles away from their guards and escape. After calling out a warning, the duty officer gave the order to open fire, killing six and wounding thirteen of the prisoners. In the cold light of day, Roberts appealed to the reporters not to report this regrettable incident. As agreed, the reporters submitted their reports, without reference to the shooting of the prisoners and Roberts countersigned their telegrams before their despatch.

The exception was Hector MacPherson, who, for political reasons, altered his countersigned report and sent it to London. He was vehemently anti-empire and attacked Rudyard Kipling as 'a foe of civilisation' who 'pandered to the innate brutality of the Anglo-Saxon race'. Not only did he betray Roberts's trust, but he exaggerated his report to tell of the slaughter of ninety bound men. When it was published by *The Standard*, there was outrage that British soldiers could murder helpless prisoners and questions were even asked in Parliament. When the truth was learned, MacPherson, who had previously incurred displeasure through his inaccurate and sensational style, had his press pass revoked and returned home in disgrace.

In contrast, Archibald Forbes relished the campaign and even managed to get himself Mentioned in Despatches. During one of the forays into the hills, the advanced section that Forbes accompanied entered a narrow and gloomy ravine. Suddenly they came under a ragged fire from both sides of the defile and several men were hit. The young soldier marching beside Forbes was hit in the thigh and fell. Forbes wrote: 'Assisted by a young soldier I cut the cloth from the fallen man's leg, and found that he was bleeding very fast. No tourniquet was accessible, nor was any surgeon in the vicinity; so, closing with my thumbs both orifices of the wound, I directed my assistant to find two round stones and get out the surgical bandage every soldier carries in the field. Just as I raised a thumb for him to introduce a stone, there came a second volley from the Afghans above. The young solder hastily ran for cover, and I had no alternative, if I were not to allow the wounded man to bleed to death, but to remain pressing my thumbs on the orifices, kneeling out in the open under a dropping fire from the native gentlemen on the rocks above. After some minutes, a detachment, climbing the crags, gradually drove the enemy away; whereupon I was able to complete my rough operation and to get my patient comfortably on a stretcher. I was naturally proud that when the surgeons came to see him an hour later, they found my device had effectively arrested the bleeding.'[2]

Roberts marched on and occupied the capital, Kabul, but without the company of Archibald Forbes. He, too, had breached the commander's stricture by sending an unacceptable report and was dismissed from the front. In the event, it did not matter greatly for the Afghan War was heading for a peaceful conclusion, albeit temporarily.

Forbes used his enforced exclusion to travel to Burma to interview the newly-crowned King Thewbaw, just before the monarch went on a blood-letting spree that eliminated his entire family. After a predictably bizarre audience, Forbes left the palace at Mandalay and sailed downriver to Rangoon. Here he received a frantic telegram from his newspaper urging him to make all speed to the latest hotspot, Zululand, where the indigenous natives had inflicted the British Army's severest defeat.

While all newspaper attention was focused on events in Southern Africa, trouble flared up again in Afghanistan. The newly-appointed British envoy in Kabul, Sir Louis Cavagnari, arrived and was disappointed that even *The Times* had not thought it of sufficient interest to report. He prophetically said, 'I am afraid there is no denying the fact that the British public require a blunder and a huge disaster to excite their interest'.[3] Three days later he and his escort were dead when a mob stormed the Residency. Within two days General Roberts was again on the march to Kabul with 6,500 men and, after a stiff fight at Charasia, occupied the capital.

Dubbed the Third Afghan War, it was covered by just one war correspondent, Howard Hensman, reporting for the *Daily News* and the Indian paper the *Allahabad Pioneer*. The Indian Government had decided that all newspaper correspondents should be excluded from this campaign and that serving officers should be employed in their place. Fortunately for Hensman this order did not reach General Roberts in time to stop the lone reporter accompanying the Field Force. The rest of the newspapers had to rely on the 'amateurs' (serving officers) like Sir J. Luther Vaughan, an old Mutiny veteran, who represented *The Times*, and also official despatches for their rather downbeat reports.

In fact, the campaign was worthy of professional attention for Roberts's command was virtually besieged at its cantonment at Kabul during the severe winter but had skilfully beaten off greatly superior numbers of Afghan army.[4] During the summer of 1880, Hensman reported a shocking reverse when General Burrow's force of 2,500 men was heavily defeated at Maiwand in a battle that saw the British lose 1,000, a quarter of whom were from the 66th (Berkshire) Regiment. The survivors fell back on the city of Kandahar and began a desperate defence. Roberts was instructed to lift the siege and left on 9 August with an impressive force of 10,000 men. In an epic march which covered 300 miles in twenty days over rugged terrain, Roberts arrived at Kandahar, where his men comprehensibly defeated the Afghan army. Howard Hensman capitalised on his exclusivity and wrote a best-selling book about the war. He later became a *Times* correspondent and spent the rest of his life reporting in India before dying in Simla in 1916.

In 1881, after he had retired from reporting, Archibald Forbes approached the War Office to claim the Afghan War Medal on the grounds that he was 'a person authoritatively attached to the Field Army, who, when with it, performed a service recorded in the C.O's Despatch'. He reinforced his claim by stating he was also a member of the 37th Middlesex Rifle Volunteers. The fact that he had gone to the aid of two wounded soldiers while under fire was met with the mealy-mouthed reply that 'Application is refused as act performed was one of humanity and not consequent on an order from a military officer'.[5] Forbes had to remain content with the dozen flashy foreign orders he enjoyed wearing.

Chapter 10

The Zulu War

Melton Prior, who had missed the Afghan War, had spent much of 1878 covering what has become known as the Ninth Frontier War against the Gaika and Galeka tribes in the eastern Cape Colony. In all ways it was an unsatisfactory campaign for a Special to cover. The distances were great, the imperial forces and their enemy were scattered and any fighting that occurred was little more than skirmishes. Prior's only moment of excitement was when he was relaxing with a friend in a house up-country. It was an uncomfortably hot evening and all the windows were wide open to catch any breeze. He later wrote, 'Suddenly, with a swish, an assegai came through the window and stuck straight upright in the middle of our table'. The guard was called out, but the culprit disappeared into the night.

Prior learned enough about the local situation and from rumours to know that there was going to be war with the neighbouring Zulus and the prospect filled him with foreboding. When he returned to London, he prophetically said to William Ingram, the editor of the *Illustrated London News*, 'You take my word for it, if we do have a war with the Zulus, the first news we shall get will be that of disaster'.[1]

Sir Bartle Frere, the High Commissioner, felt that the Zulu nation, under the military rule of King Cetewayo, was a threat to the stability of the region. After the easy subjugation of the tribes in the recent Frontier War, he and the army commander, Lieutenant-General Sir Frederick Thesiger, later elevated to Lord Chelmsford, were determined to neutralise the Zulu army.

114

Frederick Thesiger (1827-1905) had steadily and unspectacularly climbed the promotion ladder by being a diligent staff officer. In his first active service command in thirty-four years, he was sent to South Africa where he will always be remembered for the loss of 1,300 men at Isandlwana. Personally charming, he lacked leadership skills and surrounded himself with an inadequate staff. Archibald Forbes disliked him and was merciless in his criticism after the war. Thesiger lived out his life quite unable to live down the Isandlwana disaster and died of a seizure while playing billiards at his club.

Ignoring advice from the Boers and the local residents, the British were over-confident and contemptuous of this proud nation. In order to provoke an excuse to invade, Frere prepared an ultimatum, the terms of which he knew would be unacceptable to Cetewayo. When this was rejected, Chelmsford was ordered to cross the border and destroy the Zulu army and its capital at Ulundi. The invasion force was divided into three columns, one in the north near the Transvaal border, one in the south where the Tugela River met the Indian Ocean and the main centre column, which crossed the Buffalo River at Rorke's Drift.

The only British newspaper correspondent present attached himself to this main column as it laboriously crossed the rain-swollen river which divided Zululand from Natal. He was Charles Norris-Newman, employed by the London *Standard* and also, by an arrangement, the *Times of Natal* and the *Cape Standard and Mail*. He was born in 1852 and received a military education which was put to use during the Siege of Paris of 1870-71. Subsequently, he was decorated by Maréchal Louis Trochu, the military governor of the French capital.

Being something of a soldier of fortune, Norris-Newman had served with Don Carlos of Spain and later General Gordon in Egypt. He arrived in South Africa in 1877, and was employed as a journalist. His early Zulu War reports made his name and he stayed on after the Zulu defeat to report the First Boer War of 1880. By mixing his military experience with reporting, he covered the campaigns in Central Africa (1884-91) and

Matabeleland in 1894-98. He was appointed both an intelligence officer with the Rhodesian Horse and was on the staff of the Acting Administrator in 1896.

Norris-Newman later scandalised colonial society when he fell in love with Ethel Finch, a well-known local courtesan and married her on 2 March 1900. Although she had retired from prostitution, it was highly likely that she had been involved with many prominent citizens and, due to the delicacy of the situation, the newly-weds quit Africa. For two years they journeyed to Ceylon, Malaya, China and Japan, finally settling in Manchuria, where Norris-Newman was appointed English instructor with the Russian naval staff at Port Arthur. When the Russo-Japanese war broke out in 1904, he acted as a freelance Special and reported from the Russian side, witnessing the first naval attacks by the Japanese on Port Arthur. In 1907, he was intelligence officer with the Imperial Russian Service before moving to China. In the same year, he founded *The China Review,* which was the first Russian journal in the Far East. He wrote several books about the campaigns in which he had been involved and, in 1910, was living in Tientsin where he was on the staff of the *China Critic.* A combination of avoiding gossip about his marriage to a prostitute and a gift for secrecy makes his life in the Far East something of a mystery. The last reference of his later life is that in 1916, he worked for *The Gazette* in Peking.

During the first three months of the Zulu War, it was Norris-Newman's despatches that made the greatest initial impact. At the start of the campaign, he had been made welcome by the officers of the 3rd Natal Native Contingent (NNC), with whom he camped and messed. The hastily raised regiment was made up of disaffected Zulus and other tribes, who received little training. Poorly led by white officers and NCOs, and held in contempt by the British Army, they understandably gave a poor account of themselves.

Norris-Newman, or 'Noggs' as he was nicknamed, claimed he was the first man to cross the Buffalo River. It was a tense time for the river bank was shrouded in early morning mist which could

Above left: Henry Crabb Robinson – special correspondent for *The Times* during the Napoleonic Wars.
Above right: George Steevens, regarded as the most talented of the reporters, who died during the Siege of Ladysmith.
Below: William Russell writing in his tent during the Crimean winter of 1854-55.

Above: Felice Beato was the first photographer to capture the reality of war. Interior of Taku Fort 1860. Below left: Roger Fenton's photographic van in the Crimea, 1855. Below right: William Simpson photographed by Fenton.

Above left: Thomas Bowlby of *The Times*, who was the first reporter to be killed, China 1860.
Above right: Melton Prior the leading artist/reporter of the era.

Above left: Roger Fenton – Pioneer War Photographer.
Above right: Archibald Forbes displaying his foreign orders, but no British medals.

Above: 'The Stuff of Nightmares': Prior's illustration of the Ashanti King's sacrifice place.
Below left: Januarius Aloysius MacGahan: Bulgaria's unlikely national hero.
Below right: Archibald Forbes in Serbia as drawn by his friend Frederic Villiers.

Above: The death of the Prince Imperial - the scoop that fell in their laps.
Below: William Russell (third from left) watch British troops loot the Kaiserbargh during attack on Lucknow in March 1858.

Above left: Archibald Forbes's 'Ride of Death' to be first with the news of the defeat of the Zulus.
Above right: The last known photograph of General Charles Gordon.
Below left: Bennet Burleigh, of the *Daily Telegraph* – 'A lusty example of Glasgow vehemence'.
Below right: Edward Frederick Knight, adventurer, novelist and correspondent of *The Times*.

Top: Melton Prior's drawing inside the British square at Ulundi, June 1879.
Above left: The fearsome Sirdar of Egypt – General Sir Herbert Kitchener, the reporter's nemesis.
Above right: Alexander Murray – Viscount Fincastle – who won the Victoria Cross while reporting for *The Times*.

Above left: Churchill's indomitable aunt, Lady Sarah Wilson, the *Daily Mail*'s reporter during Siege of Mafeking.
Above right: Winston Churchill reporting for the *Morning Post* in the Boer War.
Below: Bennet Burleigh of the *Daily Telegraph* brings Field Marshal Lord Roberts the news that Bloemfontein has surrendered.

have concealed a Zulu force. In the event, there was no opposition and the great column lumbered eastwards into Zululand. Apart from one sharp skirmish, in which the 3rd NNC were prominent, there was no sign of the mighty Zulu army. After nearly ten days, the column went into camp just twelve miles from their starting point, at a place called Isandlwana.

Intending to move on shortly, Lord Chelmsford saw no need to fortify the sprawling camp that covered the slopes of a prominent rocky butte, which gave an excellent lookout point over the surrounding country. Instead, he sent out mounted patrols to scout the immediate area and a large reconnaissance force to search the country to the south east. The latter consisted of colonial units, including the 3rd NNC. 'Noggs' Newman faithfully chose to follow his adopted unit, which probably spared his life. After a few hours scouting, about 1,000 Zulu warriors were spotted and a message was sent back to Chelmsford requesting reinforcements. Upon receipt of the message, Chelmsford felt that the main Zulu force had been discovered and ordered half his command to prepare to leave during the night. The rest of the camp was to remain but to be ready to follow shortly. What happened the following day goes down as the greatest military defeat suffered by Britain during her colonial wars.

By the time Chelmsford travelled the twelve miles from the camp to where his colonial scouts were waiting, it was about 6.30 a.m. For the next frustrating six hours, small scattered groups of Zulus were spotted over a wide area in the surrounding hills and the tired soldiers tried to pursue them, but with little success. As the morning wore on there was a criss-crossing of messengers travelling between the camp and Lord Chelmsford. The news coming from Isandlwana was barely credible; the camp was under attack. Unwilling to believe this, Chelmsford and his staff dismissed this news with a sarcastic: 'Actually attacking our camp! Most amusing!'[2]

Finally, they did decide to return to camp to check these persistent messages. It was dusk as they rode into view of the base and were confronted with a sight that shook them to the core. In the gloom they saw that the bustling, well-equipped site they had left so recently had been reduced to a shambles of flattened tents, overturned wagons, hundreds of smashed boxes and barrels, ripped grain sacks, broken bottles, scattered papers, tangled ropes and debris of all kinds. This, however, paled at the sight of men stripped of their uniforms in all of postures of death, mutilated in some way and with their entrails spilling out of slashed abdomens.

All the draught animals, oxen and horses, had been hacked to death and even the little terriers that the officers kept did not escape the slaughter. Of the 1,500 men left in camp, over 1,300 lost their lives, including the entire 1st Battalion of the 24th (Warwickshire) Regiment and a couple of companies from the 2nd Battalion. Not a single officer had survived. Norris-Newman wrote: 'The corpses of our poor soldiers white and natives, lay thick upon the ground in clusters together with the dead and mutilated horses, oxen and mules, shot and stabbed in every position and manner, and the whole intermingled with the fragments of our Commissariat wagons, broken and wrecked and rifled of their contents. The dead bodies of men lay as they had fallen, but mostly with only their boots and shirts on, or perhaps a pair of trousers or a remnant of a coat. In many instances they lay with sixty or seventy empty cartridge cases surrounding them, thus showing they had fought to the last.'[3]

All those present would never forget the terrible night they were forced to spend amongst the dead at Isandlwana, laying on grass sticky with blood and brains, fearful that the Zulus would attack again. They also noticed a glow in the night sky from the direction of Rorke's Drift and were fearful for the survival of the men left to guard the stores and hospital at the old mission. Just before day-break, Chelmsford ordered an early start, anxious that his men should not see the full horror that had befallen their comrades in the cold light of day. They crossed the Drift back into Natal and were overjoyed to find that the 130 men left behind had managed to hold off an attack by 4,000 Zulus. Although it was of no strategic value, the victory at Rorke's Drift was a great boost to the shattered morale of Chelmsford's command.

Pausing only to gather the bare bones of this action, 'Noggs' Newman rode hard for the telegraph at Pietermaritzburg, where he found that the news had already been received. He filed his report to *The Standard* and, twenty days after the event, it was read by an incredulous public. The reason the report took so long to arrive was that the telegraph was not yet connected to South Africa so all reports had to be carried by ship from Cape Town to St Vincent in the Cape Verde Islands, the southernmost extent of the telegraph.

The public demanded to know how a British camp, defended by hundreds of rifles, artillery and rockets, could be overrun by savages armed with spears and clubs? A hastily assembled enquiry exonerated Chelmsford, who placed the blame on the late Colonel Durnford, the ranking officer left in the camp. The general local opinion was that the findings of the Board of Enquiry smacked of a cover-up. The sensational news of the Isandlwana debacle prompted the newspapers to divert their star reporters from India and for others to be sent out from Britain.

Once again Melton Prior was on his way back to the country he had left so recently, leaving behind a very discontented wife. *The Times* sent Francis Francis, and *The Standard* despatched F.R. MacKenzie to augment Norris-Newman's efforts. Charles Fripp a young and combative artist was sent out by *The Graphic*. He produced many sketches for publication but is probably best known for the most widely used painting of the Zulu War, the dramatic last stand of the 24th Regiment at Isandlwana which he displayed at the Royal Academy in 1885. Of all the war artists, he was the most accomplished. He was also a founder member of the Artists Rifle Volunteers, which was commanded by the doyen of Victorian art, Frederick, Lord Leighton.

Amongst those hurrying from India was Archibald Forbes of the *Daily News*, on what was to be his last war assignment. Frustratingly for him, the only transport he could find was a slow tramp steamer that seemed to call at every port down the east coast of Africa. Until these correspondents arrived, 'Noggs' Newman enjoyed a free rein and accompanied the troops who returned to Isandlwana on 14 March to salvage anything useful and to bury the dead. The bodies were in a bad state, however, and could not be touched. His graphic report of the haunted and desolate battleground kept public interest simmering until the anticipated reprisals began.

What the Specials found when they arrived was hostility from Chelmsford and his staff and a demoralised army. Forbes was scathing in his attack on what he saw as bungling and ineptitude by the leadership and particularly targeted Lord Chelmsford for his fiercest criticism. Melton Prior, now a seasoned veteran of several wars, used his experience to ensure he enjoyed as much comfort that a hard campaign would allow. Following a tumble from his horse, which damaged his knee, he hired a sturdy wagon. This he loaded with his favourite tinned and potted foods and several cases of brandy and whisky together with a soda making machine. He later wrote: 'I had no fewer than five horses, two in the shafts, one for myself, one for my servant and one spare horse. I followed the army through all its marches in my travelling carriage, and on the eve of the Battle of Ulundi I was the only man who had a tent; all the others lay down in the open.'[4] Hardly something that enamoured himself to either the military or his fellow pressmen.

The first opportunity that Prior had to see any action was when Chelmsford led a force to relieve Colonel Charles Pearson's column that had become pinned down at the hill-top mission at Eshowe, some thirty miles into Zululand. They had crossed the Tugela River at its mouth at the same time as Chelmsford led his centre column over Rorke's Drift. They had fought their way to Eshowe and there they learned of the defeat at Isandlwana.

Instead of retreating, Pearson chose to stay put, a decision that brought hunger, sickness and death. Between 23 January to 3 April, twenty-six men died from enteric and dysentery while being encircled by little more than a watching force of Zulus. Chelmsford felt that the relief of Eshowe was a priority and he assembled a substantial force which he personally commanded. With the prospect of a certain battle, it was somewhat surprising that Melton Prior chose to remain in Natal. He gave as his reason a dream he had had in which he saw his burial at Eshowe. As if to reinforce this premonition, he received a letter from his mother in which she, too, had seen his death in a dream. Not wishing to let down his employer, Prior enlisted the services of Chelmsford's secretary, Colonel John Crealock, a capable artist and 'the services of a private individual named Porter. When the fighting did take place ... my specially appointed artist was one of the first killed.'[5] This is something of mystery as the only fighting that took place was the Battle of Gingindlovu and no civilian, named Porter or otherwise, was a casualty. Maybe Prior was exaggerating for the sake of a good story.

One who was there was 'Noggs' Newman, who viewed the battle from within the heavily defended laager. Forsaking his pencil and notepad, he joined a civilian driver on top of one of the wagons and joined in the shooting, as 2,000 Zulus tried in vain to break the British square. This was fought within sight of Eshowe, and later that afternoon, 'Noggs' Newman rode ahead and scooped his fellows by being the first man into the besieged fort. MacKenzie, of *The Times*, was also there and took part in the bloody mounted pursuit when the Zulus broke and ran, leaving some 400 dead on the surrounding hills. With Eshowe relieved, Chelmsford returned to Natal to complete his arrangements for the second invasion. But before this could take place, there was the unfinished business of interring the dead at Isandlwana.

On 17 May, Forbes and Prior were on hand to record this melancholy event. One of Prior's most famous pictures appeared in the *Illustrated London News* under the title *Fetching away the Wagons*. It did not, however, show the true horror of the scene for the long grass he drew concealed the bones and mummified remains of the dead in all attitudes of death. He wrote in *The Illustrated London Times*: 'The sight I saw at Isandlwana is one I shall never forget. In all the seven campaigns I have been in ... I have not witnessed a scene more horrible. I have seen the dead and dying on a battle-field by hundreds and thousands; but to come to a spot where the slaughtered battalion of the 24th Regiment and others were lying at Isandlwana, was far more appalling. Here I saw not the bodies, but the skeletons of men I had known in life and health, some of whom I had known well, mixed up with the skeletons of oxen and horses, and with wagons thrown of their side, all in great confusion, showing how furious had been the onslaught of the enemy.'[6]

Forbes wrote one of his more thoughtful pieces. He reported that, 'The dead lay as they had fallen, for, strange to relate, the vultures of Zululand that will reduce a dead ox to a skeleton in a few hours, had apparently never touched the corpses of our ill-fated countrymen'.[7] Instead, the bodies had taken on a mummified appearance with leather-like skin stretched over fleshless bones. There were no official photographers covering the war, but a great number of images were taken by local men, including John Lloyd of Durban, who took a series of the wrecked camp at Isandlwana.

Forbes spent several weeks with Colonel Evelyn Wood's column, which was camped at Khambula in the north. His command were seen as being the most effective and energetic, having fought a decisive battle against the Zulus in defence of their camp. On several occasions Forbes accompanied Colonel Redvers Buller and his mounted troops on cattle raids and Zulu hunts. They were a mixed bunch of local men and frontier riff raff, made up of all types and nationalities. It needed a strong leader to keep them in line and, in Buller, they had just the man. Forbes described him as 'a stern-tempered, ruthless, saturnine man, with a gift of grim silence'.[8] Despite his disdain of the press, the newsmen recognised that Buller was newsworthy and built him up as 'The Bayard of South Africa'. It was Archibald Forbes, who further penned a rather purple-tinged account of Buller: 'Leading his men at a swinging canter, with his reins in his teeth, a revolver in one hand, and a knobkerrie he had snatched from a Zulu in the other, his hat blown off in the melee, and a large streak of blood across his face, caused by a splinter of blood from above, this gallant horseman seemed a demon incarnate to the flying savages, who slunk out of his path as if he had been – as indeed they believed him – an evil spirit, whose very look was death.'[9]

How different from the bloated and indecisive man he was to become when he was made army commander at the beginning of the Boer War twenty years later.

Another of the personalities that Forbes met was Prince Louis Napoleon, who was serving in an unofficial capacity on Chelmsford's staff. He was the only son of the late Napoleon III, who had been exiled to England following the Franco-Prussian War. He became a graduate of the Royal Military College at Woolwich but was not permitted actually to serve in the British Army. Nevertheless, he and his mother managed to persuade the authorities to allow him to travel to Zululand and observe the war as an extra aide-de-camp on Chelmsford's staff. Once in Zululand, he could not resist the chance to test his bravery and badgered his superior officers until they allowed him to accompany Buller's command on several scouts. During these forays, Louis had displayed an alarming tendency for recklessness by breaking away from the patrols, sword held high, to pursue isolated natives. During conversation with him, Forbes told Louis that the last time he had seen him was in 1870, from the Prussian side, when he and his father had come under fire and was seen galloping away. Forbes had had a poor opinion of the prince, whom he once described as 'a clothes horse', but he came to change his view during the short time he knew him in Zululand.

After painstaking preparation, the Second Invasion began on 31 May. Chelmsford must have thought that all precautions had been taken against any further disaster, but he had not reckoned on the vanity of the Prince Imperial. It was the late morning of 1 June that Melton Prior exchanged pleasantries with the prince who, accompanied by another staff man, Lieutenant Jaheel Carey, and six troopers of Bettington's Natal Horse, were on their way out of camp for a routine survey for a suitable camp site. Hours later as evening approached, Prior rode out of the camp to find a good background for a drawing.

'I had not gone very far when I saw Colonel Buller and General Wood riding together, and in the extreme distance I saw a man galloping madly towards them. I was not near enough to hear exactly what took place, but it turned out to be Lieutenant Carey returning from the deplorable disaster which occurred in the village of Itiotiozi ... The General asked "Where are you coming from?" He (Carey) was so exhausted, confused and nervous that he could hardly speak, but at last he said that they had been attacked by the Zulus when resting in the village and had to bolt.

'He was immediately asked, "Where is the Prince Imperial?" and holding down his head, with some hesitation, he replied he did not know. No words can express the horror of General Wood and Colonel Buller when they realised that an officer who had gone out on expedition senior to the Prince actually replied that he did not know what had become of him.'

Meanwhile, Archibald Forbes was dining with some officers and fellow Specials when Colonel Harrison poked his head through the tent flap and announced that the prince had been killed. At first no one took Harrison seriously and someone even threw a bread roll at him. When it sank in, there was great consternation for this had the hallmark of a serious scandal. For the reporters present, however, it was manna from heaven; a major scoop had landed in their laps.

Gradually the story emerged that the patrol, at the Prince's insistence, had descended into a wide valley and stopped for a rest by an abandoned kraal. Just as they prepared to mount up and resume their patrol, they were ambushed by a small band of Zulus. It happened so quickly that there was no time to offer any resistance and it was every man for himself as they pulled themselves onto their horses and spurred away. Two troopers were quickly shot and killed before they could mount. Louis's horse was panicked by the commotion and took off with the prince desperately hanging onto to the holster attached to his saddle. After 150 yards, the strap broke and Louis went sprawling. In an instant, the warriors were on him, and although he got off three shots with his revolver, he was overwhelmed and stabbed to death.

His companion, Lieutenant Carey, having ridden out of range, pulled up and looked back but the prince was already dead. Carey was accused of cowardice and given a field court-martial. Lieutenant Jaheel Carey gained much public sympathy through the support the press gave him. The army's knee-jerk reaction had been to make Carey the scapegoat for the Prince Imperial's death, but, once the facts were known, it would emerge that those in higher authority were culpable of a degree of negligence. Also, the Prince's mother, Empress Eugenie, made it known that she did not blame Carey for her son's death. The press, led by William Russell's *Army and Navy Gazette*, took up his cause and the charge was not sustained. Carey was allowed his promotion to captain and he rejoined his regiment, until peritonitis took his life just three years later.

It was not until the next morning that a search party was able to retrieve the bodies.

Prior wrote: 'Many of the correspondents were allowed to accompany the little force of cavalry under General Marshall, which was sent to find and recover, if possible, not only the body of the Prince Imperial, but also of the others who had not returned to camp the previous evening.

'There were the French correspondent of the Paris *Figaro*, Archibald Forbes of the *Daily News*, Mackenzie of *The Standard*, Charles Fripp of *The Graphic*, and myself. The search party spread out over a large area, as it was not known where we might come across the bodies of the unfortunate men. I was riding by the side of Forbes, when, a short distance on our left, we saw one of the troop holding up his rifle and calling out loud. Forbes immediately said, "There it is, Prior. Come on, ride for it!"

'I followed hard on his heels and was the fourth man to arrive on the spot. There I saw the Prince Imperial lying on his back, stark-naked, with a thin gold chain round his neck, to which was attached a locket containing the portrait of his father, the late Emperor Napoleon the Third. The Zulus had stripped him, and taken every particle of clothing, but, looking upon this gold chain and locket as a fetish, had respected it, and left it still round his neck.

'The French correspondent, leaning over with tears streaming down his face, took an English penny from his pocket and placed it over the Prince's eye (the one which had received a spear-thrust) in the hopes of closing it.

'On carefully examining the body it was found that he had been stabbed twenty-one times, and the bodies of the two troopers of Bettington's Horse were found at only a few yards distance, also covered with assegai wounds.'

There was a nick in the abdomen, as was the Zulu custom, but no evisceration. Forbes recalled that the wounds bled afresh as the body was moved.

The Prince Imperial's death provoked an enormous amount of press coverage and the impact on the British public was even greater than that of the Isandlwana disaster. Apart from the human interest aspect of a popular and dashing foreign prince dying for England, and a grieving widowed mother befriended by Queen Victoria, there was the point that there were several correspondents on the spot, whereas there was only one, 'Noggs' Newman, at Isandlwana. By the time Melton Prior's sketches had reached London and gone through the engraving process, it would be two months after the event that they were published. Fortuitously for *The Illustrated London News*, it coincided with the lavish funeral of the Prince at Chislehurst in Kent.

Meanwhile, Chelmsford's advance on the Zulu capital, Ulundi, ground on at a sluggish rate. He had learned that the British Government was replacing him with General Sir Garnet Wolseley and Chelmsford was determined not to be denied a final victory over the Zulus. One aspect that was not reported, as it would have reflected badly on the British Army, was the behaviour of some of the raw recruits who had been sent as replacements. There had already been incidents during the relief of Eshowe when nervous soldiers blazed away at their own side thinking they were being attacked. During the advance on

Ulundi, Prior witnessed a repetition of this type of panic when hundreds of rounds were expended. He later wrote, 'A more disgraceful scene I have never witnessed, more particularly when we realised that six rounds of canister were actually fired by the artillery, without having seen a single enemy'.[10] But such was the desire to show the British in a good light, the Specials all exercised a self-censorship when it came to anything as fundamental as steadfastness amongst their own soldiers. It actually took the belated arrival of William Russell to throw light on the unacceptable behaviour of the British 'squaddie'.

Charles Fripp, *The Graphic*'s talented but excitable special artist, had a confrontation with two senior officers as the column approached Ulundi. After a reconnaissance patrol during which there had been a skirmish with the Zulus, Colonel Lord William Beresford and his men were retiring across a river. Redvers Buller had spotted the diminutive figure of Fripp still sketching on the Zulu side of the river. The short-tempered Buller yelled for Fripp to return instantly or be sent to the rear as a prisoner. Reluctantly, Fripp obeyed but challenged Buller's right to order him about. Just then Beresford rode up and was amused to see the bantam-sized artist square up to the towering Buller. Good-humouredly, Bill Beresford threatened to horsewhip Fripp if he did not show more respect to a senior officer. At this, Fripp launched himself at Bill and it took the combined strengths of Forbes and Prior to drag Fripp from the amused Beresford. After this, they became the best of friends.

Finally, on the morning of 4 July, after covering 100 miles in four weeks, Chelmsford's Column formed a huge square on the plain before Ulundi. Forbes was amazed that the Zulus did not take advantage of the chaos created in manoeuvring so many men into formation. In fact, he made a wager that the Zulus would not attack that morning and his rash bet cost him £100. When Cetewayo's magnificent *impis* did charge, it took less than half an hour of Martini-Henry, Gatling and artillery fire to break their spirit. They made a stirring sight that moved even old sweats like Forbes; 20,000 warriors chanting and rattling their assegais against their stiff cow-hide shields as they came swishing through the grass as they charged to their destruction.

During the height of the battle, Melton Prior made a shocking discovery. His sketch pad containing all his campaign notes and sketches of the present battle had gone missing. In despair, he sank to his knees and burst into tears, until a passing staff officer, Captain Sir William Gordon-Cumming, consoled the distressed Special and gave him his own sketch pad. Sir William Gordon-Cumming was a Scots Guards captain who served on the staff during the Zulu War. He later gained notoriety when he became the main player in the 'Great Baccarat Scandal', which involved the Prince of Wales. In 1891, Gordon-Cumming sued Arthur Wilson for slander over an accusation that he had cheated at baccarat during a house party at which the prince was a guest. During the course of the game, in which the prince was banker, Wilson's son, supported by five other guests, accused Gordon-Cumming of cheating. He was persuaded to sign a paper confessing his guilt and made to promise that he would never play cards again. This was done on the understanding that the matter would be hushed up but it soon became part of London gossip. Gordon-Cumming had little alternative but to sue for slander. After a nine-day trial, during which the Prince was attacked by the press, Gordon-Cumming lost his case. This resulted in his being shunned by his peers and he was thrown out of his London clubs. Furthermore, he was forced to resign his colonelcy and was expelled from the army. There has always been some doubt about Gordon-Cumming's guilt and the impartiality of the trial.

Of the battle, Prior recalled: 'I ran down to where the 21st and 58th Regiments were heavily engaged with some Zulus, said to be 6,000 strong and 30 deep, who were charging … this corner but did not succeed in breaking it; the terrific fire of our men made them stagger, halt and fall back a straggling mass, leaving a heap of dead and dying on the ground. I have read since various statements as to how near the enemy got to our square, and it often stated that twenty to thirty paces was the closest, but I can say that I personally went out and reached the nearest one in nine paces, so their onslaught was pretty determined.'

Meanwhile, Forbes was everywhere, furiously scribbling away. Indeed, he hardly noticed being hit and bruised by a spent bullet.

As the Zulu attack wavered and they fell back, the mounted troops and cavalry were let loose to pursue with devastating effect. There followed a rush amongst the officers and correspondents to be first into Ulundi, which was well ablaze from rocket fire. The first man to enter the Zulu capital was the exceptional horseman Lord William Beresford – and he was forever known after as 'Ulundi' Beresford. Melton Prior nearly became one of the few British casualties at Ulundi, repeating his experience of the Ashanti War when he dawdled alone in the burning capital. He was engrossed in sketching when he suddenly spotted a Zulu sneaking up on him, assegai in hand. Abandoning his artwork, Prior dug in his spurs and cleared a blazing fence to safety.

All the correspondents then set about writing up their notes or completing their sketches. Forbes approached Lord Chelmsford and requested that his report should be included in the despatches he felt sure were leaving shortly. Having a short fuse and a dislike for Chelmsford, he was irritated by the latter's reply that he would not risk sending a courier with the news of the victory until the following day. He pointed out, not unreasonably, that the countryside was still full of roaming bands of Zulus and it was too dangerous. Forbes was outraged and blurted out, 'Then, sir, I will start myself at once'. Afterwards he admitted, 'I was sorry for myself the moment I had spoken'.[11] With the nearest telegraph some 100 miles away at Landman's Drift, it seemed an act of bravado. The gamblers amongst his acquaintances started placing bets and insisted on taking Forbes's £5 stake as he was not expected to be seen again.

In a generous act, Forbes took Prior's sketches and some staff messages before setting off at dusk. 'It was somewhat gruesome work, that first stretch through the sullen gloom of the early night, as I groped my way through the rugged bush trying to keep to the trail of the wagon wheels. I could see the dark figures of the Zulus against the blaze of the fires in the destroyed kraals to the right and to the left of my track, and their shouts came to me on the still night air. At length I altogether lost my way, and there was no resource but to halt until the moon should rise and show me my whereabouts. The longest twenty minutes I have ever spent in my life was while sitting on my trembling horse in a little glade of the bush, my hand on the butt of my revolver, waiting for the moon's rays to flash down into the hollow. At length they came; I discerned the right direction, and in half an hour I was inside the reserve camp of Etoganeni imparting the tidings to a circle of eager listeners. The great danger was past.'[12]

Forbes really was taking a chance for only recently an officer and trooper had been killed on the same track. Using the fortified posts that had been established to protect the column's line of supply, Forbes was able to change horses six times. Artillery Lieutenant Henry Curling was stationed at Fort Marshal and wrote to his mother: 'Forbes the correspondent got here at daylight having ridden all night through dangerous country. He hopes to get to the end of the wire about 50 miles off this evening. Anyhow, he is far ahead of all the other correspondents. He is a great, strong, coarse looking man able to undergo any amount of fatigue and to put up with any amount of snubbing. These specials are a terrible nuisance. They expect to be welcomed everywhere and in fact come whether you welcome them or not. One feels at the same time that it is dangerous to be uncivil to them. They are obliged to be pushing, unsnubbable men; no others would get on at all.'[13]

At about 3p.m. the following day, an exhausted and dishevelled Forbes reached Landman's Drift, having travelled 110 miles in twenty hours. The telegraph had just been extended to the Cape so news now reached London within twenty-four hours. Having sent his report, Forbes then rode on to Durban, where he mailed his full story and Prior's sketches. Incredibly, he had ridden 295 miles in just fifty-five hours.

Forbes's report was the first to reach Britain and was read out in both Houses of Parliament. It brought him even greater fame and his exploit came to be dubbed in the newspapers as 'The Ride of Death'. There was even a suggestion that he should receive the Victoria Cross. More modestly, Forbes applied for the campaign medal to add to his impressive collection of foreign awards. It was his nemesis, Lord Chelmsford, who firmly blocked this award, giving as a reason that Forbes had not carried the official report and the telegrams he had carried were of a more personal nature.

With the war all but over, Chelmsford handed over command to Wolseley and returned home to a mixed reception. He was feted and honoured by the Establishment but unmercifully attacked by the press. In particular, Forbes, his ego bruised, was stung into writing a series of vitriolic articles attacking the noble lord which sparked off a fierce exchange in print with some serving officers who resented any criticism of the military by outsiders. In the event, the debate ensured Chelmsford was never again given an active command.

Exhausted and disillusioned, Archibald Forbes retired from reporting and spent his remaining twenty years writing and lecturing about his exploits until his death in 1900. His last delirious words were of battle: 'Those guns, man, those guns, don't you hear those guns?' Rudyard Kipling thought him to be the 'chiefest' of all reporters, while a mellowed William Russell wrote, 'That incomparable Archibald, he has left no one to equal him'.

William Russell arrived along with Wolseley, who was left with little more than to hunt down and capture Cetewayo, whom the reporter later met in Cape Town. Russell showed he could still court unpopularity by telling the truth. In October he reported that British troops were not just getting drunk and brawling but actually housebreaking and robbing with violence and referred to an increase of convicts wearing the Queen's uniform. In the town of Heidelberg, for instance, soldiers had even stolen the town hall clock. Wolseley was predictably annoyed, not so much about the behaviour of his men, but that the British public should be told of it. He later wrote: 'Russell has established a notorious reputation with the Army, which was never to be erased, and which affected its subsequent relationship with journalists.'

Russell did accompany Wolseley's successful expedition against Sekekuni's Pedi tribe on the Transvaal/Zululand border in late 1879. It was a campaign beset by extremes of climate; days of long hot marches and nights of freezing temperatures interspersed with violent electrical storms. Several men and animals were killed and Russell's stay in South Africa ended when his horse, spooked by a lightning bolt, threw and severely injured him. It was an injury that ultimately led to him being confined to a wheelchair but not before he was able to write about one more war.

For a war of such a short duration, the six-month Zulu War had captured the public's imagination as no other colonial conflict has before or since. For the newspaper readers it was a great adventure encompassing the initial Isandlwana disaster, the gallant Rorke's Drift defence, a formidable Zulu foe and a final comprehensive victory. The Specials laid on the jingoism thickly, so much so that the cracks in the great imperial juggernaut were covered over; it would be a couple of decades before a more objective style of reporting would take its place.

The victory over the Zulus, which did little but cause hardship and a civil war, was followed by a humiliating nine-week war against the Boers in Transvaal. Known as the First Boer War, it started in November 1880 after the Boers had been told that Britain would not relinquish her control over the former Transvaal republic. General Wolseley had handed control over to one of his protégés, General Sir George Colley, who had been with him in Ashanti. A good and intelligent man, Colley lacked combat experience and had no answer against the highly mobile sharp-shooting farmers, who were able to match him in manpower.

With the prospect of war, several of the newspapers sent out their correspondents. Once again, Melton Prior packed his baggage and set sail for South Africa, the third time in three years.

He was joined by Charles Fripp of *The Graphic* and John Cameron of *The Standard*. The *Daily Telegraph*, for some bizarre reason, employed Arthur Aylward, a fervent Irish nationalist and therefore rabidly anti-British. In the event, he would find much to relish in a campaign that exposed their vulnerability. The press arrived as the British began to suffer a series of heavy defeats at Bronkhorstspruit, Ingogo and Laing's Nek, as well as being besieged in seven of their garrisons.

Charles Norris-Newman was still sending reports to *The Standard* and covered the British attack on the Boer positions at Laing's Nek, which controlled the main road between Natal and Transvaal. Advancing uphill, the attack was made piecemeal and the Boers were able to repel the mounted infantry who attempted to outflank the enemy. Labouring up the steep slopes the red-coated soldiers found that they were enfiladed by the Boers, who caused many casualties. This abortive attack was notable as the last time the British wore red tunics while the 58th (Rutland) Regiment was the last to carry their Queen's and Regimental Colour into battle.

'Nobbs' Newman, although officially dissuaded by General Colley from reporting the war from the Boers' view, nevertheless made the long journey to join the enemy camp in order to gain a balanced perspective. Arthur Aylward, the republican-minded correspondent, caused such indignation in Natal he was threatened with lynching. Consequently, he too left to join the Boers but without Newman's avowed intention of balanced reporting. Aylward travelled to Leydenberg where he took up arms and helped the Boers in their attack on the British fort. This did not stop him from returning to England with the signing of the peace treaty.

It was quite a risk Newman was taking and he had to rely on the Boers accepting him as a neutral. He described the general feeling of bitterness against 'the common foe'. He met three doctors, two French and one German, and they swopped experiences they had had in Paris during the Franco-Prussian War. The Boer camps Newman visited were made up of laagered wagons, from where the mounted Boers would carry out their attacks. He finally reached the camp of Commandant-General Joubert at Laing's Nek, where he learned of the signing of the peace terms.

After the Laing's Nek debacle, General Colley sought to occupy a nearby hill that would dominate the Boer positions. Unfortunately, Colley had not thought through his plan and was ill-prepared to fend off the Boer counter-attack. Under cover of darkness, Colley led about 400 men up the steep flanks of the hill known as Majuba. Amongst those who accompanied the men of 58th and 92nd Regiments was John Cameron, whose account was recognised as the most accurate. Once on the summit, the troops were thinly deployed around the flat plateau in what appeared to be an unassailable position.

In the morning, the Boers, having got over the initial shock of the British gaining the high ground, began firing accurately and probing for weak spots in the defences. After five hours of continuous firing, the Boers gained the summit and some of the new recruits of the 92nd began to give way and descend the hill. Gradually the British were pushed back until they made a last stand on a knoll. Finally, they too, were forced over the side. General Colley was the last to follow his retreating troops and was shot through the head. The Boers wreaked havoc on the exposed backs of the helpless British as they tried to evade the ceaseless firing. Dressed in their bright red tunics, they made easy targets at such a short range. Belatedly learning their lesson, the British Army clothed their soldiers in khaki on future campaigns.

John Cameron wrote of the final moments: 'With fierce shouts and a storm of bullets the Boers poured in. There was a wild rush with the Boers close behind: the roar of fire, the whistling of bullets, the yells of the enemy, made up a din which seemed infernal. All round, men were falling, there was no resistance, no halt – it was a flight for life. At this moment I was knocked down by the rush and trampled on and when I came to my senses the Boers were firing over me at the retreating troops who were moving down the hill. Upon trying to rise, I was taken prisoner and led away.'[14]

Thomas Carter of the *Times of Natal* wrote of his attempted escape and capture: 'Our poor fellows broke and rushed for the crest in the rear. I ran with them, being only four or five yards behind the line that had made the last stand. How anyone gained the ridge at the rear and escaped to camp, down the precipice there, a fall of thirty feet clear, and then on and over enormous boulders and bush, a good quarter of a mile further yet to go before the foot of the hill was reached under the bullets that rained down on us from all sides – I don't know. Four men dropped by my side as I ran with the crowd across the basin, before even reaching the head of the precipice. Fortunately there was a kind of heather growing out of the side of the precipice. I can only speak for myself and I managed to save myself from injury in jumping down and catching this herb. Then immediately I found I was with two or three others, who came after me, exposed to a dreadful fire as we scrambled over the rocks. The bullets rained like stones, and several poor fellows, panting and bleeding, were struck as they tried to scramble away.

'I determined to give up running, as I could tell by the way the bullets came that the Boers were all around us, though I could not see them myself, having thought to follow a dry donga shrouded in a bush, taking shelter as best I could in a dry gulley covered with slabs of rock.'[15]

Carter sheltered here for half an hour before he was discovered by the Boers. Taken to the Boer commander, he showed his pass and was allowed to descend to the British camp.

The Boers showed humanity to the wounded and released Cameron to go and fetch medical aid from the British camp. The toll for this final British defeat was over 200 dead and wounded. When Cameron wrote his account, he shared his notes and rough sketches with Melton Prior, who drew several pictures used by the *Illustrated London News*. Prior repaid this gesture when he was able to signal the already mounted Cameron that peace terms had been signed, thus giving the reporter the head start he needed to scoop the opposition. So ended four years of punishing campaigning in South Africa from which the British emerged with precious little credit and which directly led to a greater conflict eighteen years later. Thomas Carter summed it up: 'A miserable ending to a miserable war.'

Chapter 11

Egypt and the Sudan: Part I

British involvement in Egypt and the Sudan was, as in Afghanistan, strategic rather than economic. Pressure from France, Belgium and Italy, who were scrambling for a stake in Africa, and the perceived threat they posed to British control of the Suez Canal, forced the UK to fight an intermittent war that lasted nearly twenty years. Frederic Villiers described it as 'a happy hunting ground for the war correspondent', and it certainly attracted a tough, rough and ready type of correspondent who was as interested in boosting their own image as they were in reporting.[1] Egypt was still part of the Ottoman Empire but enjoyed almost complete autonomy under the control of the Khedive (ruler). Over the years, corruption and misgovernment had forced the Egyptians to sell their stake in the Suez Canal and to borrow heavily from the British and French. By 1879 the debt to these European powers was an incredible £94 million and, at their insistence, the Khedive was forced to abdicate and an international debt commission was set up to preside over Egypt's economy. Many Egyptians resented this humiliation and, led by the officer corps in the army, a series of revolts broke out.

By late 1881, Colonel Ahmed Arabi became Minister of War and felt strong enough to challenge the interference of Britain and France in Egypt's affairs. He assumed power and gathered a popular following with demonstrators carrying flags with the slogan 'Egypt for the Egyptians'. Diplomacy failed and the British sent a large naval force to the port of Alexandria, where anti-European rioting broke out resulting in about fifty deaths.

No campaign at that time would have been complete without the presence of Melton Prior, who was given only four hours' notice by the *Illustrated London News* proprietor, William Ingram, to catch a ship to Alexandria. He had just enough time to call at a chemist on the way to the station to buy a toothbrush and a cake of carbolic soap. His wife would be informed and his baggage sent on. It was yet another contribution to the final collapse of his marriage.

All Europeans, including the small press contingent, took refuge on the ships. As a consequence, Arabi ordered the port's fortifications to be increased and strengthened. The British demand that this work cease was ignored and Admiral Sir Beauchamp Seymour ordered his fleet to leave harbour and take up battle stations. For the newsmen present, this was the first time they could report on a purely naval engagement and much was made of this rather one-sided battle. At 6.30 a.m. on 11 July 1882, eight ironclads and five gunboats began a bombardment which did not cease until 5.30 p.m., when the last fort was destroyed.

Melton Prior was on board the commander's flagship, HMS *Alexandra*, which sustained over sixty hits from the shore batteries. He made sketches of the gun-crews in action and was aware of the near catastrophic explosion that was averted by the prompt action of Gunner Israel Harding. An Egyptian shell landed with its short fuse burning by a magazine containing twenty-five tons of gunpowder. Responding to the cries of alarm, Harding rushed up from the deck below, picked up the fizzing shell and dropped it in a nearby tub of water. For his life-saving gallantry, Harding was awarded the Victoria Cross.

Prior's fellow Specials, Frederic Villiers and John Cameron of *The Standard*, were billeted aboard the old gunboat *Condor*, which, after the initial 'softening up' by the big ships, was ordered to sail in close and attack one of the forts. With its defences destroyed, Alexandria fell.

William Russell, who arrived with Sir Garnet Wolseley's expeditionary force, was scathing in his report to his own journal, the *Army and Navy Gazette*. He hated the bluster and jingoism of the British, led by a press he had come to despise. He clearly saw that the British were driven 'by the burning lust after Egypt which has been chiefly aroused by the stimulus of the Suez Canal'.[2] History would repeat itself in 1956. He also saw that the Arabi Revolt was a popular uprising and not just a military coup, as it had the support of the educated classes as well as poor. General Wolseley was adamant that Russell was not to accompany his force, so the veteran newsman was finally forced to leave the stage he had dominated for so many years.

In 1895, he became the first reporter to be honoured with a knighthood and the CVO. In his retirement, he married an Italian contessa and she was with him when he died at their Kensington home in 1907.[3] Russell was honoured with a memorial bust and plaque in St Paul's Cathedral, which reads: 'The first and greatest of war correspondents.' It was unveiled by Field Marshal Sir Evelyn Wood VC, who was one who believed that Russell's reports had done much to save what was left of the army before Sebastopol.

A former Indian Mutiny comrade of Wolseley's was General Sir Henry Havelock-Allen VC. Havelock (later Havelock-Allen) had been awarded the Victoria Cross during the first battle for Cawnpore in 1857. Although undoubtedly a brave man, the fact that it was his father, General Havelock, who recommended him for the award, went down badly with his fellow officers. Havelock had a gift for writing, relished tight situations and was constantly looking for a war in which to be involved, hence his volunteering as a special correspondent. He was present at the surrender of Emperor Napoleon III and the French army at Sedan during the Franco-Prussian War. During the Russo-Turkish War in 1877, he reported from the Russian side in the battles of Shipka Pass and the Siege of Plevna.

Ill health forced his retirement in 1881, but when the Anglo-Egyptian War broke out in 1882 he made his way to the British Headquarters in Ismailia, telling a war correspondent he knew: 'Don't for goodness sake mention me in your despatches, for my wife thinks I'm somewhere on the Riviera, but I could not resist coming here to see the fun!'

He petitioned the British commander, Sir Garnet Wolseley, for a role on the staff, but the general refused. Publicly, Wolseley had described Havelock in the Mutiny as the bravest man in India but was his usual waspish self when he wrote in private to his wife: 'Havelock is still here as mad as ever; I received a letter from him yesterday, begging to have it sent home as it was a request to be re-employed, etc., etc., in his usual strain. I am extremely sorry for him, and I feel for him very much, but still feel that he can never be employed again: he is not sane enough to argue with.'

Despite this rejection, Havelock somehow managed to take part in the Battle of Tel-el-Kebir, following the Highland Brigade and riding into the Egyptian defences armed with just a riding crop. His thirst for danger led to his death on 30 December 1897 when he rode ahead of his escort and was killed by an Afghan bullet.

Meanwhile, as Billy Russell departed the stage, another altogether different player entered. Bennet Burleigh was a great bluff, loud-voiced Scotsman, whose exploits in Egypt made him a favourite with the British public. Unlike many of his fellow journalists, he did not keep a diary or write his memoirs, so his formative years are shrouded in mystery.

According to his own account, he was born in Glasgow in 1840, one of six siblings. At the age of twenty he was working as a shipping clerk when he got one of the family's domestic servants pregnant and was forced into a shotgun marriage. The outbreak of the American Civil War gave him the opportunity to escape his responsibilities and he made his way to the Confederacy, where he volunteered for the Confederate Navy to fight for the South's cause. His ship attacked Union ships in Delaware Bay until his military career was cut short when he was captured and spent most of the war in a Northern prison camp. Bennet Burleigh (he changed the spelling from 'Burley') was captured and imprisoned in Fort Delaware prison. He managed to escape by tearing up the floorboards of his cell and dropping into the sewer beneath. Later he and a few comrades captured a steamer on Lake Erie conveying Confederate prisoners and were pursued by a Union sloop. He was captured and charged with piracy. While the court decided whether to hang him or keep him in prison, Burleigh escaped again and crossed the border to safety in Canada. Afterwards, he cut his journalist's teeth reporting for various American newspapers. It was not until he reached his early forties that he took up war reporting and arrived with General Wolseley as the representative for the wire service, the Central Press Agency.

After Alexandria had fallen, the British sought the main Egyptian army, which numbered 22,000 and was on a well-entrenched ridge between Cairo and Ismailia at a place called Tel-el-Kebir. After several days of skirmishing, Wolseley ordered his command of 17,000 men to leave their camp at Kassasin during the early hours of 13 September and to march in complete silence the five and a half miles to Tel-el-Kebir. Typically, the reporters were not informed and, once they had learned that the army was on the move, had to catch up and attach themselves wherever they could.

Both Cameron and Villiers joined the Highland Brigade; the latter was rather miffed to find that Prior had done the same. Burleigh found a place with Drury Lowe's Cavalry Brigade and was looking forward to being involved in the approaching battle. As dawn broke the British were within a few hundred yards of the enemy line. Fixing bayonets, the British advanced by rushes until they were close to the smoke-shrouded parapet. A final charge on both flanks then sent the British into the enemy trenches. Well to the fore were Cameron and Prior, who were soon pinned down in a trench as the brutal hand-to-hand fighting swept over them. Finally, the ferocious use of bayonets and rifle butts forced the Egyptians back until they broke and fled.

This was the moment the cavalry had waited for and Burleigh joined in the pursuit and slaughter of Arabi's defeated army. He made his reputation by being the first to telegraph his report from Cairo, when the Cavalry Brigade preceded Wolseley's entry into the capital. His account was lapped up by the British public who enjoyed his colourful first-person style, which became the reporting fashion for the next dozen years. William Russell, however, was highly critical and delivered a scathing attack against the arrogance, boasting and partisanship of the new breed of reporter. With the exception of two or three, he was sickened to read the reports of this brief and unjust campaign.

Russell was not alone in feeling queasy about Tel-el-Kebir. One of Wolseley's staff, Colonel William Butler, a fellow Irishman, who rose to become Major-General Sir William Butler, was married to the celebrated battle artist, Elizabeth Thompson. He did not approve of his wife's painting, *After the Battle*, which depicted Wolseley standing up in his stirrups surrounded by his staff, including Butler, at the moment on victory at Tel-el-Kebir. The battle was neither glorious nor necessary in Butler's view. 'To beat those poor felhaeen soldiers was not a matter of exultation ... and ... the capture of Arabi's earthworks had been like going through brown paper ... it gave the god Jingo a new start.'[4] This painting no longer exists for it was cut up on the death of William Butler, probably as a belated gesture to his wishes. All that remains is the centre group of Wolseley and his staff.

A legacy of the victory was that it began to involve a reluctant Britain in the inherited thorn in Egypt's side, the Sudan. After the suppression of the Arabi revolt, most of the correspondents returned home. Melton Prior undertook a brief lecture programme that included a lantern show at the Savage Club in the presence of the Prince of Wales.

During 1882-83, insurrection surfaced in the Sudan in the form of Mohammed Ahmed, better known as the Mahdi, who rallied the tribes to rise and overthrow the Khedive's rule. Gladstone's government washed their hands of this troublesome and unwanted province and refused to send any British soldiers. Instead, the Khedive was left to raise an army from the remnants of the one the British destroyed at Tel-el-Kebir and local Sudanese conscripts. The command was given to an ex-Indian army staff officer, Colonel William Hicks, who had neither experience in commanding a fighting force nor, indeed, of combat.

With most of the country in revolt, Hicks left Khartoum on 9 September 1883 with a 10,000-strong force and went in search of the Mahdi. He was accompanied by three correspondents. They included Frank Vizetelly, the veteran special artist, who had ridden with Garibaldi and Lee and had been besieged in Paris. There was also Edmond O'Donovan, the wild and unpredictable correspondent for the London *Daily News* and his young companion, Frank le Poer Power. O'Donovan had persuaded Power, the restless son of a bank manager and cub reporter for the *Daily News*, to accompany him to the Sudan for a taste of adventure.

Fortunately for Power, he fell ill during the march and was forced to return to Khartoum. He was the last white man to see Hicks's rag-tag army as it disappeared into the desert wastes of Kordofan. Between the 3rd and 5th November, the Mahdi's army overwhelmed and slaughtered everyone in Hicks's command. The outside world would not learn of this defeat for another three months. O'Donovan was killed during the battle but Vizetelly's fate remained a mystery. A year after the massacre, *The Illustrated London News* received uncorroborated news that their special artist had been taken captive and was alive in the Mahdi's camp. It was further rumoured that he was incarcerated in a small cage and kept barely alive. By 1895, however, Archibald Forbes was moved to write that Vizetelly's fabled luck had run out and he concluded that all hope had gone for his survival.

Hicks's defeat made the British government take notice of what was happening, but it was still reluctant to commit British troops to fight in the Sudan. Instead, it decided to evacuate all non-Sudanese troops and civilians. Fatally, it appointed General Charles Gordon as the Governor for the Sudan to oversee the withdrawal.

The public had made 'Chinese' Gordon the most popular hero of his time. A complex man who was a mixture of fighter, saint and mystic, he personified the ideal Christian warrior. A veteran of the Crimea and Opium Wars, he had commanded a Chinese force between 1863-64 and fought some thirty-three actions against the numerically superior Taipings during that country's civil war and effectively crushed the formidable rebellion.

Returning home to a hero's welcome, he chose to devote his leisure time to helping the poor, especially waifs and strays, whom he taught, fed and clothed.

In 1873, he travelled with the famous explorer Sir Samuel Baker and opened up vast regions of the equatorial Nile. This directly led to his appointment as Governor of the Sudan in 1877. Besides fighting slavery and administrating this huge region, he continued to explore the inhospitable headwaters of the mighty river until tropical diseases undermined his health and he was forced to resign.

After postings in the Cape and Mauritius and a year's spiritual sabbatical in Palestine, Gordon was persuaded to return to the Sudan where it was hoped his knowledge and experience would be invaluable in extricating the Egyptians from this rebellious province. Gordon, however, had other ideas and refused to abandon the Sudanese to Mahdism. He did begin to evacuate some of the civilians and tried to make peace with the Mahdi. When these overtures were rejected, Gordon decided to defend Khartoum, confident that the British would send a strong force to defeat the Mahdi and save the city.

While Gordon was travelling to Khartoum, there were further reverses in the east of the country. Another Egyptian army under the command of the disgraced former British Army colonel, Valentine Baker (brother of Sir Samuel), marched from the port of Trinkitat on the Red Sea to lift the siege of the town of Tokar, some twenty miles inland. Valentine Baker (1827-1887) attained success early in his career and, by the age of thirty-three, commanded the prestigious 10th Hussars. A glittering future seemed assured and by 1874 he was Assistant Quartermaster-General at Army headquarters in Aldershot.

Seemingly happily married, Baker's life was thrown into turmoil in 1875 when he was accused of indecently assaulting a young lady in a railway carriage. He was found guilty on flimsy evidence, but public outrage, led by Queen Victoria, brought about a fine of £500, a year's imprisonment and dismissal from the Army. Having served his sentence, he joined the Turkish army and fought against the Russians, attaining the rank of lieutenant-general. Anxious to re-establish himself with the British, Baker offered his services in Egypt and was given the thankless task of commanding the gendarmerie. Although the men he commanded were little more than a rabble, Baker ignored instructions and sought a battle that would put him back in favour with the British.

Along with his 4,000 ill-trained and reluctant soldiers was a considerable number of correspondents, including the newly-appointed *Daily Telegraph* man, Bennet Burleigh, John Cameron, Frederic Villiers and Frank Scudamore of the *Daily News*. Melton Prior had to pull out as he suffered an injured leg and so missed a narrow brush with disaster.

On 4 February, near the village of El-Teb, Osman Digna led his fanatical Mahdist followers against the dispirited Egyptians. The result was a thorough rout, with some 2,500 of Baker's command hacked to death. Somehow Baker extricated the survivors, including all the press, and retreated back to Trinkitat.

Frank Scudamore, who was experiencing his first battle, recalled that he was hardly kitted out appropriately, wearing 'a blue serge suit with the trousers tied below the knees, navvy fashion, with soiled dress ties'.[5] During the retreat, he twice narrowly escaped death. A Dervish brandishing a large spear ran towards him. Scudamore cocked his revolver and pulled the trigger, only for the weapon to misfire. Frantically, the Special repeatedly pulled the trigger until, in desperation, he flung the useless revolver at his assailant and hit him in the chest. This was enough to divert the Dervish's attention and he plunged his spear into an unfortunate passing Egyptian soldier.

The other escape happened when Scudamore stopped to help a wounded man onto his horse. Before he could remount and carry them both to safety, the horse bolted, leaving the reporter at the mercy of the Dervishes. Fortunately, William Maxwell of *The Standard* was close by. Slipping his foot from a stirrup, he called to Scudamore to take hold and half dragged his colleague to safety. When Maxwell left journalism, he joined British counter-intelligence and became involved in cat-and-mouse games with the Germans during the build-up to the First World War.

This defeat prompted the British occupying force, under the command of General Sir Gerald Graham VC, to be sent from Cairo to relieve Tokar. Once more the same correspondents, who now included the restored Melton Prior, accompanied the expedition. Just three weeks after Baker's defeat, there was another battle fought at El-Teb in sight of the rotting remains of the Egyptian army. This time the British square stood firm and, despite some desperate fighting, managed to repulse the determined charges of the Dervishes. The reporters were both alarmed and impressed by the fanaticism of the natives who, even when wounded, still continued to fight.

Frederic Villiers had a first-hand experience of this when the dying warrior he was sketching suddenly pulled himself to his feet and went for the Special with a knife. Fortunately a nearby soldier rescued Villiers with a well-aimed shot. Melton Prior had a similar experience. The British were later accused of slaughtering the wounded on the battlefields of the Sudan, but so many of their comrades had been attacked by seemingly helpless natives that it became a matter of self-preservation. Certainly those correspondents present subscribed to that opinion.

General Graham marched onto Tokar which he found unoccupied. He then returned to the port of Suakin before setting out again to do battle with Osman Digna at Tamai on 13 March. The Dervish warriors came from a local tribe that wore their hair in a tightly frizzled style, earning them the nickname 'fuzzy-wuzzies' from both soldiers and Specials. Graham formed his command into two separate squares and advanced towards the enemy positions.

The correspondents were split between the two, with Burleigh, Prior and Villiers in the leading square. At a crucial moment as the Dervishes charged, the facing side of the square became detached from the other three sides. The soldiers of the 65th (York and Lancaster) gave way and fell back and became mixed up with the Royal Marines. It looked as if defeat was certain. Bennet Burleigh, revolver in hand, called out for the men of the 65th to reform, turn and fight, which they managed to do. Villiers recalled hearing Burleigh's booming voice above the din of battle crying: 'Give it to the beggars, let 'em have it boys! Hurrah. Three cheers – Hurrah!'

Little by little, the British managed to close the gaps, killing those warriors inside the square and fending off the waves of fanatics. Prior was busily sketching when a Dervish hurled a spear in his direction, narrowly missing him before skewering a soldier just behind. Villiers alternated between firing and sketching. He observed: 'The regulation revolver is not much good against Fuzzy Wuzzy; he seems to swallow bullets and come up smiling.'[6] Finally, Osman Digna retreated, leaving the British victorious, but at a cost; more than 200 had been killed or wounded. Their sacrifice, however, was to be in vain, for Graham was ordered to return to Suakin and concede the interior to the Mahdists. For his outstanding contribution in rallying the line, Bennet Burleigh matched Archibald Forbes by being Mentioned in Despatches.

Prime Minister Gladstone felt that Charles Gordon had exceeded his instructions and did nothing from March until August. Belatedly, bowing to public clamour stirred up by the press, a relief column under the command of General Garnet Wolseley was sent. After he had fallen ill during Hicks's expedition, Frank Power had found himself stranded in Khartoum, the only journalist present. He offered his services to *The Times*, which was grateful for the exclusive coverage it received during the unfolding drama. In addition, Power was the only man, apart from the garrison commander, who could send first-hand reports to the government in Cairo. As a consequence, he was appointed British Consul; quite a change of fortune for the twenty-five-year-old cub reporter. His reports were pessimistic about the capital being able to withstand an attack as there were only 2,000 men to hold a perimeter of four miles against an estimated 60,000 Mahdists. Both the Government and *The Times* gave Power permission to leave Khartoum whenever he felt fit. Instead, he stayed and reported the ecstatic reception given to General Gordon when he entered Khartoum on 18 February 1884.

Power soon fell under the spell of this charismatic soldier and became his spokesman to the British public. It was his reports that highlighted the need for British involvement and made Gordon the icon of the age. He was moved to write on 1 April: 'We are daily expecting British troops. We cannot bring ourselves to believe that we are to be abandoned by the government. Our existence depends on England!'[7] During the long months of the loose siege, Power was put in charge of the river paddle boats and undertook many scouts and raids for cattle and grain.

By the end of August, all telegraph lines had been cut and in early September the Dervishes had inflicted 800 casualties on the defenders in their first determined attack. In desperation, Gordon decided to send his aide, Colonel J.D. Stewart, and Frank Power down the Nile with messages to urge on the Relief Column he felt sure was on its way. A heavily armoured steam launch named *Abbas*, escorted by two large steamers manned by fifty riflemen, left Khartoum on 10 September. At Berber it was felt safe enough to send the escort back to Khartoum. *Abbas* steamed on until she struck a rock at the fifth cataract but all aboard managed to escape and continued in a small whaler. At Merowe, Power and Stewart decided to set off across country and landed in order to negotiate with some local tribesmen for camels and safe passage. It is thought that, having paid with gold, Power and his companions were murdered for the rest of their money and their bodies thrown into the river.

Meanwhile, Wolseley was organising his column and, on 20 September, sailed down the Nile towards Wadi Halfa at the second cataract. The members of the press were left to make their own arrangements to cover the huge distances and, inevitably, the 'old sweats' managed very nicely. Frederic Villiers used his good relationship with Wolseley to sail on the general's own launch, *Pelican*. His rival, Melton Prior also travelled in comfort on board the small steam launch owned by his proprietor's nephew.

148

The 600-mile journey passed without incident until they reached the rapids at the second cataract. Here the launch hit a rock and its passengers were forced to leap onto a large rock. In doing so, the unathletic Prior slipped and fell into the torrent. Fortunately he was quickly hauled out by a nearby party of boatmen. Despite his prompt rescue, a report appeared in one of the London papers that he had been drowned and *The Illustrated London News* prepared to send a replacement. Mrs Prior, despite her unhappy marital status, was sceptical and sent a telegram demanding more details. Her husband was able to reply, 'No details stop Am all right'.[8] Prior then joined the rest of the press corps, whose travel arrangements had been placed in the hands of Messrs Thomas Cook.

Melton Prior was not the only Special to escape death in the Nile. Frederic Villiers and Charles Williams of the Central News Agency were tipped into the river with the former losing every piece of kit, being left with just the clothes he stood in. As progress against the current was slow, Wolseley decided to send a 2,000 strong detachment to march across the Bayuda desert, so cutting across the narrowest point of a huge loop in the Nile. Even so, the journey would take twelve days and all water supplies would have to be carried. Despite misgivings on the part of some of the reporters that the column might meet with the same fate as that of Hicks, the Specials went where they thought the best story would be found.

For two of their number, it was one story too far. On 17 January, the British engaged about 10,000 Dervishes at the rocky gorge of Abu Klea. Once again, it was to be a close-run thing with the British staring disaster in the face when the Dervishes penetrated a gap in the square as they had done at Tamai. This time it was the camels that had been herded into the centre of the square that slowed the Dervishes and allowed the British to push them out. During murderous hand-to-hand fighting, the British suffered seventy-four dead and ninety-four wounded. All the reporters in the square had front row seats for the fighting and, no doubt, took part themselves.

Bennet Burleigh wrote: 'The charge of the Arabs carried many of them into the centre of our square ... There death and havoc rioted for two or three minutes, whilst our men moved off from the inextricable mass of wounded, dying and dead camels. It was an awful scene, for many alas! Of the wounded left behind ... perished at the hands of the merciless Arabs who ran hither and thither thirsting for blood ... At this stage, seeing the Arabs were no respecters of person, I myself took up a Martini-Henry, but the third cartridge stuck, and I had to resort to my revolver.'

After months with little to report, they set to with a will to write up their despatches.

After burying their dead and taking care of the wounded, the column set off for the nearby Nile. Prior, Burleigh and Pearce decided that they would take the chance and ride to Gakdul to file their reports. Prior later confessed that he had an ulterior motive for going as he felt that the weakened column would be overrun if the Dervishes attacked again and he stood a better chance by making a run for it. Spurring their ponies to a gallop, the three reporters had only covered a few hundred yards when they found themselves in bush swarming with Dervishes. As they cleared this danger they saw about fifty yelling horsemen charging towards them. Without delay, they wrenched their mounts' heads about and went pell-mell back to the British lines, accompanied by a hail of lead. Incredibly, they were not hit but their ponies all sustained bullet wounds.

The square began its last slow advance over the final four miles to the Nile with everyone suffering from lack of water. At the village of Abu Kru, they halted to fight off another attack. It was during the exchange of firing that the newsmen lost two of their colleagues. Nearly all the reporters were hit and either had minor wounds or were bruised by spent bullets. Prior was hit on the instep and Burleigh had his neck grazed. Prior's friend from Majuba Hill, John Cameron, was shot in the lung as he accepted a tin of sardines from his servant as he sheltered amongst the camels. Within a few minutes Cameron had died. St Leger Algernon Herbert of the *Morning Post* took a bullet between the eyes and was instantly killed. He had been warned by Frederic Villiers that the red tunic he wore would make him a tempting target and so it proved. Both Specials were buried in a mass burial pit and a service was read for them.

Frederic Villiers wrote: 'In this expedition which had been so destructive of man and beast the war correspondents suffered no less severely than their brethren in uniform. Out of eight who started with Stewart, four were killed and one was wounded, making our casualties more than 50 per cent – a circumstance which alone is quite indicative of the character of the fighting.'

Three steamers sent by Gordon arrived two days later with news that Khartoum was on the point of falling. Despite their weakened state, General Wilson embarked a company of infantry and sailed for the besieged city. When they reached it on the 28th they were heavily fired on from the shore and it was clear that the Mahdi had taken Khartoum. In fact the British were just forty-eight hours too late to save Gordon from the martyr's death he sought.

It would be another month before news of Gordon's death reached the British public. As soon as he officially learned of it, Bennet Burleigh undertook a highly risky ride through hostile country to Dongola, from where he wired his newspaper. The *Daily Telegraph* produced a special Sunday edition on 23 February and beat the official news by thirty-six hours. Burleigh was not above employing some low methods to beat his rivals. Once he had sent his copy, he persuaded the telegraph operator to send passages from the Book of Genesis to keep the wire busy for the next twenty-four hours. Through his determination, bravery and cunning, Burleigh had established himself as a front-rank correspondent.

The British Government had no intention of defeating the Mahdi in order to establish themselves in the Sudan and, after some more fighting in the east of the country, Wolseley was ordered to break up the column and return to Cairo. He had emerged from the campaign with an enhanced reputation, despite failing to save Gordon. The newsmen had been generally supportive and given the ambitious general plenty of publicity. Wolseley had appeared more conciliatory but he confided with his wife in a letter: 'Confound all this breed of vermin – Shall I never be strong enough to be honest and tell these penny-a-liners how I loathe them and their horrid trade?'[9]

For the newspapers, the Gordon drama had been a heaven-sent story which had kept the public enthralled for months. It had come at some cost, for in the three years of campaigning they lost seven of their reporters in action and through disease. Their names are remembered on a memorial tablet in St Paul's Cathedral.

Bennet Burleigh kept the pot boiling by exposing deficiencies in the Ordnance Department. During the hand-to-hand fighting, British soldiers had been dismayed to find that their bayonets often became bent and twisted, that the Martini-Henry rifle overheated and the soft brass Boxer cartridges caused jamming and misfires. In fact, these problems had been apparent during the Zulu War, but nothing had been done to rectify them.[10]

Charles Williams also attacked General Wilson for not making more of an effort to reach Gordon and even accused him of cowardice, a remark that resulted in a court action for libel. Frank Power was not forgotten, for Queen Victoria granted an annual pension of £50 to each of his sisters. Ironically, having seen off the British, and at the height of his power, the Mahdi succumbed to typhus and died in June.

Chapter 12

Egypt and the Sudan: Part II

As if taking a well-earned rest from years of continuous campaigning, the late 1880s and most of the 1890s saw a period of peace abroad for Britain. Domestic affairs dominated the news with the debate of Irish Home Rule bringing down yet another government. The year of 1887 saw an outpouring of public affection and rejoicing as Queen Victoria celebrated the Golden Jubilee of her reign. In 1888, the newspapers were filled with the reports of a series of gruesome murders in London's Whitechapel and the perpetrator was graphically dubbed 'Jack the Ripper'.

Elsewhere, there were a couple of significant inventions for the newsman. Tolbert Lanston invented the monotype, a typesetting machine, and the American, George Eastman, perfected his Kodak camera, with its easily loaded roll film. As this latter, highly portable invention became more readily available, so war correspondents took to including one in their campaign kit. This was not for newspaper publication purposes but as a memory aid for their reporting and to illustrate the books that invariably were written after a war.

Although this was a fallow period for the war correspondent, there were some minor wars to report. In late 1885, the intrepid rivals Melton Prior and Frederic Villiers sailed for Burma, where the anti-British King Thebaw had provoked a fight. The campaign, known as the Pagoda War, involved just thirteen days of spasmodic fighting and is only really remembered for inspiring Rudyard Kipling to write his verse, *The Road to Mandalay*. Kipling also wrote *The Naulahka*, in which he illustrated Britain's lack of understanding of its Eastern empire and the numerous skirmishes it fought to keep it intact: 'And the end of the fight is a tombstone white with the name of the late deceased, And the epitaph drear: "A Fool lies here who tried to hustle the East".'

The war brought discredit to the British and Indian armies due mainly to a personal vendetta carried out by *The Times'* disgruntled correspondent, Edward Moylan. On 21 January 1886, the newspaper published Moylan's report of the execution of three Burmese insurgents by firing squad. What made his report so shocking was that the apparent behaviour of the Provost Marshal, Lieutenant Colonel Willoughby Hooper, who had 'a love of ghastly executions'.[1]

The report ran: 'The Provost Marshal, who is an ardent amateur photographer, is desirous of securing views of the persons executed at the precise moment when they are struck by the bullet. To secure this result, after the orders "ready", "present" have been given to the firing party, the Provost Marshal fixes his camera on the prisoners, who at times are kept waiting several minutes in that position. The officer commanding the firing party is then directed by the Provost Marshal to give the order to fire at the moment he exposes his plates. So far no satisfactory negative has been obtained and the experiments are likely to continue.'

Edward Kyran Moylan was born in 1848 and called to the Irish Bar in 1864. In 1880 he was appointed Attorney General of the British West Indian island of Grenada. Three years later he was removed from office for committing perjury and disbarred. He then became representative with the British Burma Trading Company and sent to that country. When hostilities broke out he was appointed *The Times'* Burma correspondent and was well-placed to report the campaign.

After the brief period of fighting, the country was initially ruled by General Harry Prendergast VC, the British commander of the Army of Occupation. Moylan soon fell foul of the authorities when he refused to submit his reports for official censorship as laid down by Field Service Regulations. Prendergast expelled Moylan from Mandalay and he returned to Rangoon, from where he wrote a stinging report about his treatment by the general. *The Times'* editor, George Earle Buckle, used his influence as a friend of Lord Randolph Churchill, the Secretary of State for India. In turn, Churchill put pressure of the India Viceroy, Lord Dufferin, to have Edward Moylan reinstated in Mandalay.

He soon renewed his campaign against Prendergast, claiming that he had let most of the Burmese army escape. With no facilities for maintaining large prisoner of war camps or the manpower to secure the difficult jungle country, Prendergast's options were limited. He did, however, have twenty-two *dacoits* (bandits) tried and executed under the command of Lieutenant Colonel Hooper and his Assistant Provost Marshal, Lieutenant Burrows. The latter forced a Burmese prisoner to watch as five insurgents were shot and then put him in front of the firing squad until he revealed the identity of other rebels. This was actually witnessed by Melton Prior who informed Moylan. When Prendergast learned of this incident, which was tantamount to torture, he reprimanded both Hooper and Burrows. Lord Dufferin felt the incident deserved more than a reprimand and ordered that both men should appear before a court martial, He also relegated Prendergast's role and replaced him with another senior officer.

Moylan continued to plot against Prendergast's replacement until Lord Dufferin recognised Moylan's true character. Realising that Prendergast had been unfairly maligned, Dufferin tried to have him reinstated and even produced a pamphlet which was distributed to eighty influential British public figures, which exposed Moylan's use of *The Times* to make mischief. As Moylan was also a representative of the British Burma Trading Company, his motives were somewhat opaque and this later came to light in a dispute over the Mogok ruby mines in Upper Burma. Despite this, when Moylan died in Rangoon in 1893, *The Times'* obituary described him as 'a brave investigative journalist'.[2]

One of the most enterprising of the new correspondents was Lionel James. He had been born in Teignmouth in 1871, the son of a Royal Artillery colonel. When he was sixteen, he was sent to India and employed on an indigo estate in Behar. He began to play polo and acquired a string of ponies. He also began an association with the military when he joined the Behar Mounted Rifles. Finding he had a talent for writing, he had a couple of stories published in English-language newspapers. In 1894, James over-stretched his finances when he bet on his horse to win a race at Allahabad and landed heavily in debt. In order to settle with his creditors he embarked on his long career as a leading war correspondent. He started with the Calcutta-based *The Englishman*, and covered the relief of the fort at Chitral for Reuters. In 1897, he accompanied the storming of Malakand Pass in the Tirah Campaign, and was Mentioned in Despatches for his active participation.[3]

There were plenty of minor operations on India's North West Frontier, but none were significant enough to send a Special to report. Instead, newspapers increasingly employed serving officers as their reporters. This arrangement worked to the mutual benefit for both sides. It saved the newspapers considerable expense in sending their Specials to remote and inaccessible regions and it enabled officers, whether their regiments were engaged or not, to gain some publicity in order to further their careers. It was recognised that the only way for an officer to see any action was to serve on the staff or as a war correspondent. The military establishment were also happy in the knowledge that anything written would not be critical and, indeed, would show them in a good light. The only drawback to this arrangement was that the writing was bland and lacked the narrative sparkle of the professional Special.

Some of the officers employed included Robert Baden-Powell, then of the 13th Hussars, who was the *Daily Chronicle* correspondent for the Third Ashanti War of 1895. Also, Alexander Edward Murray, Viscount Fincastle, *The Times'* man with the Malakand Field Force in 1897, who certainly saw action close up and was awarded the Victoria Cross for attempting to save a wounded officer under heavy fire. Captain G.J. Younghusband

and his explorer brother, Francis, also reported for *The Times* in the dramatic relief of the remote fort of Chitral in 1895. In typical war correspondent fashion, Francis was the first man ahead of the relieving force to enter the beleaguered garrison.

Edward Frederick Knight reported the Hunza-Nager campaign of 1891 while holding a commission in the Indian army. He went on to cover many wars for *The Times* and became regarded as one of the more literary of the soldier correspondents. He led a highly adventurous life. At the outbreak of the Franco-Prussian War, he volunteered for the French army but was turned down as an alien. Afterwards, he bought a boat and explored rivers and coasts in the Caribbean and South America. This led to an unsuccessful attempt at treasure-hunting for pirate booty in Trinidad. During his career as a Special, he covered most of the wars of the 1890s, including the French annexation of Madagascar in 1894.

The Times instructed Knight to travel to Madagascar where the French had established a sort of protectorate years before. The Hova tribe, under their queen, had revolted and driven all the French from the island. The French Government reacted by sending a formidable expeditionary force to subjugate the Hovas. Knight soon discovered that the French had banned any correspondents accompanying their troops, including their own newsmen, and forbade any correspondent from landing at any port in Madagascar. Despite these restrictions, *The Times* decided to send Knight to the capital, Antananarivo, to cover the fighting from the Hova side.

Evading all attempts by the French to keep him from landing, Knight, with the help of the captain of *Dunbar Castle*, managed to row ashore on the east coast of the island. He then had to travel by foot some 600 miles to the capital through uncharted jungle and constantly threatened by hostile tribes. More than once, Knight had to resort to threats and gunfire to extricate his small party from perilous situations until, suffering from fever, he reached the capital. He found that the 50,000-strong Hova army had been sent to Majunga, where the French were expected to land.

Knight was not allowed to follow, but kept *The Times'* readers fascinated with his reports from this strange and remote island. The capital was split between the pro- and anti-queen factions and for a while there was bloodshed between the two. There was also a distinctly anti-white sentiment which prompted Knight and the British consul to prepare for a siege at the consulate. Knight's military experience came into play as the sandbags, arms and supplies were collected. In the event, the threat never came to anything. When the French finally landed, the vastly superior Hova force simply melted away. When the French did enter Antananarivo, they numbered just 3,000 as most of the force had been killed or laid low with fever and dysentery as they laboured through the jungle swamps. The Hova army at last made an effort of resistance and there was a brief fight before they capitulated. Knight later wrote: 'I was sending articles to *The Times* in which I exposed the corruption and treason of those in charge of affairs here, who were crippling the defence and betraying the Queen.'

He also commented on the censorship, or rather lack of it, imposed by the Hova government. 'There was a queer system of censorship at Antananarivo. One of the chief censors came to the Consulate once a week to read over such letters as we proposed to send. He used to cut a passage here or there out of the most innocent family letters: thus he erased the crosses at the foot of the letter addressed by a mother to her child, because he imagined these to be in cipher and could not believe that the marks represented kisses.'[4]

Knight was not the only British correspondent who had managed to evade the French authorities. The redoubtable Bennet Burleigh was also present and even managed to interview the Queen. Like Knight, he was not impressed by the rabble that comprised the Hova army and was on hand when the sickly French force occupied the capital. He did, however, leave quickly when he learned that the French had said that they had no intention of shooting him – but they intended to hang him!

With the invasion over, Knight made his way to the coast,

carrying the despatches of the French commander, General Duchesne, and caught the next Castle steamer home.

The best known of the soldier-reporters was Lieutenant Winston S. Churchill of the 4th Hussars, who had ambitions beyond the army and the Fourth Estate.

Churchill's first foray into reporting was in Cuba in 1895, for which he was paid £5 for each letter he sent to *The Graphic*. He accompanied the Spanish army in its efforts to crush the simmering rebellion that had flared up again. Impoverished Spain had poured money and men into Cuba in an effort to keep control but, at a distance of 5,000 miles, it was like holding 'a dumb-bell at arm's length'.[5] During a march through the central highlands, Churchill celebrated his 21st birthday by coming under fire for the first time. He later wondered if another young correspondent, Hubert Howard of *The Times*, whom he later came to know and admire, had been with the attacking rebels as Howard had chosen to follow and report from the insurgents' viewpoint.

The following year Churchill again persuaded his tolerant colonel to allow him time off to accompany the Malakand Field Force in an expedition against the hostile Mohmand tribe in some of the most rugged terrain on the North West Frontier.

Through his mother's influence Churchill was employed by the *Daily Telegraph*. Also accompanying the army was the ubiquitous Melton Prior and both had the opportunity to observe action close-up. Churchill joined a group of Sikh infantry as it scaled the steep sides of a valley to search a village. As they entered, they came under heavy fire from about 200 tribesmen and began to take casualties. Forced to retreat, they were caught in the open.

Churchill saw a wounded white officer dropped by his men as they were put to flight by a party of Pathans. The officer was then hacked to death by a tribesman, which prompted Churchill to draw his sword and charge forward to take on the murderous Pathan. Seeing him approach, the tribesman picked up a rock and hurled it at the *Telegraph*'s man on the spot. Churchill then sensibly changed his mind about single combat, drew his revolver and blazed away. It was with some difficulty that Churchill and his comrades managed to extricate themselves and reach the safety of the main column.

Trouble spilled over into the nearby Tirah region and the following month the British sent a huge force into this inhospitable region. There were several British reverses before the Afridi tribesmen were subdued. Both Melton Prior and another emerging Special named René Bull, of *Black and White*, had a narrow escape. They were heading for the main theatre of operations with a supply column when they left to explore a deserted village with two officers. Suddenly, the group was ambushed and dived for cover behind some rocks. Armed only with revolvers, they quickly fired off all their rounds and would have been overwhelmed had not a party of Sikhs on escort duty arrived and driven off the tribesmen.

René Bull was born in Dublin in 1872 and became a cartoonist and illustrator of note. His war reporting lasted just two years, starting with the Tirah Campaign, followed by Omdurman and finally the Boer War, where he was wounded and invalided back to England.

This was Melton Prior's third campaign during 1897! At the beginning of the year he had been in the Transvaal and observed the abortive Jameson Raid, which directly led to outbreak of the Boer War. While in Johannesburg he saw the enormous number of rifles and machine-guns stowed away ready for the 'Uitlanders', the non-Dutch residents, to rise with the help of Dr Jameson and his 800 horsemen to overthrow the Boer government. Prior found himself swept along with the emotion of the situation and sided with the would-be rebels. With news that Jameson's band were fast approaching, Prior and one of the ring leaders rode out to meet him. Prior wrote:

'But we found instead of his coming in that the news we had received was all false. Jameson had come; had been opposed by the Boers; had lost the fight, and he and his followers were being marched as prisoners to Pretoria, with the exception of a number of killed and wounded.' Instead, Prior visited the ground where the Boers had laid an ambush, and made several sketches which he sent back to London.

He recalled: 'There is no doubt that it was a miserably conducted revolution, and at times I feel the ringleaders ought to have been shot or hanged for muddling it so … We deserved to be much worse treated by them [the Boers] than we were … The Boers treated us very well indeed. The ringleaders were rounded up, or rather instructed to present themselves for arrest by a Lieutenant of Police. I was at the Club when he turned up and arrested a dozen, and at the same time had a drink with them. He then told me that at one time he had received instructions to arrest me, but later on the order was cancelled.'[6]

Prior was then sent to cover the Tirah Expeditionary Force on India's North West Frontier. Fought between October 1897 and January 1898, it saw some of the largest concentrations of troops for yet another frontier outbreak. Prior arrived in time to witness one of the epic episodes in the many fights between the tribes and the British Army; the storming of the Dargai Heights. In order to make the route safe, the tribesmen had to be dislodged from the ridge at Dargai. Prior wrote and sketched the battle. 'The Gurkhas had advanced and been beaten back: the Sikhs had also been beaten back, and Sir William [Lockwood] finding the enemy were holding the crest of the hill and the Schragrukotal Pass very fiercely, was, I should imagine, slightly puzzled. The guns were shelling the position, but nothing seemed to move the enemy from their sangers, and at last he signalled to Colonel Mathias of the Gordon Highlanders that this position in front of him must be taken at all costs. Colonel Mathias, as coolly as on parade, turned to his men, and the word was passed down, that "the general has signalled to us that this position must be taken at all costs. The Gordon Highlanders will take it!"

'The men received this order with ringing cheers, and, as their pipes began to skirl, they rushed to the attack. They were under a furious fire, the bullets rained thick upon them, but they went on climbing upwards until at last they carried the stronghold in what has been described as "superb style". During this onslaught

Piper Findlater, though wounded in both legs, continued playing the pibroch. He was awarded the Victoria Cross. Once the heights were taken the enemy fled in all directions.'

The campaign was over very tough terrain with the tribesmen constantly firing at the British camps. Prior recorded a tragic loss: 'I was riding round the edge of a mountain with a sheer descent of 2,000 feet, when one of my mules in front of me, with two cases of whisky and stores and some of my clothes, made a false step, or rather a stone gave way under its hind-foot, and the next moment he was toppling over, and I had the misfortune to see him and my whisky bumping from ledge to ledge till he reached the bottom. I did not mind losing the mule or the clothes, but the two cases of whisky – that was an irreparable loss!'[7]

The Thirty Day War between Greece and Turkey created a great deal of attention at the time as there was much support and enthusiasm for all things Greek. After what was called the 'unfortunate war', Greece was bankrupt from a political and military point of view, something that hurt her pride and prestige. Lionel James of *The Times* described it as 'the quaintest tragi-comic picnic in which I ever participated'.

Frank Scudamore and Edward Knight were officially attached to the Greek side. Such was the casual attitude taken in the area they covered they were able to cross the bridge dividing the two sides and take afternoon tea with the Turkish commander, an old friend from Constantinople. When the fighting began in earnest, they took refuge in a windowless room in the fort, where they wrote their reports of the day's fighting. By the light of a couple of candles balanced on sacks, the two scribbled away for hours as the candles burned down to stubs. A Greek officer appeared in the doorway and nearly suffered a heart attack. Snuffing out the candles, he quickly led the two Specials away explaining that the room was the ammunition store and that the sacks contained explosives.

Richard Harding Davis, the talented American correspondent for *The Times*, reported from Velestinos, in Thessaly on the east coast of Greece. He was joined by John Bass, an American reporter. They had found refuge in an almost deserted village, breaking into the house of the departed mayor.

In his droll manner, Davis described their occupation: 'He [the mayor] had fled the town, as had the nearly all the villagers; and as we liked the appearance of his house, I gave Bass a leg up over the wall around his garden, and Bass opened the gate, and we climbed in through his front window … and made discoveries of fresh treasure-trove. Sometimes it was in the form of a cake of soap or a tin of coffee … All of these things, and the house itself were burned to ashes, we were told, a few hours after we retreated, and we feel less troubled now at having made such free use of them … The Turks came in, and, in accordance to their quaint custom, burned the village and marched on to Volo.

'The battle, which lasted two days, opened in a sudden and terrific storm of hail. But the storm passed as quickly as it came, leaving the trenches running with water, like gutters in a city street after a spring shower; the men sopped them up with their overcoats and blankets, and in half an hour the sun had dried the wet uniforms, and the field-birds had begun to chirp again, and the grass was warm and fragrant again … From time to time an officer would rise up and peer down into the great plain, shading his eyes with his hands, and shout something at them, and they would turn quickly in the trench and rise on one knee. And at a shout that followed would fire four or five rounds rapidly and evenly, and then, at the sound from the officer's whistle, would drop back again and pick up the cigarettes they had placed in the grass and begin to leisurely to swab out their rifles. Down on the plain below there was apparently nothing at which they could shoot except the great shadows of the clouds drifting across the vast checker-board of green and yellow fields, and disappearing finally between the mountain-passes beyond …

'What impressed us most of what we could see of the battle then was the remarkable number of cartridges the Greek soldiers wasted in firing into space, and the fact that they began firing at such long range that, in order to get the elevation, they had placed the rifle butt under the armpit instead of against the shoulder.

Their sights were at the top notch. The cartridges reminded one of corn-cobs jumping out of a corn-sheller, and it was interesting to see a hundred of them pop up into the air at the same time, flashing in the sun ... They rolled by the dozens underfoot, and twinkled in the grass, and when one shifted his position in the narrow trench, or stretched his cramped legs, they tinkled musically. It was like wading in a gutter with thimbles.'[8]

The main focus of the war was on the island of Crete, where the four Great Powers, Britain, France, Italy and Russia, had intervened to govern the turbulent island until a governor-general could be installed. The imposition of an export tax was all the excuse a Turkish mob needed to attack Christians, including the hated British. On 6 September 1898, they slaughtered 500 Christians and besieged about 130 soldiers of the Highland Light Infantry in the Customs House by the waterfront of the capital Candia (later Heraklion). The British Vice-Consul perished when his house was burned down after the mob had set the town on fire.

The Times' correspondent witnessed a scene that resulted in the award of a Victoria Cross. He reported: 'Instantly, the whole of the houses round the harbour opened fire on the Customs House and English patrol. Every window held two or three riflemen, and the fire is described as something appalling. The patrol immediately got into the Customs House and started to return the fire. There was a guard of forty-five Highlanders near the telegraph office and forty of these were brought down to reinforce, but they came via the tunnel and archway through the town wall just behind the Customs House, losing several men ... The *Hazard's* [HM gun-boat] men behaved magnificently, and I hope they get something out of it. Their doctor should get the VC. His clothes were shot through in at least a dozen places whilst he was helping the wounded, and he escaped marvellously without a scratch.' Naval Surgeon William Maillard was indeed recommended for the Victoria Cross and he was presented with it by the Queen at Windsor Castle on 15 December 1898.[9]

There now appeared on the scene a new type of Special – the scholar reporter. At the age of forty-one, Henry Wood Nevinson was a late entrant into the peculiar world of the war correspondent. He was born in Leicester in 1856 into a strict Methodist family and attended Oxford and Jena Universities as a classics scholar. It was while studying at Jena that he became a great admirer of Germany. Surprisingly, given his religious background, he developed a great interest in military matters. Later, he put this enthusiasm to use as he worked amongst the poor in London's East End, when he formed a youth cadet company. He took a Guards drill course and passed with ninety-eight per cent marks, something he was more proud of than anything else in his life. He kept an interest in his cadets for fifteen years and only missed the weekly assembly when he was abroad. Nevinson, at that time, was mild, shy and unsure as to what he wanted to do. He held radical views, supporting Irish Nationalism, workers' causes (he lived and worked amongst the iron workers in the Black Country and the hoppers in Kent), and, later, the Suffragettes. For a time, he even flirted with the Anarchist Movement.[10]

In order to make a living, Nevinson began writing book reviews and contributing to the arts page of the *Daily Chronicle*. As a classics graduate, he loved Greece, so when the Greeks in Crete demanded their independence from Turkey he was ready to champion their cause to the extent of trying to organise a British volunteer company. When this failed, he was asked by the *Chronicle* to act as its representative and so began a war reporting career that spanned over twenty years. The Greek effort to free Crete from Turkish rule was put down and attention switched to the borders between the two adversaries. Nevinson travelled extensively to remote frontier areas in the mountains and was the first witness to the fighting. He had his baptism of fire during an abortive Greek attack on a Turkish frontier post and became addicted to the spectacle of war. He would later offend his pacifist friends by saying that he would not care to live in a world in which there was no war. Like so many of the Specials who reported from some of the world's unhealthiest regions, he contracted malaria, which would affect him for the rest of his life.

It was during this brief conflict that he met men with whom he would share danger in the world's hot-spots over the next two decades. William Maud of *The Graphic* became a particular friend until his premature death in Aden in 1903. There was John Black Atkins of the *Manchester Guardian*, later to become editor of that paper and the 'soured' veteran *Chronicle* correspondent, Charles Williams.

Nevinson also met someone who would later cause him a considerable moral dilemma in the Dardanelles campaign of 1915 – Ellis Ashmead-Bartlett. As a seventeen-year-old, the latter was accompanying his pro-Turkish father, the MP Sir Ellis Ashmead-Bartlett, when the Turkish warship on which they were sailing was captured by the Greeks and taken to Salonika. Other correspondents included George Warrington Steevens, making his debut and representing the *Pall Mall Gazette*. He was soon to be acknowledged as the outstanding reporter of his day before his premature death just three years later. Also present was Frederic Villiers, who could claim to be the first to use a movie camera, the cinematograph, in the field. Unfortunately, the cumbersome machine failed to provide anything worthwhile. Undeterred, Villiers would try again the following year in the Sudan. Upon Nevinson's return to London, he was taken on permanently by the *Daily Chronicle* and he wrote his first book, *The Thirty Day War*.

Also making his Special debut was Oxford don, Ernest Bennett, writing for the *Manchester Guardian*. He was registered with the Turks, but was captured by the Greeks and threatened with execution. Fortunately he was recognised by a Greek officer who had known him at Oxford.

Elsewhere in the world, conflicts arose. For decades, America had been absorbed with the subjugation of the tribes of Indians who had resisted the westward pressure to settle the vast lands beyond the Missouri. Now that was accomplished and the country was gaining in wealth and power, a mixture of crusading morality and the need to function like a great nation swept the country. There was a ready outlet for these needs right on her doorstep in the shape of Spain's unhappy and impoverished 'Jewel of the Antilles', Cuba. In early 1898, the United States wrested the last of Spain's New World Empire from her grasp. In an unequal contest lasting three months, Spain lost Cuba, Puerto Rico and the Philippines.

As this was the first time United States had fought an overseas war, it was naturally followed with greater interest by the American press, who felt they lagged behind the European nations with their colonial escapades. Despite the prospect of a war in the Sudan, British newspapers did send some correspondents, including Charles Fripp of *The Graphic*, who journeyed to the Philippines. With him went one of the first 'real' war photographers, M.T. Cowan of the new photo magazine the *Navy and Army Illustrated*. It was a short-lived magazine that reproduced excellent photographs of life in the armed forces, scenes from wars around the world and ripping yarns extolling British pluck. In Cuba, the American writer Richard Harding Davies wrote for both the *New York Journal* and *The Times*, as he had done during the Greco-Turkish War. Henry Nevinson's colleague George Lynch was sent by the *Daily Chronicle* and Percival Phillips represented the *Daily Telegraph*.

Edward Knight of *The Times* returned from Egypt and the Sudan and was immediately sent by his paper to Cuba. He wrote: 'I spoke a little Spanish and I was the only English correspondent to whom the authorities in Madrid would grant permission to go to Cuba had induced *The Times* to seize the opportunity of being the one English paper that had a representative on the Spanish side in the island.'

The only way he could reach Cuba was to travel to Key West at the tip of Florida and catch a neutral ship bound for Havana. Unfortunately, the local commander forbade all neutral ships to land Knight as he had seen the army camps during his trip through Florida. Striking up a friendship with Harry Scovell of the *New York World*, Knight was able to sail in the small vessel that the paper had supplied to enable their man to pick up news of the American blockading squadron.

Thinking his long wait at Key West was at an end, Knight sailed into Havana harbour under a white flag of truce. Once again, bureaucracy prevailed and Knight was told he could not be permitted to land from an enemy ship. Another few weeks were spent in Key West until he had the idea of being dropped by Scovell in a small skiff off the coast of Cuba and rowing ashore.

Having been dropped just three miles off the Cuban coast by Scovell's boat, Knight attempted to paddle ashore in what was little more than a punt. Very quickly the rough seas swamped and capsized his tiny boat. Clinging to the upturned hull, Knight spent some fourteen hours in the water until the wind changed and blew him in towards land. He had more uneasy moments when he saw the triangular black fins of sharks begin to circle. Fortunately, he reached the shore, narrowly missing being dashed on rocks, and was pulled to safety by a Spanish patrol. Knight had lost all his belongings and was arrested as a spy until *The Times* was able to confirm his credentials. He then experienced the misery of being in a blockaded city with dwindling supplies of food. Many of the poorer inhabitants were dying of starvation and disease in the streets and in the surrounding countryside.

Towards the end of the war there was an informal truce between the Spanish and the insurgents. Knight took advantage of this and visited one of the rebel camps in the hills outside the city. He was impressed and wrote: 'The men were sturdy mulattoes, clad in the white canvas rebel uniform, worn and ragged; but their accoutrements were in good condition, their carbines were clean and they presented a soldierly appearance ... It was evident that they had been well drilled and that a strict discipline was enforced. Their rifles and side arms were in much better order than those of the Spanish troops.'[11]

When it became known that the Spanish naval squadron from Santiago had been destroyed and that the one expected from Spain had been sent to the Philippines instead, Cuba surrendered and Knight was able to return to London.

The war, however, was an American 'show' and was covered by some 200 journalists. In many ways it was a war created for the newspapers, as exemplified by the oft-told story that the newspaper tycoon, William Randolph Hearst, actually pushed the United States into the conflict. He had sent the artist, Frederick Remington, to Cuba, who telegraphed that everything was peaceful and that there would be no war. Hearst is alleged to have telegraphed: 'Please remain. You furnish pictures. I will furnish war.'[12]

War correspondents had to be prepared to go when and where their masters ordered them. At the end of February 1896, Edward Knight was summoned from his favourite club by Moberly Bell, the manager of *The Times*. He was to go at once to Cairo and accompany Sir Herbert Kitchener's expedition to re-conquer the Sudan and avenge the death of Charles Gordon. Knight recalled: '*The Times* at that time had a way of giving its correspondents the shortest possible notice when packing them off to distant parts of the world.'

Knight joined the Egyptian army and was present at the Battle of Firket where he witnessed the resilience and determination of the Dervish. Knight wrote: 'On the other hand some of these indomitable warriors disdained to flee; stubbornly remaining behind the rocky ridges, they coolly fired upon us until our Sudanese had fallen on them and killed them. Quarter was given such as surrendered but many of the wounded Dervishes acted as is their wont. A wounded man would lie still as if dead until one of his foemen passed him – a British officer by preference – when he would raise up his gun and shoot him treacherously in the back.

'I saw one wounded Dervish attempt this trick. I had ridden close to him and looked upon his upturned face on which not a muscle quivered; he was to all appearances dead, but after I had proceeded some thirty yards I heard the unmistakable whistle of a passing bullet intended for myself. On looking round I saw two black soldiers who had witnessed the incident run to the wounded Dervish and empty their rifles into his body.'[13]

The long awaited reoccupation of the Sudan did not get going until the summer of 1898 and was led by the Sirdar of Egypt,

Major-General Sir Herbert Kitchener, a military commander who brought relations with the press to a new low. At first, he refused permission for any reporter to accompany the expedition south of Aswan, but was forced to relent when the newspaper proprietors put pressure on the Government. He managed to get his own back by restricting their use of the telegraph to just 200 words per despatch. Two correspondents cleverly managed to get around this as their newspapers, the *Times* and the *New York Herald*, agreed to pool their stories as they had done previously in the 1876 Balkan War.

The reporters would write 200 words each to form a complete 400-word report. Kitchener famously displayed his contempt of reporters when he pushed by a group of them standing outside his tent, with the instruction, 'Get out of my way, you drunken swabs!' He reinforced this attitude by refusing to give them any assistance or information whatsoever. Despite these obstacles, the newspapers were represented by some twenty-six specials. Although they did not know it at the time, this was to be the last of the old style set-piece battles, and a twilight was settling over the age of optimistic jingoism.

The usual veterans were present: Prior, Burleigh, Scudamore and Williams. Villiers brought along his cinematograph and, to the amusement of his colleagues, a sturdy, green-painted bicycle, which he preferred to the doubtful quality of the local four-legged transport. The newer intake included William Theodore Maud of *The Graphic* and, for *The Times*, Hubert Howard. The most talented was George Warrington Steevens, of the new popular newspaper, the *Daily Mail*, which enjoyed a readership of a half a million. Steevens, like Henry Nevinson, was a classics graduate who had been destined for a glittering academic career as an Oxford don.[14] Instead, he turned to journalism, where he came to the attention of Alfred Harmsworth, a young and ambitious newspaper proprietor, who started the *Daily Mail* in 1896. Steevens was a fervent Imperialist and possessed a capacity to write descriptive prose that was entertaining as well as accurate. Although he had a tragically short career, he raised the status of the *Daily Mail*. He was also one of two correspondents who Kitchener tolerated and actually liked. This may have been because of a somewhat over-the-top interview Steevens wrote in which he highly praised Kitchener and ended with the sentence: 'You feel that he ought to be patented and shown with pride at the Paris International Exhibition; British Empire: Exhibit No.1, *hors concours* (unrivalled), the Sudan Machine.'

Later in his life, Winston Churchill acknowledged Steevens as a great influence on his own writing style. Churchill, himself, was most anxious to take part in the Sudanese campaign and applied for a staff position. To his mortification, Kitchener turned him down and made it known that he would not accept this young subaltern under any circumstance. He had not reckoned on the Churchill family's network of influence. The Prime Minister, Lord Salisbury, had read and enjoyed Churchill's recently published debut book, *The Malakand Field Force*, and was persuaded to use his influence in getting Churchill attached to the British cavalry regiment, the 21st Lancers. Another friend, Oliver Borthwick, the son of the proprietor of the *Morning Post*, proposed that Churchill should write about the campaign, in the form of personal letters to evade the censor.

Will Maud of *The Graphic* wrote: 'From a war correspondent's point of view, what a happy hunting ground the Soudan is. Since the year 1895 a campaign in that country has been an annual affair. Although the Upper Nile cannot be honestly recommended as a summer resort, there are so many solid considerations to be set against the boiling heat, the choking dust, the tinned food, and the fleas and flies, that I never head of a man who refused the chance of going there.'

Progress into the Sudan had been made easier with the construction of a railway to Atbara, about 150 miles downriver from Khartoum, and it was from this springboard that Kitchener would advance for a final showdown with the Khalifa's army at Omdurman, the symbol of Mahdism. The correspondents regaled their readers with details of the slow build-up to the anticipated great battle, which the eager public saw as revenge for Gordon's death. Perhaps they were awed by Kitchener's temper and power to have them removed from the column, or whether they genuinely admired his skill as a commander, but most of the specials wrote glowingly about this formidable man. Without doubt, the advance proceeded smoothly thanks to Kitchener's painstaking preparations.

The Specials did not have much to report and spent much of their leisure time inventing cocktails from the vast supplies of drinks they brought with them. One of their concoctions was called an 'Abu Hamed', which consisted of gin, vermouth, Angostura bitters, lime juice and soda.[15] It was claimed to have been the creation of Frank Scudamore, who was appointed 'honorary mess steward' by Steevens. Scudamore furthermore endeared himself to all by bringing along an ice-making machine. Steevens and Scudamore were one half of the mess they formed with Will Maud and newcomer, Lionel James of Reuters. Frederic Villiers, on the other hand, swore by the therapeutic powers of Scotch whisky, having swallowed almost a whole bottle after sharing his bed roll with a scorpion.

There was not a lot to report during the lengthy build-up, so the bored reporters mischievously looked for something more light-hearted to write about. One of their targets was the lone British cavalry regiment, the 21st Lancers. It was just about the only regiment in the British Army not to have gained a battle honour and had been bestowed with the satirical motto, 'Thou shalt not kill'. This naturally made the men of the Lancers anxious for an opportunity to throw off their unwanted reputation.

Unfortunately, the bored hacks did not help to instil pride in the regiment in the eyes of the public. George Steevens and others wrote uncomplimentary pieces about their scouting methods in which they endangered themselves in a frantic effort to find glory. Also, their appearance, through little fault of their own, was risible. The ludicrous-looking desert garb and equipment made them figures of fun, with the outsized quilted neck guard hanging from the tropical helmet which gave the appearance of mounted coalmen or stevedores. Festooned with cross-belts, bandoliers, water bottles and knapsacks, the Lancers were mounted on tough little Syrian ponies, whose resilience made up for their wild appearance. Steevens wrote: 'It was their first appearance in war ... they were the only regiment in the British army which had never been on active service ... At this first glimpse of British cavalry in the field, they looked less like horsemen than Christmas trees.'

Winston Churchill was a frequent visitor to the Steevens mess, as he preferred the amiable company of the Specials to those of his fellow officers of the 21st. The feeling was mutual, as the regiment rather resented Churchill being foisted on them and gave him the menial command of the Officers Mess Caravan, consisting of a mule and two donkeys. Churchill confided: 'These are little people. I can afford to laugh at them. They will live to see the mistake they have made.'

One correspondent who did write complimentary pieces about the regiment was the twenty-seven-year-old Honourable Hubert Howard, the second son of the Earl of Carlisle. In order to show their appreciation, he was invited to ride and mess with the officers. Although not a soldier, Howard had some cavalry experience as he had led a troop of volunteers called the 'Cape Boys' in the Matabele War of 1896 and had been severely wounded in the leg.

It was during one of the 21st Lancers' scouts that Howard helped save the life of Lieutenant Raymond de Montmorency, soon to win the Victoria Cross at Omdurman. Approaching a seemingly deserted village, de Montmorency rode forward alone to check. Suddenly a small party of Dervishes appeared and fired at him. Although not hit, he was forced to dismount and take cover. Howard spotted that the officer was in danger of being cut off from his troop. Together with two men, Howard charged, firing as they went and drove the Dervishes away.

After a lengthy build-up, the two armies finally faced one another at dawn on 2 September. The 20,000 strong Anglo-Egyptian army faced west in an arc, with its backs to the Nile. Moored behind them were six gunboats, with all guns pointing towards the advancing army of the Khalifa.

Steevens wrote: 'The noise of something began to creep in upon us; it cleared and divided into the tap of drums and the far-away surf of raucous war-cries. A shiver of expectancy thrilled our army, and then a sigh of content. They were coming on. Allah help them! They were coming on.

'It was now half-past six. The flags seemed very distant, the roar very faint, and the thud of our first gun was almost startling. It may have startled them too, but it startled them into life. The line of flags swung forward, and a mass of white flying linen swung forward with it too. They came very fast, and they came very straight; and then presently they came no farther. With a crash the bullets leaped out of the British rifles. It began with the Guards and Warwicks – section volleys at 2,000 yards; then, as the Dervishes edged rightward, it ran along to the Highlanders, the Lincolns, and to Maxwell's Brigade. The British stood up in double rank behind their zariba; the blacks lay down in their shelter-trench; both poured out death as fast as they could load and press trigger. Shrapnel whistled and Maxims growled savagely. From all the line came perpetual fire, fire, fire, and shrieked forth in great gusts of destruction.'[16]

What an extraordinary sight they made, something that would never again be witnessed. Like some vast medieval horde, 50,000 banner-waving foot soldiers and horsemen advanced like a storm-cloud towards the awe-struck invaders in a suicidal mass frontal attack.

The specials were distributed amongst the defenders as they sought the best vantage points. Frederic Villiers had erected his cinematograph on the aft deck of a gun-boat and had a splendid view of the advancing Dervishes. He had just started to turn the crank on the camera, and so would become the first man to capture a battle on film, when disaster struck. As the guns commenced volley firing, so the deck plates were shifted by the vibration, causing the camera tripod to collapse and the camera to open, thus exposing the film. Undaunted, Villiers fell back on his trusty sketch pad.

The first phase of the battle was really a one-sided affair. Concentrated artillery and machine-gun fire ensured that the Dervishes got nowhere close to Kitchener's men. Through the dust and gun-smoke could be seen the plain covered with the dead and dying. Steevens reported: 'It was the last day of Mahdism and the greatest. They could never get near, and they refused to hold back. By now the ground before us was all white with dead men's drapery. Rifles grew red-hot; the soldiers seized them by the slings and dragged them back to the reserve to change for cool ones. It was not a battle but an execution.'[17]

Eventually, there was a lull as the attacks grew weaker and the firing petered out. Kitchener then ordered an advance parallel with the river towards nearby Omdurman. The Dervish army of some 50,000 had been defeated by an Anglo-Egyptian force of 25,000, but had suffered 23,000 casualties compared with 330 from the British-led force.

The 21st Lancers, with both Howard and Churchill onboard, was ordered forward to harass the retreating survivors. This was the opportunity the glory-starved regiment had long awaited and when a thin ragged line of Dervishes was spotted, the charge was sounded and the Lancers dug in their spurs. As Churchill later wrote, 'We started to trot, two or three patrols galloping out in front towards the higher ground, while the regiment followed in mass – a great square block of ungainly brown figures and little horses, hung all over with water-bottles, saddle-bags, picketing-gear, tins of bully beef, all jolting and jangling together; the polish of peace gone; soldiers without glitter, horsemen without grace; but still a regiment of light cavalry in active operation against the enemy … Everyone expected that we were going to make a charge. That was the one idea that had been in all our minds since we had started from Cairo.'[18]

Too late, the Lancers found that they had been lured into a trap; for the ragged line disguised a dry water course concealing about 2,000 Dervishes. The momentum of the charge took the 310 cavalrymen into the midst of the enemy. Hacking and stabbing, there followed a desperate and bloody struggle before the survivors could extricate themselves. Churchill and Howard were in the thick of it and the former's subsequent account made exciting reading:

'The collision was prodigious. Nearly thirty Lancers, men and horses, and at least two hundred Arabs were overthrown. The shock was stunning to both sides, and for perhaps ten wonderful seconds no man heeded his enemy. Terrified horses wedged in the crowd, bruised and shaken men, sprawling in heaps, struggled dazed and stupid, to their feet, panted, and looked about them ... Stubborn and unshaken infantry hardly ever meet stubborn and unshaken cavalry ... The Dervishes fought manfully. They tried to hamstring the horses. They fired their rifles, pressing the muzzles into the very bodies of their opponents. They cut reins and stirrup-leathers. They flung their throwing- spears with great dexterity. The hand to hand fighting lasted perhaps one minute. Then the horses got into their stride again, the pace increased, and the Lancers drew out from among their antagonists. Within two minutes of the collision every living man was clear of the Dervish mass.'

In those few minutes of fighting, the 21st Lancers lost twenty-one men dead and fifty wounded, some severely. Although the charge achieved nothing, the press latched onto it as being more newsworthy and spectacular than the unequal contest between spear and machine-gun. In Steevens' words: 'The blunders of British cavalry are the fertile seed of British glory.' The charge was a glorious folly which finally established the 21st Lancers and gave them their long awaited battle honour of Omdurman.[19]

Two Specials rode out onto the corpse-covered plain to explore the scene of the recent carnage. Suddenly, they were confronted by a grizzled warrior, who pulled himself up and came at them with a spear. One of the hacks turned and galloped back to the safety of the column. The other, Bennet Burleigh, had problems turning his horse and had to draw his revolver. In his excitement, he managed to empty his weapon, hitting everything except his adversary. At the last moment, Captain Nevill Maskelyne Smyth, of the 2nd Dragoon Guards, rode out of the column and killed the Dervish, who managed to wound him with a spear thrust. For this act, Maskelyne was awarded the Victoria Cross and in the citation he was described as saving 'a camp follower', a description which must have wounded the collective pride of the Fourth Estate, and Burleigh's in particular.[20]

The next phase of the battle was the advance on Omdurman. Unfortunately, the attempt to move in formation soon came unstuck and the right rear brigade, the 19th Sudanese Regiment, became detached and isolated. Both Steevens and Scudamore got wind of this and galloped across from the main body to join its commander, Colonel Hector MacDonald, a hard-swearing former sergeant in the Gordon Highlanders. As he was always ready for a drink and a chat, the two Specials had found the rough and ready soldier more agreeable company than the rest of the officer corps. MacDonald greeted the two correspondents with: 'Gentleman, I am delighted to welcome you and I think I can show you some good sport.'

As the gap between themselves and the rest of the column widened to about a mile, they were suddenly charged by a regiment of Dervishes waving black banners. Quickly facing about, MacDonald was able to bring all his firepower to bear, but his men blazed away until all their ammunition was exhausted. They then resorted to the bayonet and managed to fend off the attack until reinforcements arrived. MacDonald's brigade and the reinforcements then managed to repel another charge and re-join the main column. Despite Kitchener's poor handling of his command during this part of the advance, he was able to enter Omdurman without any further resistance.

Scudamore added to his popularity by offering some cold lagers to his parched colleagues, including Hubert Howard, who was naturally elated after taking part in the 21st's charge, crowing that he had had the time of his life. Being teetotal, Howard had to decline and be content with drinking muddy river water.

The British artillery was still firing the occasional shell at the domed tomb of the Mahdi. Tragically, it was there that Hubert

Howard met his death from 'friendly fire', having just survived the mad cavalry charge. Along with some companions, Howard had gone forward to explore, when a shell burst amongst them. Frank Rhodes, a *Times* colleague, was badly wounded in the shoulder and Frank Scudamore's pony was killed. Howard was instantly killed by a piece of shrapnel. In the confusion of battle, nobody had told the artillery to cease firing. The 21st Lancers was particularly upset by Howard's death. Not only had he been an agreeable companion but he had taken part in the charge and would have been relied upon to report glowingly on the regiment's performance.

The death and wounding of the two correspondents of *The Times* made it imperative to make alternative arrangements for their reports. The manager of *The Times* approached Winston Churchill, who declined, so they accepted the reports of Bennet Burleigh by arrangement with the *Daily Telegraph*.

On entry into Khartoum, Burleigh helped release Charles Neufeld, a European who had been held in fetters by the Khalifa for twelve years. Gathering some farriers and engineers, Burleigh had the chains removed from the unfortunate prisoner, after which Neufeld referred to Burleigh as the 'King of War Correspondents'. This description was not, however, one widely held by his fellow correspondents, who had been victim to his unashamed quest for a 'scoop'. Henry Nevinson was one of Burleigh's victims when his luggage was thrown off as their train was just about to depart.

Another example of his cunning was the departure from the Sudan of all the correspondents. Burleigh joined them as they steamed up the Nile to Shepherd's Hotel in Cairo. Catching a boat to Brindisi, they all then caught a train for London. At the last moment Burleigh jumped off, declaring that he was going to stay behind. It later transpired that he returned to Cairo to report what became known as the 'Fashoda Affair', which involved the French attempting to claim the upper Nile for their own and thwarting Britain's own plans to open an uninterrupted route down the Nile and through to Cape Town. By interviewing soldiers who had taken part in this intervention, which ended peacefully, Burleigh and the *Daily Telegraph* were able to publish exclusively this potentially grave international incident. The reaction by his fellow correspondents was one of anger tinged with envy.

Now that the reconquest of the Sudan had been successfully achieved, there was a scramble amongst some of the Specials to return home and write up their lucrative accounts of the war. Four correspondents, unbeknown to the others, rushed to write up their notes for a quick publication. Within a few weeks, George Steevens emerged as the victor with his best-selling account, *With Kitchener to Khartoum*, which beat his rivals Bennet Burleigh, Winston Churchill and Ernest Bennett. Despite Kitchener's obdurate attitude, these war correspondents had managed to write enough to keep the public satisfied.

As with the conclusion of all wars, there was time and space to write in greater detail and to expose any shortcomings. Bennet Burleigh once again criticised poor equipment, in particular the soldiers' boots, which did not stand up to desert conditions and fell apart. When this question was raised in the House of Commons, the War Office's reaction was to state that the boots were high quality footwear but that the work done by the British troops had tried them too severely. George Steevens wrote in the *Daily Mail*: 'It is a strange sort of answer to say that a military boot is a very good boot, only you mustn't march in it.'

Ernest Bennett repeated previous allegations he had made in the *Manchester Guardian* that the wounded Dervishes had been killed or left to die on the battlefield; this, despite the experience of the determined wounded to kill any enemy who came within range of where they lay. Bennett temporarily left journalism and joined the Oxford University Volunteers at the start of the Anglo-Boer War. He was commissioned and served in the Oxfordshire and Buckinghamshire Light Infantry and took part in the campaigns with Generals Roberts and Kitchener. He returned to war reporting with the *Manchester Guardian* and covered the 1911 Italian-Turkish in Libya and the Balkan War the following year.

Although they may not have realised it at the time, the Specials had just covered the last of the old-style colonial wars, where primitively armed natives broke themselves upon the squares of sophisticatedly armed soldiers. From now on warfare would become more deadly and reporting increasingly difficult.

Chapter 13

The Anglo-Boer War

The foundations for another war with the Boers had been laid many years earlier. The Zulu and First Boer Wars had signalled British intentions to control all of Southern Africa but it was the discovery of huge gold deposits in the Boer republic of Transvaal that spurred the British to try and absorb Transvaal and the Orange Free State. In 1896, Cecil Rhodes, with tacit British agreement, had launched the ignominious 'Jameson Raid', led by his assistant, Dr Leander Starr Jameson. The expected uprising failed to materialise and Jameson and his misguided followers were arrested. This acted as a clear warning to the Boers that the British were prepared to take their country by force and prompted the newly wealthy republics to arm themselves with the latest French and German weapons. With diplomatic negotiations exhausted and British troops concentrated near the border, war was declared on 18 October 1899.

British forces in the whole of South Africa at the beginning of hostilities numbered just 14,500 and were heavily outnumbered by the 50,000-strong Boer army. Britannia, however, was at the zenith of her powers and she felt she could easily deal with 'a bunch of unruly farmers'. Henry Nevinson was in the country to cover the negotiations and travelled to both the Transvaal and the Orange Free State to interview such Boer leaders as Kruger, Reitz, Smuts and Joubert, all of whom greatly impressed him.

Nevinson doubted the rightness of the British cause but felt, nevertheless, that he should report from the British side. He was given a pass and allowed to ride through the Boer lines into Natal, where the main British force was stationed at the town of Ladysmith.

There he met up with some familiar faces; Will Maud of *The Graphic*, George Steevens, Bennet Burleigh and his *Telegraph* colleague, Robert MacHugh, Lionel James and Frank Rhodes of *The Times*. Of course there were Melton Prior and George Lynch of the *Illustrated London News*, William Maxwell of *The Standard*, Harry Pearse of the *Daily News*, Arthur Hutton of Reuters, as well as several others. They, too, had been evacuated from the Transvaal, where they had been covering the ultimatum, and had caught the last train out to Natal.

Lionel James has left a rather patronising description of some of his fellow Specials, including 'Bennet Burleigh, a lusty example of Glasgow vehemence', and Melton Prior: 'But for the genius of his imaginative pencil, he was the prototype of the thousands of colourless citizens who daily flock between Suburbia and the City.'[1] With the exception of George Steevens, whom James regarded as a genius, he did not rate his fellow correspondents very highly. He did have a soft spot for Frank Rhodes, who was a placid, sweet-natured man in contrast to his dynamic and celebrated younger brother, Cecil.

James was from a military family and had been brought up mainly in India before going on to become one of the foremost Specials of the Edwardian age. His entry into journalism was precipitated by his bankrupt horse-racing stable and a lost wager. In 1894, he bet heavily on his own horse in a meeting at Allahabad which landed him in debt. In order to settle with his creditors, he took a job with a Calcutta journal and was sent to cover the Chitral campaign. He enjoyed the experience and soon joined Reuters, covering the North West Frontier campaigns of Mohmund, Tirah and Malakand. In exceeding the call of duty, he became involved in the fighting at the Malakand Pass and helped rally wavering British soldiers, for which he was Mentioned in Despatches. From 1899 to 1913, he was the principal war correspondent of *The Times*.

Within days, the Boers had crossed the border and fought the

British in two battles, at Elandslaagte and Talana. The fighting at Elandslaagte was only twenty miles from Ladysmith and reported by Steevens, Nevinson, Lynch, James and Prior. When the battle began, Prior noticed that he was in the midst of heavy rifle fire and that his colleagues and soldiers alike had hastily moved away from him. Bennet Burleigh yelled at him: 'Confound your white helmet, Prior; you are drawing all the fire!' It had not occurred to him that his nice new white tropical helmet was making a clear target. Prior reasoned: 'If I took it off my bald head would act like a heliograph to them … Fortunately I had a waterproof cloak, so I took my helmet off, carried it under my arm, and flung the coat over my head; then crouched as low as I could, like the rest were doing, by the side of ant-heaps. This certainly had the right effect, for the shells left me and chose another objective.' He later dyed his new headgear with tea, a trick he learned from the soldiers.[2]

In a sudden evening storm, the British infantry, led by Colonel Ian Hamilton, managed to dislodge the Boers from a series of ridges. At the moment of victory, Nevinson wrote, 'Wildly cheering, raising their helmets on their bayonets … Line after line of khaki figures, like hounds through a gap, came pouring into position, shouting fiercely: "Majuba, Majuba".'[3] This was a particularly poignant moment for Hamilton to savour, as he had been badly wounded at Majuba Hill. The Boers descended to where their horses were tethered and for the first time prepared to ride away when they took the full impact of a cavalry charge by British dragoons and lancers. The result was a complete victory for the British and the only one they would enjoy for many months.

There followed a series of reverses, with weary and demoralised soldiers seeking refuge in Ladysmith as the Boers began to command all of Natal north of the Tugela River. As the noose tightened around Ladysmith, Burleigh said to his old comrade, 'Prior, my boy, it is all over, we are beaten and it means investment. We shall all be locked up in Ladysmith.'[4] Unable to persuade Prior to accompany him, Burleigh bade his farewells and boarded a train south before the Boers completely surrounded the town.

Prior felt it was his duty to stay where he felt the action would be and, for the first time, experience being besieged. Soon enough he came to regret his decision. Henry Nevinson also spurned the chance to leave. 'We could not tell how long the siege might last, but there we were in the very front line, and for a war correspondent that is the choice of all positions in the world. How could we abandon it? Or how could we even think of quitting those famous British and Irish regiments gathered there at the centre of peril? It appeared to me unimaginable, and evidently others of my colleagues thought so too, for only one of them attempted to go.'[5]

Burleigh, wily old hack that he was, knew that he would be kicking his heels in Ladysmith, unable to get his reports through to his paper. Besides, his *Telegraph* colleague, MacHugh, had elected to stay and could cover any news from inside Ladysmith. Burleigh immediately attached himself to the large relief force arriving from Britain and India under the command of General Redvers Buller.

It is of interest that in early 1900, the controversial Lieutenant Harry 'Breaker' Morant acted as despatch rider for Burleigh. Morant was an Anglo-Australian drover, horseman, poet, soldier and convicted war criminal whose skill with horses earned him the name 'The Breaker'. In 1902, while serving with the Bushveldt Carbineers, he participated in the summary execution of several Boer prisoners and the killing of a German missionary. His actions led to his controversial court-martial and his execution for murder.

Within weeks, the Boers had besieged the British in Ladysmith, in Kimberley on the border with the Orange Free State, and at Mafeking where Transvaal, the Cape Colony and Bechuanaland met. This is where the Boers made a great strategic mistake by taking their eye off the main objective. If they had contained the British in these towns and sent their main force into the Cape, they would have had virtually the whole country under their control and deprived the British of their supply port and naval base. Instead, they wasted their considerable strength and numerical advantage on mounting these sieges.

Although strategically unimportant, the Boers initially positioned 10,000 men around Mafeking. The town was defended by just 600 Rhodesian troopers and civilians pressed into service. They were commanded by Colonel Robert Stephenson Baden-Powell, who had been instructed to try and divert the Boers by harassing their flank and rear. Instead, he chose to defend the small dusty railway town and to draw the enemy into committing themselves to a siege. In this respect, he was entirely successful. With so few men to defend a large perimeter, he came up with some ingenious ruses to fool the enemy. These included dummy artillery and a searchlight that was carried from one strong-point to another to give the impression there were many searchlights. The most bizarre was the non-existent barbed-wire fences. Poles were planted around the perimeter and everyone who approached them had to pretend to step over the 'barbed-wire'. The Boers were totally taken in. Baden-Powell organised cricket matches, cycle races, balls and concerts and generally behaved like the archetypal eccentric soldier he was.

There was, however, a dark side to this outward display of British élan. Despite it being surrounded, it was still possible to get in and out of Mafeking and some British correspondents made the journey to report on the position. As the siege progressed, Baden-Powell refused to allow them to leave as he was worried that they would expose his treatment of the black population. In order to keep going during the six-month siege, he had cut the food rations to the blacks to a starvation level so that the whites would have enough rations to see the siege through.

One of the Specials was a conscientious twenty-five-year-old named Angus Hamilton, on his first assignment for *The Times*. He found the sight of starving blacks too much to bear and wrote a report condemning their plight. Having managed to get it smuggled out, the report was 'spiked' by his editor on the grounds that it would reflect badly on the myth of Baden-Powell and Mafeking. In fact, the whole country had been swept by 'Mafeking fever' and anything reported that was critical or controversial would have been howled down by the public. Instead, Hamilton bowed to his employer's wishes and sent optimistic and upbeat despatches. Although he went on to report other wars, he was a troubled young man who succumbed to the pressures of his profession. In 1913, he committed suicide by cutting his throat in a New York hotel during a lecture tour.

The other correspondents bottled up in Mafeking were Emerson Neilly of the *Pall Mall Gazette*, Vere Stent of Reuters, F.D. Baillie of the *Morning Post* and Edwin George Parslow of the *Daily Chronicle*. They all came through the siege unscathed with the tragic exception of Parslow, who became a victim of murder. With little to do of an evening except drink, Parslow got into a drunken argument with an unstable artillery officer, Major Murchison. Insults were swopped until Murchison settled things by drawing his revolver and shooting Parslow. Although Baden-Powell sentenced him to death, he was reprieved because of his service during the siege. After the war, Murchison was taken back to Britain to serve a prison sentence for manslaughter.

Also present was a remarkable woman reporter, Lady Sarah Wilson, who reported for the *Daily Mail*. She was the youngest daughter of the 7th Duke of Marlborough and aunt of Winston Churchill. The *Daily Mail* recruited her after one of its correspondents, Ralph Hellawell, was arrested by the Boers as he tried to get out of Mafeking to send his despatch. Lady Sarah neither asked for or received preferential treatment and was a popular figure during the siege. Not popular enough, however, for she was excluded from a large all-male dinner thrown by her colleagues for Baden-Powell and his staff. She would, nonetheless, have been included in Rudyard Kipling's description of war correspondents he observed during the Mafeking campaign as having 'the constitution of a bullock, the digestion of an ostrich and an infinite adaptability to all circumstances'.[6]

When General Buller sailed for South Africa on the *Dunnottar Castle*, he was accompanied by sixteen gentlemen of the press, including Winston Churchill, who had resigned his commission having decided his future lay in politics. Failing to win a seat at Oldham in the summer by-election, Churchill concentrated his efforts on self-publicity. The outbreak of the Anglo-Boer War was a heaven-sent opportunity for him to get his name before the public. He had been made an offer to represent the *Daily News* and, using this as a lever, managed to strike a lucrative deal with the *Morning Post*. The proprietor, Oliver Borthwick, took him on for an incredible £250 per month plus expenses and allowed Churchill to keep the copyright for his writing.

Like most of the Specials, Churchill did not deny himself a good supply of alcohol and tinned luxuries. He hauled all of these up towards the front line in Natal where he established himself at the railway town of Escourt. Using his network of friends in the military, he managed to get a ride on an armoured train which was heading towards Boer infested country. He later wrote that, 'Nothing looks more formidable and impressive than an armoured train; but nothing is in fact more vulnerable and helpless'.[7] During the return journey, the Boers derailed the train, taking the troops and Churchill prisoner. Churchill could not have orchestrated a better publicity campaign. When he eventually made his way back to Natal after his escape from imprisonment in Pretoria, he discovered that the British newspapers had been filled with his escapades and found that his name 'had resounded at home'.

Buller was pleased to see him back and overruled a War Office order that no soldier could act as a war correspondent by granting Churchill a commission in the South African Light Horse. He could not offer him army pay as well as his *Morning Post* salary, and it is not known if Buller was aware that Churchill was earning £50 a month more than the commander-in-chief! The rest of the press corps howled their disapproval, but Churchill was impervious to their slings and arrows as long as he got his way.

While Buller's relief force became stalled at the Tugela River, to the west, General Lord Methuen set out to relieve Kimberley. He led 8,000 troops and they followed the railway line that ran parallel with the western border of the Orange Free State. Amongst those accompanying this column were Frederic Villiers, Edward Knight of *The Times*, Julian Ralph of the *Daily Mail*, and an ex-private soldier, Edgar Wallace, working on his first assignment for Reuters. Ralph observed the Battle of Magersfontein and articulated what it was like to fight the Boers: 'The Boers are an invisible foe. Our men never once saw them, and yet were unable to raise hand or foot without being riddled with bullets … Our men fell just as ripe fruit does from a shaken tree.'

Frederic Villiers had been lecturing in Australia and had arrived on the ship carrying men of the New South Wales regiment. Leaving his wife in Cape Town, he travelled to join Methuen and reached his command just as the Highlanders were retreating from the British defeat at Magersfontein. It was during this stalled advance on Kimberley that Villiers came under fire from men of the Suffolk Regiment who mistook his Cape cart for one used by the local Boer commander. Fortunately, all Villiers suffered was a nasty fright.

Edward Knight was not so fortunate. It was towards the end of the battle at Belmont that a Boer raised a white flag. In response, 'Dogger' Knight stood up only to be shot by a dum-dum bullet in the right arm, which later had to be amputated. Undaunted, Knight soon learned to write with his left hand. Unsurprisingly, he found the newly available portable typewriter a boon.

Methuen's column went on to fight the battles of Modder River and Stormberg, in which he took appallingly high casualties. The combination of these casualties and the reverses that Buller was suffering in Natal came to be called the 'Black Week'. This directly led to a call for civilian volunteers to fill the shortage of manpower. It was no longer a war fought by professionals but one that now involved the whole nation. The mood became one of defiant jingoism as newspapers responded with even stronger patriotic prose and some downright lies.

The war created great interest at home and abroad with most publications sending their reporters – until there were about 300 correspondents representing papers and magazines from around the world. *The Times* alone sent twenty reporters, headed by Lionel James. Wishing to distinguish themselves from the rest of the journalistic herd, *The Times'* men took to wearing a toothbrush stuck in the band of their hats as a sort of club identification. The American correspondent Richard Harding Davis wrote, 'If you were a *Times* man you wore a toothbrush; if you were not a *Times* man you didn't dare do it. No, sir!'

Amongst the more obscure journals represented were such titles as *Illustrated Sporting and Dramatic News, Pen and Pencil* and the *Darlington North Star*. Also the *British Medical Journal*, which would have much to write about the appalling lack of adequate medical facilities and supplies, which led directly to the high death rate caused by disease. By the end of the war, two thirds of casualties had been caused by disease. A *Times* correspondent, W. Burdett Coutts, exposed the scandal of the lack of effective medical care and the large-scale typhoid epidemic. This resulted in an influx of volunteer civilian doctors including one of the great celebrities of the period, Sir Arthur Conan Doyle, who offered his medical services and wrote about the appalling conditions he encountered.

His contemporary, the great Imperialist, Rudyard Kipling, also arrived to throw his weight behind Britain's determination to defeat the Boer and was persuaded by General Roberts to co-edit a propaganda paper in the Orange Free State, called *The Friend*. As the year approached the new century, the besieged Specials in Ladysmith had to endure boredom and squalor with occasional bursts of violence.

Lionel James of the *Times* neatly summed up the four month-long siege: 'November – Novelty, December – Ennui, January – Desperation, February – Resignation & Starvation.'[8] Unable to send out news, James decided to use carrier pigeons. Unfortunately, these were intercepted by the Boers, who wrote to thank him for an enjoyable meal!

The town and surrounding strongpoints were under fire at any time during each day. Many believed that Boer informants in the town were giving the enemy artillery targets to fire on. Amongst those targeted were the hated members of the Jameson Raid, of whom there were several in Ladysmith, including the leader himself, and Frank Rhodes of *The Times*.

One day Melton Prior and Henry Nevinson rode out to visit the British southern strongpoint at Caesar's Camp under the command of Colonel Ian Hamilton. As they paused to water their horses in the Klip River, a shell burst above them. Fortuitously, the shrapnel splashed all around them but left them unscathed.

At the beginning of the siege, Prior made his sketches and then copied them on tracing paper. These he folded as small as he could, 'about the size of a compass', and paid a native runner £50 to take them through the Boer lines to Colenso. Unfortunately, the courier was killed, so Prior repeated the process. This time the native was caught and beaten. A third one did manage to get through but the exercise had cost a fortune. It was then arranged for an organised and regular postal service to be used, under the auspices of the military censor, costing £15 per letter.

George Steevens, rigid with boredom, created a gently satirical paper called the *Ladysmith Lyre*, which was followed by the *Ladysmith Bombshell*. The *Lyre* only lasted for three editions due to the untimely death of its proprietor. Enteric, or typhoid, had reached epidemic proportions by the end of the year and had afflicted Steevens. William Maud shared a house with Steevens and was told by the doctor that his friend was dying. It was suggested that Steevens should be told in case he wanted to make any last arrangements. Poor Maud broke the news, which took Steevens by surprise because he thought he was over the worst. Having left his last instructions, Steevens asked that the bottle of champagne he had been saving for when they were relieved should be opened. They touched glasses and bade farewell to each other in a rather stiff British way. Three hours later George Steevens was dead. It was necessary to bury the body as soon as possible, so that night a sad group of Specials accompanied the coffin to the ever-growing cemetery and, in a brief ceremony, buried one of the most highly regarded journalists of his day. Unable to function properly as a Special, Maud volunteered for service and acted as ADC to Colonel Ian Hamilton. He, too, was laid low with enteric but survived and was invalided back to England.

When word of Steevens's death reached the correspondent's arch-enemy, Lord Kitchener, he was genuinely saddened and remarked to Vernon Blackburn: 'I was anxious to tell you how very sorry I was to hear of the death of Mr Steevens. He was in the Sudan, and of course, I saw a great deal of him and knew him well. He was such a clever and able man. He did his work as correspondent brilliantly, and he never gave the slightest trouble – I wish all correspondents were like him … He was a model correspondent, the best I have ever known and I should like you to say how greatly grieved I am at his death.'[9]

In 1901, Will Maud was sent to Macedonia after the kidnapping of an American missionary, Ellen Maria Stone, and her pregnant friend, Katerina Stefanova-Tsilka. Both were held for an enormous ransom by a Macedonian independence group. In what has been described as 'America's first modern hostage crisis', it was an affair that attracted wide coverage in the media. After six months of intensive negotiations, the Turkish government paid the ransom and the hostages were released. As for Maud, he had never fully recovered his health after Ladysmith and in 1903, on his way home from reporting the war in Somalia, he died in Aden.

Other reporters also had adventures. George Lynch of *The Illustrated London News* got wind that a soldier on outpost duty had wandered close to the Boer lines and had had a conversation with an enemy picket. He decided he would try the same thing and get a story from the Boer perspective. Riding south, he reached the reputed location but could not see any sign of the enemy. He kept on riding until it occurred to him that he might get clear and go all the way to Buller's column. Dismounting, he managed to walk unchallenged through the Boer lines but, just as he thought he was home and dry, he was stopped and captured. Imprisoned in Pretoria, Lynch fell sick and was repatriated home to Britain after a month. Once he had recovered, he was sent out to China to cover the Boxer Rebellion.

One Special, Arthur Hutton of Reuters, did successfully evade Boer patrols and made his way across the Tugela River to reach the British lines. There he joined Churchill and Bennet Burleigh, who were among the Specials who followed Buller's attempts to force a way through the strongly held Boer positions north of the Tugela River. It was on the Tugela that a new branch of journalism appeared for the first time in a theatre of war: the newsreel.

William Kennedy Laurie Dickson was born in 1860 in France to English-Scottish parents. In 1879, following the death of his father, Dickson's mother took him and his sisters and emigrated to the United States. Her son soon showed an aptitude for photography and engineering and joined Thomas Edison, the pioneering inventor. With Edison's encouragement, Dickson designed the world's first practical 35mm movie camera.

In 1895, Dickson left Edison and, with two friends, founded the America Mutoscope and Biograph Company, designing and patenting a huge, electrically driven camera which produced high quality films. Two years later, Dickson came to England and set up the British Biograph Company, which enjoyed some success with films of European royalty, beach scenes and parades.

It was the Boer War, however, that really put the company on the map. Dickson travelled on *Dunnottar Castle* with General Buller, Winston Churchill and the large party of war correspondents. Because Dickson was not regarded as a war correspondent, he could not get accreditation to travel with the Army and had to rely on persuading Buller to issue him a special pass. This did not, however, entitle him to draw army rations or forage for his horses. Consequently, much of his time was spent scrounging just to stay alive. He attached himself to the only unit that showed him any sort of forbearance, the Naval Brigade, who were often called upon to bale him out of some desperate situations. Dickson also established a good rapport with Lord Dundonald, who commanded the mounted irregulars, like Churchill's South African Light Horse, and who, on several occasions, obliged with mock charges and manoeuvres for the camera.

When the Dublin Fusiliers suffered carnage at Colenso, Dickson and his two assistants, Seward and Cox, helped the stretcher parties bring in the many casualties. (The camera Dickson used was very heavy and bulky, hence the necessity for assistants. Indeed, it was big enough to provide shade for shelter at lunch.) Dickson also extensively used a stills camera and the images he sent back to Britain were syndicated to several publications including the popular weekly magazine, *With the Flag to Pretoria*, published by the Harmsworth brothers.

Besides filming the Naval Brigade bombarding Boer positions, Dickson's first real war film was that of the ambulances crossing a pontoon bridge spanning the Little Tugela River. They were bringing back the dead and wounded from the ill-fated attack on Spion Kop. It was one of his most effective reels as it shows British infantry in the foreground covering the retreat, the long line of ambulances and mounted figures snaking across the mid-ground with the sinister shape of Spion Kop in the background. Realising the significance of what he was filming, Dickson shot three reels to be on the safe side in case of accident. In the event, all three have survived. When his films arrived back in London and were processed, they were shown to packed houses at the Palace, a music hall theatre in the Strand.

Dickson and his colleagues endured many hardships, including having his cart twice ransacked by passing British troops. Misfortune was compounded when both Seward and Cox contracted typhoid. Leaving his camera with his navy friends, Dickson took his assistants 600 miles back to Durban for proper medical care, having little faith in the British field hospitals. Happily, both men recovered.

Dickson returned to the front just before the 118-day siege was lifted. He retrieved his equipment and was given a seaman as an assistant. Evading the military police, Dickson drove into Ladysmith on a back road and was one of the first civilians into the besieged town. His first impression was of the stench of death that hung everywhere due to the many unburied dead horses and oxen. The salute of the official march past by Buller was taken by the gaunt figure of General White and was captured by Dickson's camera.

In another shot he filmed, a column of troops pass the slouch-hatted Winston Churchill, who was standing next to Dickson at the time; this was probably the very first moving image of Britain's future prime minister. Dickson was not the only cameraman to film the Boer War, but certainly the most successful. His biggest rival was Charles Urban of the Warwick Trading Company, who used the more portable 35mm hand-operated camera. This would have been the same camera that was abortively used by Frederic Villiers in the Sudan and Greece.

Lionel James managed to outwit his fellow besieged Specials as they were relieved by the first of Buller's force. Despite the still-present danger of Boer marksmen, James left under cover of darkness, reached General Buller's headquarters and was the first to telegraph the news of the relief of Ladysmith. Instead of continuing to work as a Special, James volunteered and joined the newly-raised King Edward's Horse, serving out the remainder of the war in the saddle.[10]

With Ladysmith relieved and Natal made safe, the Specials hurried to the British advance in the Orange Free State. This was led by the recently arrived General Frederick Roberts, replacing General Buller whose less than energetic efforts in Natal had caused consternation at home.

Roberts's arrival coincided with a swing in fortunes towards the British, as first Kimberley was relieved, to be followed by the Orange Free State capital, Bloemfontein. Bennet Burleigh was one of the three correspondents who rode ahead and entered the town as the Boers pulled out before riding back to tell Roberts that Bloemfontein had capitulated.

Mary Kingsley, one of few female correspondents, covered the war for the *Morning Post*. Sadly her career was short-lived – in addition to her reporting duties, she volunteered as a nurse, but contracted typhoid and died on Whit Monday, 1900.

Henry Nevinson, freed from Ladysmith and despite suffering from the effects of malaria, went in pursuit of General Roberts. He bought a cart and drove over tough terrain and covered 300 miles in ten days. Sick, suffering from lack of food and water and having two horses die on him, Nevinson, nevertheless, reached Pretoria in time to see Roberts take the surrender. He was, however, incredulous that Roberts allowed so many armed Boers to escape from his clutches. It was these who carried on a guerrilla war for another two years. Nevinson stayed on and attacked Kitchener's policy of burning Boer farms to deny the guerrillas food and shelter. As a result, his editor, Hugh Massingham, was forced to resign because the paper's anti-war sympathies had caused a decline in circulation.

William Dickson was on hand to film the annexation ceremony at Bloemfontein and its surrender by dozens of Boers. He was not so lucky with the fall of Pretoria, as he was delayed by twenty-four hours and missed the surrender ceremony. Improvising, he co-opted a soldier to unfurl a huge Union Jack on the roof of the City Hall, taking care to avoid showing the now empty square below. He then persuaded the amenable General Roberts and staff to act out their part in the ceremony. The resultant film was a huge hit with the London audiences. By the end of the war, Dickson's company had made a profit of £2,000, a huge sum for the period.

With the fall of the capital of Transvaal, Roberts handed over his command to General Kitchener, nemesis of the Specials. If they thought the censorship had been tough, it was about to become virtually impossible to get anything past Kitchener's restrictions. This, and the fact that the war appeared all but over, led to a mass exodus of the Specials. One who stayed and became both popular and notorious was Edgar Wallace of the *Daily Mail*.

His was a remarkable story of a self-educated man who, through determination and natural talent, enjoyed an exceptionally successful literary career. Born in 1875, he was a foundling brought up by a Deptford fish porter and his wife. After an elementary education, Wallace left school at the age of 12 and worked at such jobs as newsboy and labourer. Seemingly doomed to a life of menial jobs, he joined the infantry at the age of eighteen as a puny under-nourished recruit. In 1896, he transferred to the Medical Staff Corps to train as a medical orderly and was sent to South Africa. His interest in literature set him apart from his fellow soldiers and, with encouragement from the chaplain and his wife, he began to write poetry. After meeting Rudyard Kipling in Cape Town, he was inspired enough to start submitting articles and stories to the local newspapers. In 1899, he bought himself out of the Army and was taken on by Reuters.

As many of the correspondents left after Pretoria surrendered, Wallace was appointed the principal *Daily Mail* correspondent. His style was hard-hitting, two-fisted jingoism, just the thing to revive interest in a war that was losing the public's interest. He also had the knack of telling a story, which eventually led to his fortune.

Although the early days of the war had displayed gentlemanly conduct from both sides, now a decidedly nasty element had entered. The foreign press, almost universally pro-Boer and anti-British, reported a succession of atrocity stories. Wallace retaliated with adventurous tales of brave British and Empire troops usually performing some heroic but fictitious deed. Blindly patriotic, he even managed to turn a British defeat into victory, as he did when he wrote of the Boer attack on the British camp at Vlakfontein. 'It was a victory and a victory in spite of our heavy casualty list. Not only did we drive off an enemy outnumbering us three to one but by the splendid dash of our infantry we have established the irrefutable fact that, in spite of twenty months' hard fighting and tedious trekking and the lugubrious views of *The Times'* correspondent notwithstanding, the old hands are as fit and just as keen as ever. And it was a marvellous victory also.'[11]

Wallace was accused of fabricating his own atrocity stories. One in particular fuelled the flames of hatred against the Boers and led to Kitchener having Wallace escorted under armed guard back to Cape Town. He had written: 'Abandoning the old methods of dropping the butt end of a rifle on the wounded soldier's face when there is none to see the villainy, the Boer has done his bloody work in the light of day, within sight of a dozen eye-witnesses, and the stories we have hardly dared to hint, lest you thought we had grown hysterical, we can now tell without fear of ridicule. The Boers murder wounded men.'[12] Alone of all the correspondents, Wallace had no fear of Kitchener and even had the nerve to attack this stern and rigid commander for weakness in his dealings with the Boers.

As the war dragged on into 1902, Kitchener was ready to make peace and a conference was set up at a place called Vereeniging. All correspondents were denied any information regarding progress, while speculation was rife. Only the *Daily Mail* seemed to know what was going on and on 31 May, it scooped the rest of the world by its headline of PEACE. It even beat the official announcement in the House of Commons. How was this possible? The *Mail* followed its scoop with details of how Edgar Wallace had managed to penetrate military security and outwit the censor.

Wallace had begun to visit his stockbroker in Johannesburg by train, which passed through Vereeniging each day. He had also used his contacts from his Army days and persuaded a former colleague, who was a member of the headquarters staff, to stand by the perimeter wire as the train steamed by and blow his nose. If he used a red handkerchief each day, then the talks were stalemated, blue would mean progress and a white would signal success. When, at last, he saw the white handkerchief, Wallace told his stockbroker, who then sent a coded wire to his brother in London, which would be passed onto the offices of the *Mail*. This system worked perfectly and Wallace and his paper got their scoop.

One should spare a thought for the veteran Bennet Burleigh, who devised an equally ingenious code but was pipped at the post. On learning news of the peace signing, Burleigh telegraphed the *Telegraph*'s owner, Edward Lawson, the innocent message – 'Whitsuntide greeting' – which passed the censor without a problem. It took a while before the baffled *Telegraph* staff turned to the Book of Common Prayer and broke the code. The Whit Sunday text begins: 'Peace I leave with you; my peace I give unto you.' The paper published the news that terms had been agreed and that peace was imminent.

Kitchener was furious with Wallace and had his accreditation rescinded, a ban that lasted Kitchener's life. When the campaign medals were awarded for the first time to war reporters, Kitchener made a particular point of refusing one to Wallace. Unable to perform as a correspondent, Wallace took up writing novels and became the most popular writer of his generation. His best known were *The Four Just Men* and *Sanders of the River*. Despite making a fortune, he was famed for his extravagance and died penniless in 1932 while working on the script of the film *King Kong* in Hollywood.

Returning to South Africa for the peace conference was Henry Nevinson, who was appalled at the conditions in which the Boer women and children were held. In fact the scandal of the concentration camps had been exposed, not by professional journalists, but by letters to *The Times* from Miss Emily Hobhouse, who had visited in her capacity as an activist for a charity organisation. Nevinson apart, journalists were not inclined to report anything to Britain's detriment. With South Africa regarded as old news, the public were bored and were indifferent to any injustices suffered by their old enemy. They had a new monarch on the throne and looked forward to a new century of peace and prosperity.

Chapter 14

The Last Days of the Golden Age

During the summer of 1900, Britain had become involved with a unique multi-national expedition in China. A secret society called 'Righteous and Harmonious Fists', or 'Boxers' as they were known by Westerners, came into prominence with a call to exterminate all 'foreign devils' in China. They slaughtered missionaries, businessmen and Chinese Christians. Western embassies in Perking appealed to the Dowager Empress to use the Imperial Army to suppress the uprising; instead, they found that there was considerable royal sympathy for the Boxers.

The Chinese authorities demanded that the foreign ministries depart Peking and promised to furnish safeguards en route. Several of the Europeans protested that the ministers should reject their demands; chief among them was an old China-hand, Dr George Ernest Morrison, *The Times*' China correspondent. He vigorously expressed the view: 'If you men vote to leave Peking tomorrow, the death of every man, woman and child in this huge unprotected convoy will be on your heads, and your names will go through history and be known forever as the wickedest, weakest, and most pusillanimous cowards who ever lived.' In the event, his view prevailed.

With the surrounding country in an uproar and with communications cut, foreign ministers sent for troops and sailors from coastal bases to protect them. A total of 430 marines and sailors from eight different countries arrived in Peking. They set to building a defensive perimeter in the Legation part of the city.

This area housed 353 civilian men, women and children, in addition to which there were about 2,700 Chinese Christians.

From the beginning of June until their relief on 14 August, they were besieged by fanatical Boxers, baying for blood. George Morrison, like Mark Twain, became one of the few people to have the interesting experience of reading his own obituary. After the first fierce Boxer attack, the *Daily Mail* had reported that the Legations had fallen and everyone was slain. *The Times* assumed that Morrison had died and printed a glowing three column obituary but, happily, he survived, despite being wounded. He was even Mentioned in Despatches by the British Minister: 'Dr Morrison, *The Times'* correspondent, acted as lieutenant to Captain Strouts and rendered most valuable assistance. Active, energetic and cool, he volunteered for every service of danger and was a pillar of strength when matters were going badly. He was severely wounded on 16th July by the same volley that killed Captain Strouts and his valuable services were lost for the rest of the siege.'[1] After peace returned, Morrison resumed his post for *The Times* until his death in 1920.

The paper had sent John Cowan as his replacement and he joined other reporters as they accompanied the relief force of 20,000 troops made up of units supplied by Britain, Japan, Russia, the United States, France, Germany, Italy and Austria. George Lynch, an escapee from Ladysmith, was also on hand. He wrote critically of the brutal treatment of Chinese civilians meted out by the Russians, French and Germans. On one occasion, British soldiers rescued some women who had been thrown down a well by Russian soldiers. George Lynch's experience in China led him to condemn 'the vulgar aggression of the West against the East'. He wrote of the ill-treatment of Chinese civilians, including the massacre of a boatload of helpless coolies. In the First World War, he patented special gloves for the handling of barbed-wire.

Overcoming stiff resistance, the Alliance fought its way to Peking and successfully relieved the Legations.

Queen Victoria died in 1901 and with her passing, and the crowning of a new king, a different attitude began to emerge in

Britain. Accepted values became 'Victorian' and outdated. King Edward VII, known to be a pleasure-loving, jolly man, set the tone for a more light-hearted, less hidebound society.

Wars were changing too. They were becoming more far-reaching and destructive. They were beginning to involve other nations and, because of this, it became necessary for the military to control censorship more effectively than they had before. Although new technologies made a war correspondent's task easier – the typewriter, the camera, the telephone and radio – increased censorship made life more difficult and reporting was a constant round of struggle and obstruction. Censors were selective in what they allowed. What they did not like was the reporting of poor morale and bad conditions for troops while harshness and cruelty to the native population were not to be described in print.

Britain undertook a minor expedition in Somaliland. This prompted Melton Prior and Bennet Burleigh to be diverted on their return from reporting on The Delhi Durbar proclaiming Edward VII Emperor of India.

The 1903 campaign was to see many long, hot and thirsty marches punctuated with fierce fighting which ultimately failed to destroy or capture the 'Mad Mullah'. Although the old friends did not see any action, Prior found the climate good for his increasing health problems, particularly emphysema and asthma. Burleigh, in his droll way, concurred by writing: 'It is very healthy, plenty of sun, plenty of sand but the shortest road to a public house is a thousand miles long!'[2]

One correspondent who became involved in one of the fiercest fights was Will Maud of the *Daily Graphic*. He joined a column commanded by Johnnie Gough, a fellow Ladysmith siege veteran, with whom he enjoyed a good relationship. Marching through thick scrub, the column was ambushed by a superior force, which they held off for three hours. With ammunition running low, Gough ordered a withdrawal. Between writing and sketching, Maud had been helping with the wounded. Gough learned that the officer in charge of the rearguard had been wounded and went to give aid, leaving Maud in charge to continue the march. On reaching safety, Maud found out that several acts of gallantry had been performed by the rearguard and Gough had recommended two of his officers for the Victoria Cross. He also censored Maud's report for also recommending him for the Victoria Cross. In the event, Gough did receive the VC, a decision which was in part due to Maud's persistence.

Johnnie Gough was soon greatly saddened by the news that Will Maud had died of fever in Aden while on his was home to his pregnant wife. He asked his father to write to the editor of the *Daily Graphic* to suggest a public subscription to which he would contribute anonymously. Given the general suspicion that the military held for war reporters, this was an unusual and generous gesture.

In 1903, the British provoked a regrettable confrontation in Tibet. There was a strong perception that Russia had been making overtures in Tibet in order to gain dominance in the region and threaten the British Raj. Without wishing to occupy the country, the British sought a treaty with the Tibetans but, receiving no response, they crossed the border and marched on the capital, Lhasa. This was part of the 'Great Game' played out by Russia and Great Britain in which the latter sought to halt any move towards India by the eastern-expanding Russian empire. Led by Sir Francis Younghusband, who had acted as correspondent for *The Times* during the Chitral Relief, 3,000 British and Indian soldiers crossed the Himalayas to this remotest of countries. In several skirmishes, some 2,100 primitively armed Tibetans were killed.

One of the few casualties suffered by the British was Edmund Candler of the *Daily Mail*, who was on his first major assignment. In freezing temperatures on a mountain pass between Tuna and Guru, the two sides confronted each other in a close quarters stand-off. A misunderstood gesture led to the Tibetans reacting violently. Candler, who was standing on the end of the front rank, later wrote:

'The morning of the 30th (March) was bitterly cold. An icy wind was blowing, and snow was lying on the ground. I put on my thick sheepskin for the first time for two months, and I owe my life to it …

'The attack on the south-east corner was so sudden that the first man was on me before I had time to draw my revolver. He came at me with his sword lifted in both hands over his head. He had a clear run of ten yards, and if I had not ducked and caught him by the knees he must have smashed my skull open. I threw him, and he dragged me to the ground. Trying to rise, I was struck on the temple by a second swordsman, and the blade glanced off my skull. I received the rest of my wounds, save one or two, on my hands – as I lay on my face I used them to protect my head. After a time the blows ceased; my assailants were all shot down or had fled.'

Candler was repeatedly hacked and was wounded in twelve places. Fortunately his thick *poshteen* saved his life but his hand was badly wounded, resulting in amputation. The British reacted with a couple of minutes of sustained close-range rifle and machine-gun fire which left over 600 tribesmen dead. Candler was hospitalised and his reporting for the remainder of the expedition was handled by Henry Newman of Reuters. After this experience, Candler returned to teaching in India but later returned to war reporting in the First World War.

In the same year Japan and Russia went to war over one another's claims of influence in Manchuria and Korea. A war involving a giant power, Russia, and a swiftly modernising country, Japan, attracted the world's press. The British were well represented with veterans like Prior, Villiers and Burleigh, as well as some newcomers like Ellis Ashmead-Bartlett.

The Times sent Lionel James to Hong Kong where he attempted a 'first'. The paper hired a boat, installed the newly-invented wireless and went looking for news. On 14 March, James was rewarded. Off the Russian-held Port Arthur, he saw and reported the sinking of the Russian flagship by a Japanese mine. He was able to say over the airwaves, 'In the history of journalism, the first time that a message has been sent direct from the field of war activity'.[3] His triumph was short-lived, however, for he also reported two Japanese ships sunk in the same minefield. This new style of news gathering was too uncontrollable for the censor-conscious Japanese, and James's operation was banned. James concluded that there was no future for wireless as a means of reporting wars. The Japanese, on the other hand, saw its potential and used it during their operations against the Russians.

The Japanese were found to be masters of polite procrastination as the correspondents fretted in their Tokyo hotels and awaited the elusive press pass that would take them to the front. As Burleigh put it, 'We ate the bread of idleness'.[4]

Melton Prior, in particular, seems to have suffered the most from the inactivity. He arrived on 7 February and kicked his heels for six months. With nothing to report, except a severe earthquake that shook the city in May, his health deteriorated. Worry and depression caused him to lose weight and his asthma attacks became more frequent. Finally, he and Burleigh did get to Manchuria but were not allowed to get nearer the front than four miles. This final frustration and his poor health finally broke Prior and he returned home, never to travel again. His increasing despondency was heightened when his first wife, whom he still adored, was knocked down and killed by a tram. He still occasionally called into the offices of the *Illustrated London News* and, during a conversation with the new editor, was persuaded to commit to paper the story of his adventurous life. The result was a manuscript of 400,000 words! Sadly it was the last thing he did, for he died in November 1910. His funeral was a lavish and well attended affair that befitted the passing of one of the truly great old-time Specials.[5]

Bennett Burleigh's campaign ended not long after as he tried to free himself from the stranglehold the Japanese had imposed on the foreign reporters. He travelled to Tientsin and attempted to get permission from the Russians to cover events from their side. Once the Japanese found out, they withdrew his accreditation and complained to the British government until he was recalled home. Frederic Villiers was also frustrated by the months of waiting but he was finally part of a group of ten which was chosen to observe the siege of Port Arthur. These included Richmond Smith of *Associated Press*, Benjamin Norregaard of the *Daily Mail*, Richard Barry of the *San Francisco Chronicle* and a newsreel cameraman named 'Rosy' Rosenthal of the Bioscope Company. Although he and his comrades did have to travel six miles each day from their billet, he was able to see much of the bombardment and some of the Japanese attacks. He 'messed' with the *Telegraph* reporter, David James, and a fifty-year-old photographer named Ricalton. Villiers was both amused and irritated by the behaviour of the young Ellis Ashmead-Bartlett, who had served as a subaltern in the Boer War and was the son a wealthy baronet. Later he was to become a considerable correspondent, but he gave the first impression of being a condescending snob. Villiers heard him say to a Japanese officer, 'There's my card, sir – the Junior, don't you know and you can take it from me, as an officer and a gentleman, that what I tell you is correct'.[6] To Villiers and the others specials, Ashmead-Bartlett became known as 'The Toss'.

During the three months they were there, the Specials were offered every courtesy by their hosts but ended up seeing and reporting only what the Japanese wished them to see. As Villiers later wrote, 'The correspondents are practically prisoners, held, of course, with a silken cord'.[7] Even though the Boer War had been censored, the reporters had been free to wander where they liked. The Japanese took measures to prevent this happening and put all foreign reporters under strict surveillance and, in so doing, invented the modern military censor.

The veteran American correspondent Richard Harding Davies ironically summed up the Japanese polite censorship in a piece he entitled *The Japanese-Russian War: Battles I Did Not See*:

'We knew it was a battle because the Japanese officers told us it was. In other wars I had seen other battles, many sorts of battles, but I had never seen a battle like this one. Most battles are noisy, hurried and violent, giving rise to an unnatural thirst and to the delusion that, by some unhappy coincidence, every man on the other side is shooting only at you … But the battle of

Anshantien was in no way disquieting. It was a noiseless, odorless, rubber-tyred battle. So far as we were concerned it consisted of rings of shrapnel smoke floating over a mountain pass many miles distant. So many miles distant that when, with a glass, you could see a speck of fire twinkle in the sun like a heliograph, you could not tell ... whether the cigarette rings issued from the lips of Japanese guns or from those of the Russians. The only thing about the battle of which you were certain was that it was a perfectly safe battle to watch ... But soothing as it was, the battle lacked what is called the human interest ...

'Our teachers, the three Japanese officers who were detailed to tell us about things we were not allowed to see, gazed at the scene of carnage with well-simulated horror. Their expressions of countenance showed that should anyone move the battle eight miles nearer, they were prepared to sell their lives dearly. When they found that none of us were looking at them or the battle, they were hurt. The reason that no one was looking at them was because most of us had gone to sleep. The rest, with a bitter experience of Japanese promises, had doubted there would be a battle, and had prepared themselves with newspapers. And so, while eight miles away the preliminary battle to Liao-Yang was making history, we were lying on the grass reading two months' old news of the St Louis Convention.'

Like Davis, William Maxwell of the *Daily Mail* did see the distant artillery exchanges that heralded the beginning of the Battle of Laio-Yang. Unlike Davis, however, Maxwell admired the Japanese control of the newsmen, something he drew from when he was appointed Chief Field Censor on the staff of General Sir Ian Hamilton in the Gallipoli campaign of 1915.

Davis later experienced the shameless Japanese habit of patent infringement when he was asked by General Fukushima to bring his kit to the office of the General Staff. Davis complied with the general's wish and spread his kit out on the floor. Selecting the three items of the greatest value, which were the Gold Medal cot, the Elliott chair and Preston's water-bottle, the General asked to borrow them on the understanding that he wanted to copy them for his own use and would make some restitution to the officers who had invented them. Later, Davis found, to his annoyance, that the Japanese had manufactured them and issued them to officers on campaign. No acknowledgement or payment was forthcoming.

With time heavy on his hands, Davis listed the items typically carried by correspondents on campaign. Besides a bed, cooking kit and chair, he listed the following items as essential:

Two collapsible water-buckets of rubber or canvas.
Two collapsible brass lanterns, with extra isinglass sides.
Two boxes of sick-room candles.
One dozen boxes of safety matches.
One axe.
One medicine case containing quinine, calomel and Sun Cholera Mixture in tablets.
Toilet case for razors, tooth-powder, brushes and paper.
Folding bath-tub of rubber in rubber case. These are manufactured to fold into a space little larger than a cigar box.
Two towels, old and soft.
Three cakes of soap.
One Jaeger blanket.
One mosquito head-bag.
One extra pair of shoes, old and comfortable.
One extra pair of riding-breeches.
One extra pair of gaiters.
One flannel shirt, Gray least shows the dust.
Two pairs of drawers. For riding the best are those of silk.
Two undershirts, balbriggan or woollen.
Three pairs of woollen socks.
Two linen handkerchiefs, large enough, if needed, to tie around the throat and protect the back of the neck.
One pair of pyjamas, woollen, not linen.
One housewife.

Two briar pipes.
Six bags of smoking tobacco.
One pad of writing paper.
One fountain pen, self-filling.
One bottle of ink, with screw top, held tight by a spring.
One dozen linen envelopes.
Stamps, wrapped in oil-silk with mucilage (glue) side next to
     the silk.
One stick of sealing wax.
One dozen elastic bands of the largest size.
One pack of playing cards.
Books.
One revolver and six cartridges.

'In the list I have included a revolver, following the old saying that "You may not need it for a long time, but when you need it, you want it damned quick." Except to impress guides and mule-drivers, it is not an essential article. In six campaigns I have carried one and never used it, nor needed it but once, and then while I was dodging behind the foremast, it lay under tons of luggage in the hold.

'The number of cartridges I have limited to six, on the theory that if in six shots you haven't hit the other fellow, he will have hit you, and you will not require another six.'

Davis impishly added: 'But the really wise man will pack none of the things enumerated in this article. For the larger the kit, the less benefit he will have of it. It will all be taken from him. And accordingly my final advice is to go forth empty-handed, naked and unashamed, and borrow from your friends ... And of all travellers, the man who borrows is the wisest.'

Earlier, in the Sudan, George Steevens wrote something similar:

'I am not an old campaigner. The old campaigner, as you know, starts out with the cloths he stands up in and a tin opener. The young campaigner provides the change of linen and tins for the old campaigner to open.'

Two reporters who did come under fire with tragic results were Ernest Brindle of the *Daily Mail* and Lewis Etzel of the *Daily Telegraph*. Both were travelling on a junk between Schwantaitze and Erdiko in Manchuria with the intention of cruising along the Llaotung coast. Brindle reported: 'About 6 o'clock in the morning the Junk was surrounded by four sailing boats manned by Chinese soldiers, who, without explanation opened fire, their shots falling all over our boat. We were below reading and waiting and Etzel, looking out, received a fearful wound in the back of his head and expired in a few moments. The soldiers, who were dressed like pirates, said they mistook us for a pirate boat they were seeking. They afterward donned uniforms. I walked to Tienchwang to summon assistance. One of the Chinese crew was badly wounded and it is not likely he will recover.'[8]

One reporter who did manage to evade his 'minders' was *The Times'* correspondent Lionel James, now back on dry land. Tiring of watching shrapnel bursting in the distance, he hid out in the millet fields and, for five days, witnessed the Battle of Liao-Yang. Being an ex-military officer, he avoided describing the battle as a personal adventure and sent an accurate report from a purely military aspect. After a gruelling journey, he managed to reach a telegraph office and file his detailed and uncensored account, the only eyewitness report of the battle. This, however, was a minor success for the Japanese had gone a long way towards crushing that most romantic trade in journalism – the war correspondent.

Having said that, there were still some small colonial wars in North Africa to cover that gave the impression that things were unchanged. At a time when overseas possessions were the mark of a powerful nation, Spain, smarting from her defeat in Cuba and the Philippines, fought a fierce six-month fight with Rif tribesmen in Spanish Morocco, which took the lives of thousands and led to unrest in Spain itself. In 1911, the French-held city of Fez in French Morocco was twice besieged by Berber tribesmen before reinforcements could arrive from France. It took weeks of hard marching and fighting in the desert to subdue the tribes.

Italy was anxious not to be left behind in the slicing up of the crumbling Ottoman Empire. She went to war in late 1911 over the area which is now modern Libya. In a nasty and cruel war, Italy finally overcame all opposition and the Turks lost their last African province. The young British war correspondent Ellis Ashmead-Bartlett fell foul of the Italians when he revealed that unarmed Arabs had been killed at Tanguira Oasis in what was the world's first aerial bombing.[9]

All these conflicts were covered by the British press, including the now venerable Frederic Villiers. His old comrade Bennet Burleigh was ailing and the Italian victory in Tripoli was to be his swansong. He returned home to retirement in Bexhill, where he died on 17 June 1914. He may not have been the greatest writer journalism has ever seen, but he was certainly one of the most colourful.

In 1912-13, there was yet more trouble in the Balkans, with the Turks losing yet more of their empire. The war generated much public interest and an estimated 200-300 journalists from around the world covered it. Frederic Villiers was accredited to the Bulgarians and was determined to explore all possibilities of the moving image by equipping himself with a new system called Kinemacolor. He did, however, draw the line on what he felt was suitable fare for the public. When the Bulgarians hanged a couple of Turkish spies, dozens of cameramen augmented the howling crowd of spectators.

Villiers recalled this morbid circus: 'Then followed a scene that was indescribably disgraceful. The camera men – and there were legions – crawled up trees, mounted the roof of the barn, and occupied every coign of vantage. Bulgarian children, dressed in gala attire and accompanied by their fathers and mothers, crowded up to the gallows trees to gloat over the misery of these wretched men. I became so nauseated with the disgusting sight that I closed down my machine and fled.'

Villiers returned to London certain that a new and larger war was looming: 'I called my agent to fix me up with the usual syndicate, for the Great War had arrived. He almost laughed in my face. "No, my dear Villiers," said he, "never a war with Germany".'

Frederic Villiers' fellow correspondent Ellis Ashmead-Bartlett, who he had dubbed 'The Toss' in the Russo-Japanese War, had gained in experience. He was reporting from the Turkish side for the *Daily Telegraph* and joined his fellow correspondents as they accompanied a Turkish corps by rail to Thrace. With his sharp sense of humour, he wrote:

'Meanwhile, some thirty-two correspondents, photographers and cinematograph operators, representing almost every European nationality, had assembled on the station platform. Their costumes were varied, some of them grotesque. One cadaverous Frenchman, who arrived on an emaciated cab-horse, decked out with an abnormal quantity of obsolete saddle-bags, revolvers, water-bottles, filters etc., was at once christened Don Quixote, and an obese German, who followed him in, was nick-named Sancho Panza. The correspondent of the *Kreuz-Zeitung* wore the largest sombrero hat that it has ever been my lot to see, with one side looped up after the manner of Roosevelt's Roughrider, or of the C.I.V. As it rains continually this season, I imagine that he must intended to use it as an umbrella.'

The *Daily Mail* sent out a new reporter named G. Ward Price, who was still reporting when the Korean War ended in 1953. He teamed up with Ashmead-Bartlett, Martin Donohoe of the *Daily Chronicle* and Lionel James of *The Times* and they were the only correspondents to have a close-up of the decisive Battle of Lule-Burgas. Ashmead-Bartlett and his guide had great difficulty in obtaining horses, but finally found a couple who were old and broken down. They did have some vestige of energy as they were able to convey their riders from the overwhelming Bulgarian attack to the safety of the town of Lule-Burgas. There, Ashmead-Bartlett was able to report on the Bulgarian attack:

'Masses of dark-clothed figures began to appear among the trees on the low ridge of hills lately evacuated by the Turks. A great shout went up: "There are the Bulgarians!"'

'The Turkish soldiers around me commenced to ply them with

long-ranged fire, which did not check the advance for a moment. A staff officer dashed up shouting: "Everyone must clear out of the town and make for higher ground behind, where you will find our infantry entrenched. The town cannot long be held. Only the rear-guard can remain."'

Ashmead-Bartlett reached the crest of the ridge about a mile behind the town and took up a position with the Turkish artillery. From here he could clearly watch the battle unfold: 'The Bulgarians now half-surrounded the town, and had advanced half-way down the hill, where they lay firing at the entrenched battalion of Turks in the town. The latter inflicted heavy losses on the invaders, who were quite devoid of any cover. But now the Bulgarian artillery had been brought up to the crest of the ridge and commenced to shell the town and the Turkish entrenchments on the higher ground where we stood. Their fire was wonderfully accurate, but the Turks stood their ground well and refused to leave the town.

'For more than two hours this rear-guard held out heroically. About two o'clock fresh masses of Bulgarian infantry debouched from the hills and rushed down into the firing line, and the whole line dashed forward with magnificent élan. The fire of the Turkish entrenchments now rose into a sullen roar … The Bulgarians fell in scores, and the advance came to an end only a few hundred yards away from the entrenchments.

'But the defence had shot its last bolt, the ammunition was exhausted and much against its will, the heroic rear-guard was obliged to fall back.'[10]

As the Turkish army and civilians retreated, Ashmead-Bartlett was left with a familiar problem: 'It is all very well for a war correspondent to see a battle and to note carefully what has happened throughout the whole struggle and during the retreat, but his exertions are absolutely wasted, unless he is able to despatch the news to his paper without delay and before his rivals. This is the only way that a paper can obtain any adequate return for the large sum of money spent in fitting him out, buying him motor-cars and horses, and sending him to the front.'[11]

In the confusion of the retreat he found Martin Donohoe of the *Daily Chronicle*, who told him that *The Times'* man, Lionel James, had stolen a march on the rest of the correspondents by departing early and catching a steamer to Constantinople. There he would have to submit his report to the censor and, when passed, have it sent by telegraph to his paper. Determined to beat James, Ashmead-Bartlett and Donohoe spent a fruitless day trying to bribe their way on board a couple of steamers, the captains of which made outrageous demands. Finally, they found a passing steamer that would take them for free. Both realised that the Turkish censor in Constantinople would delete any mention of the huge reverse that had befallen the Turkish army, something that Lionel James would experience. Instead, they managed to evade the Turkish authorities and catch a ship to Rumania from where they could send their uncensored reports to London.

Lionel James resigned from *The Times* in 1913 after having his salary drastically reduced. At the outbreak of the First World War, he rejoined the King Edward's Horse and ended the war as a Colonel with the award of the Distinguished Service Order. When he died in 1955, at the age of eighty-four, he was described by *Punch* magazine as 'One of the Princes of the Golden Age of War Correspondence'.

Ward described the campaign as 'the last of the nineteenth century type of war, in which correspondents would be dependent on horse-transport, and accompanied by a staff of interpreters, grooms and batmen'.[12] In this short and vicious war, Bulgaria and Serbia defeated the Turks and thus ended their centuries-long power in Europe. It also precipitated the Turkish revolution when the country was taken over by Kemal Ataturk and the Young Turks who changed the face of Turkey. It was also a prelude to a catastrophic war that would alter the political and social structure of the world. Ironically, within eighteen months Bulgaria and Turkey found themselves as allies with Austria and Germany.

The long anticipated war with Germany broke out in August 1914. It found the British authorities ill-prepared in most departments except that of an effective censorship system in place. The next four years changed forever the relationship between the press and the military and the public's acceptance of what it reads in the newspapers. This radical change came about in a climate of great patriotism, national security and a need to maintain the public support for the war. British military observers of the Russo-Japanese War had been impressed by the control the Japanese exerted over the press through their strict censorship. Learning from this, a Bill was proposed but, due to much opposition, it was not enacted. Instead, the framework was established so when war was declared, it was a simple matter to put it into action.

As early as August 1914, the War Office, under the control of Lord Kitchener, established the Press Bureau with the express purpose of excluding war correspondents from the Western Front. All news would be controlled and supplied by the military. In a candid statement, First Lord of the Admiralty, Winston Churchill told a journalist that 'the war is going to be "fought in a fog" and the best place for correspondence about the war was London'.[13] How ironic that the old press-hater Kitchener and the shameless, publicity-seeking war correspondent Churchill should now both be dancing to the same tune. There was to be no question of allowing war correspondents to wander around the front line, observing conditions and discussing tactics with senior officers as they did in Victoria's time.

The Golden Age of war reporting had ended, never to return.

Appendix I

Part of Henry Crabb Robinson's report on the Battle of Friedland which brought news of the defeat of Russia, the last Continental power still in arms against Napoleon and Britain's last major ally. The Emperor of the French now dominated Europe, and Britain stood alone.

The Times
2 July 1807

It was between two and three o'clock on Saturday, the 20th, that we were filled with consternation by the vague, but loud and confident report of a total defeat of the Russians in East Prussia. The information contained in that morning's papers, had prepared us to hear of a general engagement; and the fears of impartial and judicious men were stronger than their hopes. The universal cry was, 'It is another battle of Austerlitz; another battle of Jena.'

In the afternoon, an *Hamburgh Correspondenten Extraordinary* was published, which afforded some matter for criticism, though the general fact of a victory over the Allies on the part of the French was not to be doubted. In the evening there also appeared the following article in a periodical publication, which being rather literary than political, affects a character above that of a daily newspaper:–

'The campaign is opened; but as the negotiations which preceded the renewal of hostilities were veiled in impenetrable obscurity, so the first remarkable occurrences, which have taken place are inexplicable. On the 5th of June, the Russians made a general attack upon the main army of the French, which seemed to be prepared to act only on the defensive. This attack failed; yet the right wing of the French army, under Marshal Ney, took a retrograde position, by the command of the Emperor.

'On receiving information of these occurrences, the Emperor left Finkenstein, and now it appeared that the Russians had begun to retreat. Were those previous attacks made only to mask this retreat, which had had probably been resolved upon before? Or had Massena, after having covered his flank with intrenchments on the left bank of the Narew, threatened by some movement the rear of the Russians? However this may be, from this moment the French army followed the Russians, broke through their line of operations, and united their several corps. On the 13th, their headquarters were in the bloody fields of Preussich-Eylau, while of two other columns, one had stationed itself, the day before, in Friedland (which lies to the right), and the other had marched towards Koningsberg. Whether it has been possible for General L'Estoq to maintain his connection with the Russian army, is for the present unknown. The first intelligence we have received of these remarkable incidents, is too indefinite to enable us to form easy idea of the result; but it is probable that the Russians will not be able to take a position otherwise than behind the Niemen.'

The temperate tone of this article, written apparently after the appearance of the *Hamburgh Correspondenten*, served to throw discredit upon the intelligence contained in that Paper. The article announcing the great advantages gained at Heilsberg, and the successes of the first French movements, was believed; but the two letters from Koningsberg obtained less credit.

On Sunday, I was in company with some of the first of the *Pouvoirs Constitués* of Hamburg; but, instead of expressing triumph, it was merely said, that the battle had begun favourably, &c. This might be courtesy, in order to preserve good humour in a mixed company: however, it served, to nourish some hope in our bosoms. But, on the following day, in the evening, an extraordinary sheet of the periodical publication I have before alluded to, was sent forth, containing an article which I must also give you entire:–

'We every day receive fresh intelligence concerning the misfortunes of the Russian army. On the 13th (a press *erratum* for the 14th), according to official statements, a battle took place at Friedland, in which the Russians lost upwards of 30,000, in dead, wounded, and prisoners. As the news was brought from the French head-quarters on the very day of the battle, nothing of the result was known, but that the French were masters of the field; but whether the Russians continued their retreat, or took a position, is unknown.

'This morning private intelligence has been received from a person of distinction in Danzig, dated the 19th. According to this, the French Emperor attacked the Russian army on the 15th, totally defeated it, and took 200 cannon. The number of prisoners, it is added, is incalculable, and the Russians have lost everything. Whether this is a fresh affair, or merely the battle of the 14th, is yet uncertain. Prince BORHHESE is gone to Paris with the news. Koningsberg, according to the same intelligence, was entered by the French on the 16th.

'In Berlin, on the 20th, nothing farther was known from the theatre of war, than the battle of Friedland mentioned above; but farther details were known of the various actions up lo the evening of the 11th, when the Russians were compelled to abandon their advantageous position by Heilsberg during the night. It is also confirmed that, on the 5th, Marshal Nay had been obliged, by the superior force of the Russians, to change his position.

'The effect of this article was such, as to render the next morning's *Hamburgh Correspondenten* rather a relief to our extreme alarm, than a confirmation of our fears; for though the first part of the intelligence was confirmed, and even stamped with official authority, viz. that at the battle of Friedland the Russians had lost from 25 to 30,000 men, to which were added 80 cannon, and 30 generals, yet the second report if the battle of the 15th, and or the entrance of the French into Konigsberg, was passed over in silence: and this was, in the minds of most persons, a sufficient refutation of the whole. Besides, I know that early this morning no official intelligence had arrived of the capture of Konigsberg at Hamburgh, and the journey may be made in five days; and when we further remark, that we have information from Berlin up to the 20th, when this intelligence was not known there, we may venture to assert that this is a *premature* statement. This would, however, be a very poor consolation (for if an army be defeated which covers a defenceless city, the place must of course fall, and it is of little moment when), if the same inference did not also apply still more strongly to the report of the second battle on the 15th. This also might have been known at Berlin on the 20th, and certainly would have been carefully communicated. In all probability, therefore, this whole article is but an exaggerated statement of the victory of the 14th, which is sufficiently lamentable in the report brought to M. BOURIENNE. It is almost superfluous to add, that this same article, which is published in Hamburgh on the 22nd, is said to be dated Dantzig the 19th. The person of distinction meant, is understood to be General RAPP.

'But how idle is this cavilling about dates! In a few hours, we shall probably receive fresh advices, and, I fear, we shall then find that this is fact, which appeared improbable. How often do we not experience this!

'I have not been able to learn either the exact position of the Russian Armies of Reserve, or their force; but, I understand, there is one of 60,000 at least, sufficiently near to receive the retreating army: and, if the first news only be true, we may still nourish the hope (it will not be sanguine or confident), that though Konigsberg may be taken, and the French have gained another victory, still Russia is not vanquished. Should, indeed, the defeat be total ———!!

'We must wait with patience for the more tardy and indirect intelligence which the friends of the Allies will sooner or later transmit to us. Yesterday, letters of the 7th were received from Konigsberg, by way of Copenhagen. The Russians boast of a number of successes in little engagements; and speak of the affair with Marshal Ney, on the 5th, as a victory: and, indeed, the French accounts themselves justify this assertion. It is also reported, that letters have been received from Konigsberg, dated the 17th, when the French were not arrived. This *may* be true; but unless the asserted victory of the 14th can be disproved, it will not be of much importance.

'I have thus, in *many* words, told you how little we know here. I must now add the reports of another description, which have been circulated here, were it only to tell you that they *do* exist, though no one credits them. It is said, that letters from Leipsic, dated the 15th, mention, that the battle lasted four days, and ended in favour of the Russians! Alas, it was a letter from Leipzic which made known over the whole North of Europe, and even in England, that the Prussians had totally defeated the French at Jena.

'But this is not enough; for while one wing of the Russian army is allowed to be beaten, the other, it is said, has taken Warsaw!!! – We shall unquestionably find, that in a series of engagements, which began on the 5th, and which were not ended on the 14th, there have been some advantages on the part of the Allies. A Marshal may have fallen, and a dreadful slaughter of the French may have repeatedly taken place. I have heard it sagely remarked, that hitherto the French have given us *only* the results – as if BUONAPARTE cared for any thing else! He may have lost four thousand, or forty thousand men; it is the same to him, provided the remaining force is strong enough to do the remaining duty. He is the man in the fable, who willingly gives up one eye, that his adversary may lose both. And his losses, whatever they may be, will be carefully concealed, and speedily repaired.

'I will now briefly notice a few circumstances of less importance.

'The Prince de PONTE CORVO is arrived at Berlin; and report says, that MASSENA is also expected.

'Yesterday information was received by the Duke of MECKLENBURG SCHWERIN, who resides at Altona, that his territory is declared neutral; that is, after being plundered and ravaged, till little remains to be taken away (the damage is estimated at 20 millions of dollars, an enormous sum for so small a country), the land is abandoned as unproductive. Yet the French are to retain military possession of it. The Duke is said to have joined the. Rhenish Confederacy.

'The Prussian troops in the Island of Rugen, under General BLUCHER, are now in Pomerania. After the catastrophe which has taken place in East Prussia, we have lost all interest in what may occur in Pomerania. And the British Expedition, the non-arrival of which several months ago has irreparably injured the English cause on the Continent, would now be heard of with indifference by its enemies, and with regret by its friends.

'To conclude – There has issued from Stralsund a Proclamation or Address in French, in favour of LOUIS XVIII, King of France and Navarre!!! The white flag is hoisted; and all loyal Frenchmen are promised *"une disciplince paternelle et une solde plusque double, &c."* This pay is also stated even to as, odd farthing; and the uniform is carefully described – with a special note that deserters are to inquire for the regiment of the King of France, commanded by Mons. the Duke of PIENNE. I send you the original as a curiosity.

'SOLDIERS,- Under the auspices of the loyal Sovereign of Sweden, the white flag is again hoisted. Honour calls you to assemble round this banner, a paternal discipline, and pay more than double your present pay, await you.- Peace to Europe is the object you are called upon to obtain, in the ranks of the Royal Army of France. The love of Louis XVIII. your legitimate Sovereign, is already in your hearts.- *Vive le Roi!*

'The uniform is white, the collar, facings, &c. blue, with yellow lace, blue pantaloons with the same.

'Ai soon as the cavalry is formed, the soldiers of this army will resume the service.

'Every loyal Frenchman, who shall bring over the troop he commands, or cause it to rejoin the white flag, shall consequently enjoy the same rank he already holds, agreeably to the declaration of Louis XVIII. King of France and Navarre, dated Dec. 10, 1804.

'Each deserter is to enquire for the regiment of the King of FRANCE, commanded by M. Le DUC de PIENNE. The pay for the private soldier is 5½ schellings of Pomerania, without bread (about 16 sols of France), and with two pounds of bread, 6½ schellings.

'A report is in general circulation, which, though I cannot trace it to any satisfactory authority, is so important, that I must relate it as I have received it. A revolution, instigated by the Janissaries, is said to have taken place in Constantinople. It is further stated, that the Sultan, his on, and all the immediate Ministers, have fallen victims to the popular fury; and that the nephew of the late Sultan has been proclaimed successor.

'Others add, that the French Minister SEBASTIANI and many French are among the killed.

'What has more immediately occasioned this catastrophe is not mentioned. Some are of opinion that the blockade by water, maintained by the English, and the possession of so large a part of Moldavia and Wallachia by the Russians, must have threatened this immediately populous city of a famine, the Turks have no magazines of any kind.

'I understand, that 400 waggons have been put in requisition in order to transport the divisions of MOLITOR and BOUDET to East Prussia. This circumstance, and the silence of the Hamburgh papers this morning; has raised the spirits of many here. But, on the other hand, we have instances of a delay in communicating details of victories, in order to produce a great effect by a connected relation of the whole when the work is completed. It is reasonable to suppose, that, as soon as the victory was decidedly on the side of the French, NAPOLEON made proposals of peace. How may they have been received?'

Appendix II

Henry Crabb Robinson's final report from Spain on the embarkation of the British army following the retreat to Corunna.

The Times
26 January 1809

We this day present our readers with the last letter of our Correspondent at Corunna, to which place an accident obliged him to return, after he had taken, he supposed, his final departure. This, however, had enabled us to offer an interesting picture of the situation of that town immediately preceding the engagement.

Corunna, Jan. 15, Night

I thought I had for very long period left this place, but untoward accidents have brought me again within its walls; I trust, however, but for a few hours, that I may behold it in the last moments of its dying liberty-not a scene of tumult, but the prey of quiet apprehension and gloomy affliction. The last two days have materially changed the appearance of things. Yesterday evening, the fleet of transports which had been dispersed in their passage from Vigo; began to enter the harbour, and the hearts of thousands were relieved by the prospect of deliverance. I behold this evening the beautiful Bay covered with our vessels both armed and mercantile, and I should have thought the noble three-deckers, which stood on the outside of the harbour, a proud spectacle, if I could have forgotten the inglorious service they were called to perform. In the meanwhile the stairs which lead to the water were thronged with boats, in which were embarking the British cavalry.

The English soldiery appeared to have taken possession of all public places, while the inhabitants looked on with mortification and sorrow. Tonight a more ominous scene presented itself. I had occasion to go to the Government Palace, and found the broad staircases and anti-chambers filled with English military, who had also taken possession of the Square before the Palace. Here they had kindled some half-dozen fires, (I fear with no uncostly materials) and were busily employed in a sort of gipsey-cookery. I proceeded to the quay; and the scattered lights from the numerous shipping would have been a gay scene; but for the long waving line of light which we saw and knew the enemy had kindled above.

During the whole of the day there have been skirmishes between the French and English, at less than a league distance, in small bodies; much firing but little execution. To-morrow there is no doubt that our embarkation will proceed, and the enemy will probably be prudent enough to witness this without interfering, until a large proportion of our force is thus rendered useless At the close, he will endeavour to wreak his vengeance upon the last divisions which remain. Whether the armed inhabitants will have the generosity to protect these last troops on their retreat, who will be at their mercy, we cannot tell. Should they refuse to do this, and say to us – ' You came into a mountainous province, and by the ostentatious display of your well-dressed army, drove us from the defence of our native hills – the natural fortress which God had given us was trusted to you, and you basely delivered lit up to the spoiler you might have guarded the avenues to our city, but you scorned a service which you thought was immaterial to your own safety, and behold the foe stands in the narrow paths which lead to our vallies [sic] and town – I fear that, should the volunteers of Corunna throw down their arms when they see the British flying to their ships, we shall have little right to complain of desertion or abandonment.

We are much in the dark concerning the extent of the enemy's force, as well as his present positions. It is evident that the principle upon which he acts is procrastination, and that he proposes to render the blow more sure, by delaying to strike. Among the people, the notion is very prevalent that the French have hitherto a very insignificant force. The English Officers have represented them as amounting to 20,000 men.

The next day, 16 January, the French attacked and were driven off, allowing the British troops to embark on the waiting ships with little further interference from the enemy.

Notes and References

CHAPTER 1: IN THE BEGINNING
1. H.C. Robinson *Diary, Reminiscences & Correspondence*, Vol.1 (1869).
2. The Battle of Bailén, fought in Andalusia between 16 and 19 July 1808, was a heavy defeat for the French army under General Pierre Dupont who was forced to surrender almost 18,000 men, making this the worst disaster and capitulation of the Peninsular War.

CHAPTER 2: THE FATHER OF THE LUCKLESS TRIBE
1. A. Hankinson, *Man of War* (1982).
2. W.H. Russell, *The War from the Landing at Gallipoli to the Death of Lord Raglan*, Vol.1 (1855).
3. W.H. Russell, *The Great War with Russia* (1895).
4. E. Grey, *The Noise of Drums and Trumpets* (1971).
5. W.H. Russell, *The War*.
6. ibid.

CHAPTER 3: BALAKLAVA
1. W.H. Russell, *The War*.
2. ibid.
3. ibid.
4. Philip Howard, *We Thundered Out*.
5. William Russell, *My Diary in India* (1859).
6. Hankinson, *Man of War*.
7. John Hannavy, *The Camera Goes to War* (Exhibition catalogue 1975, The Scottish Arts Council).
8. Lawrence James, *The War with Russia from Contemporary Photographs* (1984).

CHAPTER 4: EASTERN TROUBLES
1. W.H. Russell, *My Diary in India 1858-59* (1860).
2. ibid.
3. ibid.

CHAPTER 5: THE AMERICAN CIVIL WAR
1. R. Hudson (Ed.), *William Russell, Special Correspondent of The Times* (1995).
2. ibid.
3. Bradley S. Osbon, *A Soldier of Fortune* (1906).
4. Hudson, *William Russell*.
5. ibid.
6. E. Cook, *Delane of The Times* (1915).
7. Justin H. Walsh, *To Print the News and Raise Hell!* (1968).

CHAPTER 6: PRUSSIA ON THE MARCH
1. A. Forbes, *How I Became a War Correspondent* (1884).
2. ibid.
3. ibid.
4. R. Hudson, *William Russell, Special Correspondent for The Times* (1995).
5. A. Hankinson, *Man of War* (1982).
6. ibid.
7. Henri Labouchere, *Diary of the Besieged Resident in Paris* (1871).
8. A. Forbes, *Memories and Studies of War and Peace* (1895).

CHAPTER 7: INTO AFRICA'S DARK CENTRE
1. The Indian Wars were well reported in America. Among the men who died with General Custer at the Battle of Little Big Horn was newspaper correspondent Mark Kellogg of the *Bismarck Tribune*.
2. G. Wolseley, *Soldiers Pocket Book*.
3. M. Prior, *Campaigns of a War Correspondent* (1912).
4. William Winwood Reade, *The Story of the Ashantee Campaign* (1874).
5. *The Daily Telegraph*, 1 March 1873.

CHAPTER 8: THE BALKAN WARS 1876-78
1. Roger Fulford, *The Prince Consort* (1949).
2. A. Hankinson, *Man of War* (1982).
3. Melton Prior, *Campaigns of a War Correspondent* (1912).
4. F. Villiers, *His Five Decades of Adventure* (1921).
5. Frank D. Millet (1846-1912) was also an artist and writer of some repute and associated with contemporaries like John Singer Sargent and Henry James. Millet died aboard *Titanic* when she sank in April 1912.
6. Drew Gay of the *Daily Telegraph* sent for his wife with tragic consequences. When the Russians were advancing on Constantinople, he sent her to Athens for safety. Here she contracted typhoid and died.
7. A. Forbes, *Memories and Studies of War and Peace* (1895).
8. ibid.

CHAPTER 9: THE AFGHAN WARS
1. B.M. Best, *Campaign Life in the British Army during the Zulu War*, The Journal of the Anglo Zulu War Historical Society, December 1997.
2. A. Forbes, *Memories and Studies of War and Peace* (1895).

3. A. Swinson, *North-West Frontier* (1967).
4. H. Hensman *The Afghan War 1879-80* (1882).
5. The National Archives, WO32/8559 (1881). Further states, 'Civilians who attach themselves to a Field Army for their own advantage and who hold no military appointment under Government with that Army shall be deemed absolutely ineligible for a war medal'.

CHAPTER 10: THE ZULU WAR

1. I. Knight, *Zulu, Isandlwana & Rorke's Drift 22-23 January, 1879* (1992).
2. Charles Norris-Newman, *With the British in Zululand throughout the War of 1879* (1880).
3. M. Prior, *Campaigns of a War Correspondent*.
4. ibid.
5. ibid.
6. ibid.
7. A. Forbes, *Memories and Studies of War and Peace* (1895).
8. ibid.
9. ibid.
10. M. Prior, *Illustrated London News*, 12 July 1879.
11. A. Forbes, *Memories and Studies of War and Peace* (1895).
12. ibid.
13. Henry Curling letter dated 5 July 1879. Lieutenant Henry Thomas Curling, Royal Artillery, was the only officer who fought on the front line to escape from Isandlwana. *The Curling Letters of the Zulu War* by Brian Best (2001).
14. J. Cameron, *The Standard*, 1 March 1881.
15. Ron Lock and Peter Quantrill, *The Red Book – Natal Press Reports 1879*.

CHAPTER 11: EGYPT AND THE SUDAN, PART I

1. F. Villiers, *His Five Decades of Adventure* (1921).
2. W.R. Hudson, *William Russell Special Correspondent of The Times* (1995).
3. Russell married an Italian countess, Antoinette Malvezzi.
4. William Butler, *An Autobiography* (1911).
5. F. Scudamore, *A Sheaf of Memories* (1925).
6. F. Villiers, *Five Decades of Adventure*.
7. F. Power, *The Times*, April 1884.
8. M. Prior, *Campaigns of a War Correspondent* (1912).
9. *The Letters of Lord and Lady Wolseley 1870-1911* (1922).
10. B.M. Best *The Anglo Zulu War Historical Society Journal*, June 1998.

CHAPTER 12: EGYPT AND THE SUDAN, PART II

1. Willoughby Wallace Hooper, *1885-86 Burma. 3rd Anglo-Burmese War* (1886).
2. Colonel H.M. Vibart, *The Life of General Sir Henry N. D. Prendergast VC* (1914).
3. Lionel James, *High Pressure* (1929).
4. E.F. Knight, *The Wanderings of a Yachtsman and War Correspondent* (1923).
5. W.S. Churchill, *My Early Life* (1930).
6. Melton Prior, *Campaigns of a War Correspondent* (1912).

7. ibid.
8. Richard Harding Davis, *Notes of a War Correspondent* (1910).
9. *Journal of the Victoria Cross Society* No.21, October 2012.
10. Henry Nevinson's son was Christopher Nevinson, the leading figure in English Futurism and an outstanding First World War artist.
11. E.K. Knight, *The Wanderings of a Yachtsman and War Correspondent* (1923).
12. James Creelman, *On the Great Highway* (1902).
13. E.K. Knight, *The Wanderings of a Yachtsman and War Correspondent* (1923).
14. George Warrington Steevens was born in Sydenham, now part of South London, in 1869. He was educated at the City of London School and Balliol College, Oxford. In 1893, he was elected a Fellow of Pembroke College.
15. Drinks loomed large in the correspondents' lives. George Steevens even devoted an entire chapter entitled *The Pathology of Thirst* to the pleasures of finding a truly thirst-quenching concoction in *With Kitchener to Khartoum*
16. G.W. Steevens, *With Kitchener to Khartoum* (1898).
17. G.W. Steevens, *The Daily Mail*, 5 September 1898.
18. W.S. Churchill, *The River War* (1898).
19. G.W. Steevens thought that the charge was a gross blunder having sustained far heavier losses than those inflicted. In doing so, the 21st Lancers ceased to be an effective unit and were unable to be used in any pursuit.
20. Bennet Burleigh in his book *Khartoum Campaign 1898* rather plays down Smyth's exploit while enhancing his own. The other correspondent who fired off his pistol and rode to safety was Bennett Stamford.

CHAPTER 13: THE ANGLO-BOER WAR
1. L. James, *High Pressure* (1929).
2. M. Prior, *Campaigns of a War Correspondent* (1912).
3. H.W. Nevinson, *The Fire of Life* (1929).
4. Bennet Burleigh, *Natal Campaign* (1900).
5. H.W. Nevinson, *The Fire of Life* (1929).
6. A. Sebba, *Battling for the News - The Rise of the Woman Reporter* (1994).
7. W.S. Churchill, *My Early Years* (1972).
8. L. James, *High Pressure*.
9. G.W. Steevens, *From Capetown to Ladysmith* (1900).
10. L. James, *High Pressure* (1929).
11. E. Wallace, *Daily Mail*, 9 July 1901.
12. ibid.

CHAPTER 14: THE LAST DAYS OF THE GOLDEN AGE
1. Cyril Pearl, *Morrison of Peking* (1967).
2. Morrison's eldest son, Ian, became *The Times* correspondent in the Far East during the Second World War.
3. Melton Prior, *Campaigns of a War Correspondent* (1912).
4. Lionel James, *High Pressure* (1929).
5. Melton Prior, *Campaigns of a War Correspondent*.
6. Bertha Burleigh, Bennett's wife, was an artist. She designed and executed the

memorial to Melton Prior, which was unveiled in the crypt of St Paul's Cathedral by Field Marshall Evelyn Wood on 22 October 1912.

7. Frederic Villiers, *Five Decades of Adventure* (1921).

8. ibid.

9. Lewis Etzel was an American reporter acting for the *Daily Telegraph*. The US Government put pressure on the Chinese who jailed the Chinese general in charge and paid compensation to Etzel's family.

10. For all his annoying traits, Ellis Ashmead-Bartlett was the only correspondent during the First World War who persisted in writing the truth and was instrumental in halting the wastage of life in the futile Gallipoli Campaign of 1915. Significantly, he was the only accredited war reporter not to be honoured with a knighthood after the conflict.

11. Ellis Ashmead-Bartlett, *With the Turks in Thrace* (1913).

12. G. Ward Price, *Extra-Special Correspondent* (1953).

13. William Beach Thomas, *A Traveller in News* (1925).

Bibliography

Anon, *We Thundered Out, 200 Years of the Times 1785-1985*, 1985.

Arnold, Edward, *The Unveiling of Lhasa*, 1905.

Ashmead-Bartlett, Ellis, *With the Turks in Thrace*, 1913.

Burleigh, Bennet, *Empire of the East or, Japan and Russia at War 1904-5*, 1905.

_____, *Khartoum Campaign 1898*, 1898.

_____, *The Natal Campaign*, 1900.

Churchill, Winston, *The River War*, 1902.

Crowe, Sir Joseph, *Reminiscences of Thirty-Five Years of my Life*, 1895.

Davis, Richard Harding, *Notes of a War Correspondent*, 1897.

Dickson, W.K.-L., *The Biograph Battle*, 1901.

Forbes, Archibald, *Barrack, Bivouacs and Battles*, 1891.

_____, *The Afghan Wars*, 1892.

_____, *The War Correspondence of the Daily News 1877*, 1878.

Greaves, Graeden, *Wild Bennet Burleigh – The Pen and the Pistol*, 2012.

Hensman, Howard, *The Afghan War*, 1882.

Hudson, Roger (Ed.), *William Russell – Special Correspondent of The Times*, 1995.

Johnson, Peter, *Front Line Artists*, 1978.

Knight, E.F., *Reminiscences – The Wanderings of a Yachtsman and War*, 1923.

Knight, Ian, and Laband, John, *The Anglo-Zulu War*, 1996.

Prior, Melton, *Campaigns of a War Correspondent*, 1912.

Sharf, Frederic A., *Abyssinia, 1867-68. Artists on Campaign*, 2003.

Sibbald, Raymond, *The Boer War*, 1993.

Steevens, George, *Capetown to Ladysmith*, 1900.

_____, *With Kitchener to Khartoum*, 1898.

Villiers, Frederic, *Villiers, His Five Decades of Adventure*, 1921.

Wilkinson-Latham, Robert, *From Our Own Correspondent*, 1979.

Youngs, Tim, *Travellers in Africa: British Travelogues, 1850-1900*, 1994.

Index

231